The FORGOTTEN GENERAL

Painting of Major-General Sir Andrew (Guy)
Russell KCB, KCMG, 1918.

The FORGOTTEN GENERAL

New Zealand's World War I Commander
Major-General Sir Andrew Russell

JOCK VENNELL

ALLEN&UNWIN

First published in 2011

Copyright © Jock Vennell 2011

Allen & Unwin
Sydney, Melbourne, Auckland, London

83 Alexander Street
Crows Nest NSW 2065
Australia
Phone: (61 2) 8425 0100
Fax: (61 2) 9906 2218
Email: info@allenandunwin.com
Web: www.allenandunwin.com

National Library of New Zealand Cataloguing-in-Publication Data
Vennell, Jock.
The forgotten general : New Zealand's World War I commander,
Major General Sir Andrew Russell / Jock Vennell.
Includes bibliographical references and index.
ISBN 978-1-877505-07-2
1. Russell, A. H. (Andrew Hamilton), 1868-1960.
2. New Zealand—Army—Officers—Biography. 3. Generals—
New Zealand—Biography. 4. World War, 1914-1918—
New Zealand. I. Title.
940.40092—dc 22

ISBN 978 1 877505 07 2

Frontispiece image courtesy of the Deans family collection;
all other internal images courtesy of the Russell family collection.
Maps by Morag Torrington
Index by Nicola McCloy
Set in 11.5/16 pt Minion by Post Pre-press Group, Australia

Printed and bound in Australia by Griffin Press

10 9 8 7 6 5 4 3 2 1

MIX
Paper from
responsible sources
FSC® C009448

The paper in this book is FSC certified.
FSC promotes environmentally responsible,
socially beneficial and economically viable
management of the world's forests.

Contents

List of Maps

Preface

'A born leader of men, with natural gifts for the military art which fell little short of genius.'[1]

So wrote Colonel Hugh Stewart, the official historian of the 20,000-strong New Zealand Division that fought in France and Belgium in World War I. His subject: the division's commander, Major-General Sir Andrew (Guy) Russell. Seventy-seven years later, prominent military historian Dr Chris Pugsley went much further, rating Russell as not only the outstanding divisional commander among the British armies that fought on the Western Front, but the one military commander of genius that New Zealand produced in the twentieth century.[2]

Under Russell's leadership, Pugsley wrote, 'New Zealand produced the finest fighting division of all the British and Dominion divisions among the British armies in France, and perhaps the consistently finest division of any of the armies—British, French, or German—that fought on the Western Front.'[3]

Bold claims indeed, given that the New Zealand Division was only one of 60 British and Dominion divisions fighting on the Western Front by 1918, and there were many more French and German divisions. Many of these were first-class formations commanded by men of great military ability, among them Lieutenant-General Sir John Monash, who rose to command the Australian Corps; and General Sir Clive Currie, who led the four Canadian divisions.

There is no doubt, however, that by 1918 Russell had established himself as one of the outstanding divisional commanders on the Western Front. Under his leadership the New Zealand Division developed a reputation as one of the finest in the British armies that fought in World War I. In the last year of the war, and in recognition of his outstanding abilities, Russell was offered command of a full British Army corps (three to four divisions). For health, and perhaps other reasons, he was unable to accept.

Given his accomplishments, the larger question is why Russell is the forgotten general of New Zealand's military history. In part it is because of the dominance of World War II history in general, and of Lieutenant-General Sir Bernard Freyberg in particular. In part it is because of the neglect of the historians themselves. This biography aims to restore Major-General Sir Andrew Russell to his rightful place as one of this country's finest military commanders.

War service, however, occupied only a few years of Russell's long life, whether as a divisional commander in World War I or as inspector-general of military forces and member of the War Council in World War II. His other careers as successful farmer, businessman, NZRSA president and prominent defence lobbyist spanned the Depression years of the 1920s and 30s, and finally the 1940s when war came much closer to home. By any measure, Russell's achievements in these years, and the qualities of character and intellect that drove them, were extraordinary.

This project has been a challenging one. Apart from his diaries, Russell kept no personal records of his campaigns, wrote only one discoverable dissertation on military subjects, made few public speeches that have survived, and left no memoirs. By contrast, Sir John Monash, Russell's much better known Australian equivalent from World War I, left a vast collection of personal papers, articles and lectures on military subjects, a collection of his war letters, a book on Australian victories in France, and at least two biographies. Russell, however, was a prolific letter writer. This book is based on these letters; material provided by the National Library and Archives New Zealand; research at the Imperial War Museum, the Army Museum, and the Liddell Hart Centre for Military Studies in London; and on family memories. Dr Chris Pugsley's work has been of great assistance, too, in examining Russell's commands, both at Gallipoli and on the Western Front. In addition, 'The Russell Family Saga', an unpublished collection of letters and other family material compiled by Colonel Reg Gambrill in the 1970s, was an invaluable starting point.

The Russell story, however, is more than his alone. It is about the men he led for four unbroken years of war, starting with the raw and inexperienced brigade that arrived on Gallipoli in May 1915 and finishing with the élite division at the spearhead of the British counter-offensive that finally ended the war on the Western Front. In four years of war over 100,000 young men from a colonial nation of just 1.1 million—20 percent of its male population—fought overseas, and nearly 60 percent of them were killed or wounded.

Too many of them would have been the leaders of New Zealand's first post-war generation—its outstanding politicians and civil servants; its doctors, lawyers, teachers and other professionals; its successful farmers, entrepreneurs and tradesmen; its nation-defining writers and thinkers. This is their story, as much as it is that of their commander, Major-General Sir Andrew (Guy) Russell. Proud of the men he led and dedicated to their welfare, he would have expected no less.

Introduction: 'A Magnificent Feat of Arms'

As darkness fell on 6 August 1915, 1900 men of the New Zealand Mounted Rifles Brigade, under the overall command of Brigadier-General Guy Russell, slipped quietly out from the northern end of Ari Burnu on the Gallipoli peninsula.

Their task was to capture key Turkish positions in the foothills of the Sari Bair range, allowing two columns of infantry to advance unopposed up three valleys (deres) and take the main Sari Bair ridge. Speed and surprise were vital, as the foothills had to be cleared by 11 pm to give the main assault columns enough time to reach the ridgelines before dawn.

It was Russell's first offensive operation at Gallipoli, and an extremely difficult and hazardous one. His troops would have to advance in total darkness, over steep, broken country and against a Turkish garrison of unknown strength. To ensure surprise and to avoid his men firing on each other in the dark, the attack would have to be delivered in complete silence, and it was all to be done by men weakened by months of dysentery and enteric fever. Careful planning and attention to detail were critical, and Russell ensured in advance that everyone, from squadron commander to trooper, knew what their role was to be.

The mounteds' first objective, Old No. 3 Post, was an immensely strong position protected by barbed-wire entanglements and buried mines. Two lines of trenches and several strongpoints protected the southern face of the outpost, and several hundred Turkish troops were camped on the far side of the position. Right on 9 pm and as planned, the patrolling British destroyer *Colne* switched on its searchlight and shelled the outpost for 30 minutes, while the Auckland regiment crept up the precipitous south side of the hill, the noise of their approach muffled by the exploding shells.

At 9.30 pm exactly the bombardment stopped and the mounteds stormed the post before the Turks could detonate the protecting minefield. Waikato mounteds and Turks fought hand to hand in the darkened, roofed-over trenches while the Aucklanders attacked the rest of the garrison who were encamped behind the hill. They scattered wildly, leaving behind most of their weapons.

The next major objective, Table Top, was a steep-sided, flat-topped hill approached by difficult ridges and ravines, all overlooked by enemy trenches. Table Top was in turn shelled for 20 minutes before the mounteds cut their way with bayonets and entrenching tools up its precipitous sides, reaching the summit shortly before midnight.

Luck and surprise were with them. Misled by firing at Old No. 3 Post and Bauchop's Hill, most of the Turkish garrison had moved down a gully towards the fighting, leaving their trenches on Table Top unguarded—except for a trench on the southwestern edge which the mounteds quickly overran. When the Turks returned in groups to their positions, 150 of them were taken prisoner.

Further north, the Otago and Canterbury regiments met much stronger resistance at Bauchop's Hill which, like Table Top, was a mass of ridges and ravines, entrenched everywhere. The mounteds advanced up the hill, charging enemy machine guns in the scrub head on, taking row after row of Turkish trenches before finally reaching the summit around midnight. By 1 am on 7 August Russell's force was in occupation of Old No. 3 Post, Table Top, and Bauchop's Hill. Eighty troopers were dead and 230 wounded, but the vital entrances to three valleys were now in Allied hands and the way cleared for the infantry to advance on the Sari Bair ridge. Russell's report of the operation was terse and unadorned; not so that of his superiors. Generals Hamilton and Birdwood commended the thoroughness with which Russell and his brigade commanders had planned the assault and the 'determination and vigour' with which an operation critical to the success of the Allied attack had been carried out.

Australian war correspondent Charles Bean agreed, describing the night assault of the mounted brigade as a 'magnificent feat of arms, the brilliance of which was never surpassed, if indeed equalled, during the campaign'. The taking of Bauchop's Hill by the South Islanders, Bean wrote, was 'a feat of arms of which it is perhaps not too much to say that it is has no parallel in British military history'.[4]

The fighting qualities of the mounted riflemen were a critical factor in their success; the other was the calibre of their commander. Like most World War I commanders facing the grim realities of trench warfare, Russell was learning on the job. But here for the first time he was able to display his planning and tactical skills, and his ability to manage colonial troops under exceptionally difficult conditions. He would repeat the performance as commander of the rearguard in December 1915 when 48,000 Australian and New Zealand troops were evacuated from Gallipoli without losing a man.

On the foothills of Sari Bair Russell laid the foundations of a reputation that would survive the Gallipoli campaign and earn him a knighthood, along with command of the 20,000-strong New Zealand Division that he took to France in 1916. Under his leadership, it would become one of the élite fighting divisions in the British armies that fought on the Western Front in World War I.

Chapter 1

The Frontier of Debt

'Are you going to be satisfied in the future with the position of a small farmer running a thousand sheep on 2,000 acres [809 hectares], and leading a solitary life in the bush, when you might be commanding a regiment?'—Colonel A.H. Russell, writing to his grandson, Guy Russell, then a second lieutenant in the British Army on garrison duty in India.[5]

Guy Russell was born into a pioneering Hawke's Bay family with a long tradition of military and political service. His great-grandfather, Andrew Hamilton Russell the first, enlisted in the Black Watch regiment as a private in 1788 and saw active service under the Dukes of York and Wellington. He fought in the Napoleonic Wars at the Battle of Copenhagen in 1807, took part in the ill-fated Walcheren Expedition of 1809, and died of fever after the Battle of Salamanca in 1811. In recognition of his 23 years of active service, the Duke of Wellington granted his son, Andrew Hamilton Russell the second (Guy's grandfather), an army commission at the age of 16.

Guy's grandfather first came to New Zealand as a captain in the 58th Regiment (Northamptonshires) on the outbreak of the New

Zealand Wars in the 1840s. In 1859, he resigned from the army with the rank of lieutenant-colonel, bought Mangakuri station on the Hawke's Bay coast and farmed it for the next 15 years. During this time, he was appointed a civil commissioner and resident magistrate for Hawke's Bay, served in the Stafford Ministry as Minister of Native Affairs, and was appointed to the colony's Legislative Council. For some years he was also employed as a superintendent of military roads and was responsible for the construction of the Wellington–Paekakariki section of the main route north.

Guy's father, Captain A.H. Russell the third (Ham), and his uncle William (later Sir William) Russell, followed their father into the 58th Regiment before selling their commissions in the British Army and emigrating to New Zealand. In 1862, they went into partnership to farm 14,000 hectares of Maori leasehold land located in rolling hill country between the Tutaekuri and Ngaruroro rivers, 32 kilometres northwest of Hastings. Two other brothers, Herbert and Arthur, would later join them from England, Herbert taking up land near present-day Palmerston North and Arthur a bush property at Ohingaiti in the central North Island.

The brothers, however, had little capital and less farming experience, which made their early years hard going. They had raised some money from the sale of their commissions and had borrowed from family members. Each partner was also entitled to 140 hectares of freehold land as a result of their army service, and they were helped in the early years by advances against their wool clips from the banks that had lent them money. At the time of occupation, their vast holdings were mostly covered in scrub and swamp, which had to be turned by hard manual labour into grass for sheep.

Life on the new runs was primitive. Ham lived communally with two farm labourers in a two-roomed raupo hut on the banks of the Tutaekuri River, subsisting on a diet of wild pork, bread and tea. William joined him in 1862 and together the brothers worked to clear enough land to graze the first small flocks of sheep. Wool was then their sole source of income, and prices—reflecting the general boom-and-bust nature of the late nineteenth-century colonial economy—were erratic. It was also labour-intensive, as bales had to be hauled 50 kilometres downriver by horse-drawn dray to the port of Napier and there loaded onto ships moored off the beach.

In 1864, another 1416 hectares was added to the Russell holdings with the purchase of the Flaxmere lease, but it brought no relief from the problems of pioneering farming. Major floods in 1867, 1876, and 1880 caused much damage to the two properties and many others in Hawke's Bay. They also lost large numbers of lambs to wild pigs; pasture to the newly introduced rabbit pest; and crops and grass seed to rust disease and an expanding population of introduced birds.

But this was frontier New Zealand and there were other challenges to overcome, including a threat to the very lives of the Russell brothers and their families. By 1860, the settler government, backed by British troops and colonial militia, was at war with the Maori tribes of the Waikato and Taranaki over land. In October 1866, the Russells were forced to abandon their homestead for the shelter of Napier when a war party of 200 Maori from Taupo and Tarawera arrived at nearby Omaranui pa with the clear intention of attacking and capturing the town.

Two days later, a force of settler militia and 'friendly' Maori under Colonel George Whitmore made the first move, attacking the pa on the banks of the Tutaekuri River after its defenders refused a call to surrender. Forty Maori were killed, including their chief Kepa and the prophet Panapa, and another 40 taken prisoner. Whitmore's staff officer in that engagement was Ham Russell, who narrowly escaped death himself when his horse reared and threw him into the line of fire.

In 1870, the Russell brothers began negotiations to buy the two leasehold blocks from their Maori owners. William expected no opposition to this because the land was well removed from existing Maori settlements and surrounded by Crown land. A pragmatic man, he observed that many Maori had 'taken to drink' and were heavily in debt to local merchants. This made him think that they were even more likely to sell.

Lack of capital was the immediate problem. William told his brother that if they could not raise enough money from other sources—presumably the banks—he would return to England and marry a daughter of the Hodgskin family of Sherenden in Sussex. The union, however, depended on the father making a good settlement on her—'my choice to be reserved until the articles are inspected'. Within two years, William had inspected Harriet Hodgskin and married her, accepting a settlement of 5000 pounds from her presumably willing family. In 1864, his brother likewise returned to England and married Katherine Sarah Tinsley of Sedgley, daughter of a wealthy nail manufacturer, in Staffordshire.

With the capital raised from the two marriages the two properties were finally bought, but the former Maori owners—assisted by European 'native agents' and lawyers—made repeated efforts to repudiate the sale. Their grounds were that neither the agreed commission nor the 3000-pound purchase price had been paid, that the certificate of title had been obtained by fraud, and that there were defects in the original deeds of conveyance.

The Russell brothers saw these claims as attempts by local Maori and their agents to extort money from them as legal owners of the land, and fought them vigorously through the courts. In the end, they won the case, but it was not until 1885 that they were finally guaranteed legal title to Tunanui and Flaxmere.

Their financial position was eased, however, by the steady development of the land. By 1873, large tracts of manuka and fern had been cleared, ploughed and sown, and a new homestead and woolshed built. By 1875, the Tunanui and Flaxmere stations were shearing 20,000 sheep between them. In 1882, refrigerated shipping revolutionised the colony's trade with Britain, enabling farmers like the Russell brothers to export sheepmeat as well as wool. A year later, the new manager of Tunanui could claim, with some exaggeration, that the run was now 'like the Garden of Eden in a wilderness'.

Chapter 2

The Reluctant Schoolboy

'Off he went as bold as a lion and did not want me to accompany him . . . He began Latin and looked grave over it; gave a boy a bloody nose in his first scrimmage.'—Ham Russell recalls his son Guy's first day at school in England.

Guy Russell was born on 23 February 1868, the elder son and second of a family of seven (Mildred, Guy, Gwen, Gertrude, Muriel, Claude, and Evelyn) born to Ham Russell and his wife, Katherine, over the next 10 years. By the time of Guy's birth, Ham and William had moved from their primitive whare on the banks of the Tutaekuri and were farming the Russell blocks from Redclyffe, an ample two-storey homestead further down the river towards Napier.

As with most of the New Zealand frontier in the 1860s, settlement in Hawke's Bay was sparse: the roads were unpaved tracks, the rivers mostly unbridged, and social life was limited. The Russell's nearest neighbours were the Maori at Omaranui pa and a few scattered settlers at Taradale, now a suburb of Napier. Deprived of the companionship of children their own age, the Russell children turned to each other, and it was here that the foundations of Guy's close and lifelong relationship with his sisters, Milly and Gwen, were laid. It was at Redclyffe, too, that Guy and his grandfather forged the bond that endured until the colonel's death in 1900—a bond that helped to mould Guy's character and his career.

Although he was now a resident magistrate in Hawke's Bay, by 1874 Ham had had his fill of the hardships, isolation and crudities of life in Britain's most remote colony. That year he took his family back to England. They settled in Sedgley, the home of his widowed and wealthy mother-in-law Eliza Tinsley.

The voyage home, however, was marred by tragedy when their youngest child, Mary, died of dysentery in New York. Guy was then just six, but already the traits that would define the man were beginning to appear. Family members recalled that he played a leading part in the arrangements for the funeral of his infant sister. His father noted that his son did not flinch when asked to go down into a dark cellar in Sedgley; and that he endured a burn to his foot from a firecracker without complaint. After a visit to the Polytechnic in London, Guy showed 'a good deal of cool courage' in withstanding an electric shock from one of the exhibits. He had also asked to venture down in a diving bell—presumably in a deep-water tank.

In March 1876, Guy attended his first school, the Miss Hills School at Lynmouth. For the first time he was in the company of boys his own age, and his education out of the hands of governesses. His stay was to be shortlived. In 1877, bored with the staid life of Victorian England and thinking that the future of his family still lay in the Antipodes, Ham Russell brought his wife and children back to New Zealand.

They settled at Moorlands, the home originally built by his father at Flaxmere, where the family enjoyed a social life considerably better than that at Redclyffe three years earlier. There were dinner parties and luncheons, many guests and callers. Ham organised shooting parties, which Guy, now aged nine, was allowed to join.

The return lasted just 16 months. Beset by worries about finance, low returns from farming, and the 'rascally lawyers and native agents' who were challenging the title to the Russell lands on behalf of their former Maori owners, Ham sent his family back to England, settling finally at Lausanne in Switzerland. Here, supported by income from the family properties in Hawke's Bay, Ham lived for most of the next 35 years as a so-called 'gentleman of leisure'. The task of managing the Russell estates now fell largely on William, who was already heavily involved in colonial politics.

Guy remained in England to complete his education, first as a boarder at Twyford preparatory school, near Winchester—a school described by author Thomas Hughes, the author of *Tom Brown's Schooldays*, as 'a rough, badly managed, bullying place'. From a close-knit, affectionate family and an adventurous open-air life in the colonies, he was now confined within the rigid structures of the British public school system. He hated it. Letters to his parents at this time reveal an unhappy and bewildered 10-year-old boy desperate to be out of boarding school and back home with his family in New Zealand.

'I would rather than anything be out in New Zealand and riding to the post on a message or to get the letters and it always makes me sad to think of them,' he wrote to his father. 'Are all the little birds that I used to try and shoot gone away now. Is the drain running well and I hope that the fat cattle paddock's fence is getting put up better. I suppose that the hawkes [*sic*] have stopped trying to kill the lambs.' To his unbending mother, he wrote: 'I have not had one happy day since I came here. I so often feel sad.' By the last term of his incarceration, Guy's attitude to boarding school life had not changed: '[I] will be glad to leave this Black Hole of Calcutta.'

Guy gradually overcame his homesickness—if not his dislike of boarding school—and his intelligence and capacity for leadership began to surface. He passed out top of the fifth form at Twyford, and in his last year there was head of house. Guy's grandfather, whose home at Winchester was his out-of-school base, had by now formed a high opinion of his grandson's intellectual capabilities and felt that he was fitted for a career other than the traditional ones of army officer or farmer. He favoured a scientific career after taking a degree at Oxford or at the higher levels of the British civil service. Ham, equally ambitious for his son, thought a career in law the better option; alternatively a study of 'agricultural theory' and then practical experience running the family farms back in New Zealand.

Both were to be disappointed. In 1882, Guy went on to Harrow, one of England's élite public schools. Founded in 1572, Harrow had already produced many eminent men, including Captain James Cook's botanist, Sir Joseph Banks; the Romantic poet Lord Byron; novelists Anthony Trollope and John Galsworthy; playwright Richard Sheridan; prominent reformer Lord Shaftesbury; and Prime Minister Sir Robert Peel, founder of the modern police force and the British Conservative Party.

Guy Russell was now part of a world of rigid tradition that included the wearing of morning suits, straw boaters and top hats, and a curriculum focused on English history, French, the Classics (Greek and Latin), and mathematics. Social life was bounded by 'houses', each of which competed fiercely against all the others for sporting trophies. None of it made any noticeable difference to his attitude to boarding school life. 'I get to dislike this place more and more,' he wrote to his father. 'I believe I have heard you say that Uncle Arthur disliked it. I certainly detest it.'

Not surprisingly, Guy performed poorly at Harrow—to the chagrin of his father, who wanted him to be the school's leading boy and to excel academically. School reports refer to him being slovenly and neglectful, inconsistent in performance, surly in demeanour and self-centred in his approach to his duties. His form master's report in May 1885, two months before he left Harrow, commented: 'A poor creature, I am sorry to think. Won't do his best or anywhere near it.' Guy's housemaster, J.A. Cruickshank, with whom he clashed often, described him as 'a nice manly boy' but inclined to be rebellious and too easily led. Guy's comment on Cruickshank after one of their frequent rows: 'He's a mean beast at best.'

In later years, Guy would admit to a dislike of schoolmasters—probably, he admitted, because he recognised some of the same critical, controlling instincts in himself. His apathy and poor academic performance he would blame on chronic indigestion, a condition that continued to blight his life until the age of 21, when he 'pretty well overcame it'.

Guy's experience of Harrow, however, was not entirely negative. He enjoyed football and cricket, although he didn't claim to be outstanding at either. Significantly, he took a keen interest in the school cadet corps; and he read constantly, mostly novels, to the displeasure of his masters, who regarded this sort of activity 'as sinful in one so young' and positively 'criminal' if done in class. When he left Harrow he took 100 books with him, many of which had been confiscated by his form masters.

Now in his mid-teens, Guy relished the term holidays at his Uncle George's farm in Wales and at his father's new home at Lausanne. There he played tennis and went fishing, boating, horse riding, and climbing in the Swiss Alps with his father, Ham, who was a keen mountaineer, and occasionally with his sisters. Among these expeditions was a father-and-son ascent of the Matterhorn (4478 m), one of the highest and deadliest peaks in the Alps, and a severe test of skill and nerve for any but the most experienced mountaineers. With his father's enncouragement, Guy was beginning to indulge his penchant for extreme risk-taking.

Along with this physical activity, Guy had an active social life of amateur theatricals, parties and dancing, which he enjoyed to the full but only increased his dislike of boarding school. In the words of family biographer, Colonel Reg Gambrill: 'The very thought of school was anathema to him, yet he had a brilliant mind and a very strong sense of filial duty to his parents. These two factors seemed eternally at war within him.'[6]

Guy Russell emerges from his school days as an intellectually able but uncommitted student—as was his near contemporary, Winston Churchill. Churchill entered Harrow three years after Russell, but there is no evidence that they were aware of each other. The similarities of character and experience, however, were marked. Both hated their prep schools and neither did well academically at Harrow, although both read voraciously and at a level beyond their years. Both were confirmed individualists and uncomfortable with the constraints and disciplines of boarding school life.

In one of history's smaller ironies, Churchill would go on to head the Royal Navy as First Lord of the Admiralty and devise the strategy that became the disastrous Gallipoli campaign of 1915. Russell would emerge as one of the few effective commanders in that campaign, lead the rearguard that saw nearly 50,000 Australians and New Zealanders evacuated safely from its beaches, and blame his fellow Harrovian for what he considered an avoidable military disaster.

Chapter 3

The Making of a Soldier

'I understand your father to say that in going into the Army you do so with the intention of becoming a real soldier and not a drone which is content to plod on and see himself passed by men of more pluck and energy than himself. If so, the sooner you take to work the better.'—Guy Russell's grandfather, 'the Colonel', writes to him on his entry to the Royal Military College, Sandhurst, in September 1886.

When Guy Russell entered Harrow, he carried with him his family's ambitions for a career in law, science or the civil service. However, there was the management of family properties in Hawke's Bay to be considered, as well as grandmother Eliza Tinsley's business interests in England. In the event, the reports from Harrow destroyed any hopes of Guy's entrance into Oxford to study for a law or science degree, and he opted—like his father and grandfather before him—for a military career.

It was an inspired, if not unpredictable choice. After spending several months in Germany sharpening his command of the language, Guy sat the entry examination for the Royal Military College,

Sandhurst. He passed with the second-to-top marks in his intake, unlike Douglas Haig, the man destined to command all British and Dominion forces on the Western Front in World War I. Haig scraped into Sandhurst a few years before Russell with the greatest difficulty; and Henry Wilson, who would eventually rise to be chief of imperial general staff, failed the entrance exam three times before being finally admitted.

At that time, physique and prowess at games rather than intellectual ability tended to be the standard by which officer cadets of the time were selected and later promoted. Russell, at 5 feet 7 inches in height (1.72 metres) and not particularly good at games, would seem to have been disadvantaged, but a family tradition of service to the military, proficiency in French and German, and high marks in the entrance examination would have been hard to ignore.

Given the emotional turmoil of his life that year, however, Guy showed considerable mental toughness in passing at all. He was besotted with his tennis partner, Violet Brooke, who was allegedly playing him off against her other male friends, and the 'devil of jealousy' had raised its ugly head. More seriously, he had for several months watched the slow decline of his mother's health and was compelled to sit the examination just two days after her death from tuberculosis at the age of 43.

In September 1886, Guy took his place at Sandhurst and at last found his niche. With his interest now fully engaged, the young New Zealander relished the college routines and disciplines, the company of his fellow cadet officers, and his courses, both academic and practical. Among these were military history and tactics and Russell excelled in both. His overall performance was rated by his examiners as 'exemplary'.

Sandhurst in the 1880s, however, was an unpromising environment for young officers soon to face the grim realities of twentieth-century warfare. Training still focused on solid line formations, mechanical precision, a rigid dependence on order, and firing strictly in volleys on the word of command. Artillery doctrine had not moved forward since the Crimean War 30 years before, and machine guns could be written off as 'suitable only for the destruction of savages and hardly suitable for use against white men'.[7] Russell's near contemporary, Major-General J.F.C. Fuller, remembered being taught a lot of obsolete tactics and doing 'a tremendous lot of useless drill'.[8]

Although a staff college had been established to remedy the deficiencies exposed by the Crimean War, officer training had a distinctly anti-intellectual cast. Polo and pig-sticking (in India) were the occupations of choice, and any sort of book work 'quite beyond the pale'.[9] As for leadership at unit level, 'Officers were still so busy being gentlemen, in or out of gorgeous uniforms, that they had little time for their men and a total lack of concern for the latter's welfare.'[10]

Arrayed in such uniforms, Russell and his fellow cadets paraded at Buckingham Palace in June 1887 as an honour guard during ceremonies to mark the fiftieth anniversary of Queen Victoria's reign. It was all too much. After standing in the sun for five hours without food, Guy and several other young soldiers collapsed and had to be revived with the help of 'two bottles of brandy and smelling salts, a camp stool and two umbrellas, all the gifts of a sympathetic crowd'.

Guy Russell emerged from Sandhurst in August 1887 with the Sword of Honour, awarded as the best cadet of his course—the first New Zealand-born officer to achieve that distinction. In January 1888, as a freshly commissioned subaltern, he was posted to the 1st Battalion of the Border Regiment, in which two generations of Russells had already served, then stationed at Sialkot some 350 kilometres from India's volatile North-West Frontier.

Thirty years earlier, the Indian Mutiny, involving mainly Hindu troops of the British Indian Army, had plunged much of north and central India into rebellion against British rule. The uprising was eventually defeated, but Russell's intended regiment was now part of the network of garrisons that would underpin imperial control of

India. They would remain until Britain's most prized overseas territory ('the Jewel in the Crown') was finally granted independence in 1947.

Russell sailed from Portsmouth bound for Bombay via Suez where he spent an uneventful two hours ashore seeing nothing but 'dirt a la Orient'. Back aboard ship he relieved his boredom by pelting the Arab boatmen with oranges. Subsequent visits to Suez would not be so mundane. In 1915, Russell returned in command of a mounted rifles brigade defending the Suez Canal against an attack by Turkish troops, and went on to command the brigade at the debacle that was Gallipoli. A year later, he went back to Suez to form and train his country's first infantry division for service on the Western Front.

The regiment that Russell joined in northern India would have been typical of the British Army in the 1880s—officered by the sons of gentlemen who had attended élite public schools, its soldiers drawn mostly from the industrial and rural working classes. 'A rough lot,' Fuller put it, 'simple, tough, illiterate, largely recruited from down-and-outs, men who had got into trouble, vagabonds, and a sprinkling of the sons and grandsons of NCOs and private soldiers.'[11]

The reality of service with the British Army, however, did not match its early promise. In 1888, there were no major rebellions in India to suppress, or border wars to fight. For the troops there was little to fill their off-duty hours except drinking and sports; for the officers, polo, race-riding, and leave back in England for those who could afford it. Russell found the company of his fellow officers tedious and there was no socialising to be had with 'the natives' who were 'not of gentlemen standard anyway'. The dull routines of peacetime soldiering were broken only by regular pig-hunting expeditions and polo tournaments.

The young subaltern took both very seriously, relishing the thrill of the chase and the hard riding in rough country. He bought a wild, hill-bred pony—'a splendid pig-sticker but an awful man-eater'—from a fellow officer who had found him too unruly to ride. It repaid him by ripping off his little finger while he was feeding it, but it could have been worse: 'He might have got me down and trampled on me,' Guy wrote to his family,' which might have been an awkward business as these country hill-bred ponies are like the natives, regular savages.' Of his growing fondness for polo, Russell observed: 'I think the game keeps one up to the mark . . . there is more risk and [it] requires more nerve and dash than any other game.'

As in his schooldays, Russell's leave was spent mostly with the family at the Château de Perroy overlooking Lake Geneva, where his father Ham now lived with his new French wife, Stephanie Lagier. Here Guy met Lili de Saugy, a wealthy and well-connected young Frenchwoman, and embarked on the first serious relationship of his life. Details of the courtship are scarce, but Lili remembered him as 'a serious young man, at the same time gay, lively, and likeable . . . probably the best tennis player of our set, and the best dancer'. Guy attended church every Sunday, rode regularly and participated in bathing parties at the lake, where, Lili recalled, the women were kept 50 metres away from the men 'for decency's sake'.

In May 1888 came a demonstration of the self-sufficiency and independence of mind that would mark Russell's later years in senior command. He passed up the chance of leave with his fellow officers at Murree or Dalhousie, where there was female company aplenty but little else to do to pass the time. Instead, he went hunting red and black bear, musk deer and chamois in the mountains of Kashmir, accompanied only by his Indian shikari (guide) and two 'coolies' to carry essential food and gear. The all-day hunting delivered not only several trophies but a considerable boost to his self-confidence. Camped in the snow at 3000 metres, he wrote to his sister: 'I have enjoyed the whole thing immensely, and feel as if I was worth twice as much as before I came.'

However agreeable in parts, the life of a peacetime soldier did not suit the ambitious young New Zealander. From the start, he itched to be on active service—preferably on the volatile North-West

Frontier—and away from the tedious garrison life of drills, company inspections, the issuing of rations and checking of accounts. He wrote to his grandfather: 'I am bound to say that all I care about is service. I don't care a straw for the sword at my side, I only care for it in the hand.' Guy's frustrations were not helped by low army rates of pay, and what he considered to be slack standards of discipline and turnout in his regiment. 'For those who want soldiering pure and simple,' he complained to his father, 'this service is no good.'

For intellectual stimulus and emotional relief, Guy turned to a study of the Hindustani and Persian languages, and to his beloved cello. There was even the promise of another romance, for accompanying him on the piano was Miss Warburton, a young woman of mixed English/Afghani origins—'her father being the son of an Afghan princess who ran away with a Colonel Warburton during our last occupation'.

The racism and snobbery prevalent amongst the British ruling élite in India at the time was no deterrent to Guy's pursuit of Miss Warburton; nor, it seemed, was his ongoing engagement to Lili de Saugy. In a letter to a sister, he hinted that he expected soon to announce a new engagement, but for reasons unknown the promised liaison did not come to pass.

In December 1888, the Border Regiment left India for garrison duty at Mandalay in Burma, which had been declared a province of British India in 1886. Here at last was the promise of real soldiering against elusive bandit gangs called 'dacoits', which had begun a campaign of guerrilla warfare against the country's colonial rulers. Again it was not to be. Another unit was preferred over the Borders for service on the subsequent Chin Hills expedition, and Russell now expected the regiment to be confined permanently to 'chowkidar' (watchman) duty, as it had been for the last 15 years in India.

When a column of the regiment was finally deployed against the dacoits, his colonel refused to let him go because the young lieutenant was now responsible for training its mounted infantry and could not be spared. In a minor skirmish, however, Russell's company attacked a jungle village and took some prisoners, but achieved little more. The so-called 'shadows in the forest' would go on fighting the British until 1890, when they finally gave up the unequal struggle.

In May 1889, Russell was sent to join five other British officers commanding a regiment of Indian troops at Miajuri in the ruby mines district of Bernardmyo, some 200 kilometres northwest of Mandalay. He remembered it as 'a small wretchedly built little village of bamboo huts and wooden shanties perched 6,000 feet [about 2000 metres] high in a hollow surrounded by fern hills ... of the most uninteresting and ugly description'.

The region thoroughly depressed him with its eternal rain, fever and atrocious food. The situation was not improved by his feelings towards the native troops (sepoys) of his regiment, whom he described as 'a miserable apology for soldiers'. The compensations were cheap living and card games at night with his fellow officers, but he also made time to grow a rose garden and press on with his language studies. The damage, however, had been done. By March 1890 Guy was writing to his sister Milly: 'My ambition, never a strong feature, is dead, though I manage to get through a certain amount of work, more because I hate being left behind than from any wish to be in front.'

Seeing no hope of active service unless he got into one of the best regiments, Guy was tempted to leave the army. In June 1890, a bout of malaria gave him a temporary escape: too sick to continue duty at Miajuri, he was sent home to New Zealand for six months to recuperate. Returning to the country of his birth was a deliberate choice because he knew it would give him a chance to compare his present life in the army with career options in New Zealand.

Money appears to have been a major concern, although as a beneficiary of his grandmother Tinsley's will, Guy was now receiving an extra 1500 pounds a year. Even so he considered his pay as a serving officer insufficient; and the pension he would receive on retirement from service would also be inadequate if he had to depend on it to support a family.

There was the worry, too, that he would never accumulate enough capital to later take up farming in New Zealand, or anywhere else. He rated his prospects for promotion to senior rank, and therefore better pay, as poor—'nearly 20:1 against commanding a battalion'. The only way to get ahead in the army, he concluded, was being on active service or 'having friends at the War Office'.

But if the peacetime British Army offered Guy Russell few financial rewards and outlets for his energies and talents, he still preferred the military life to any other. Also, by this time other qualities that would help shape the future battlefield commander were beginning to surface—among them a passion for efficiency and good discipline. From India, he had written criticising the slovenly discipline in his battalion; and from Burma, of his determination to have the smartest company in the regiment. A sense of his fitness for higher command was also emerging: 'I am sure I have more ability to command than the average fellow, and that I am more practical,' he wrote to his father. These qualities, he felt, had been largely dormant until now.

Meanwhile, sick leave in New Zealand was beginning to pall and the prospect of staff college in England held no attractions ('this eternal theory without practice'). Guy Russell wanted to be where there was some prospect of real soldiering, possibly in South Africa: 'I see the makings of a squabble with the Boers by today's telegrams and wish I was at home [England], for it would have been a good opportunity should anything turn up, as my health is now quite right.'

In December 1890, Guy's sick leave came to an end and he was ordered to rejoin his regiment, now home from Burma, at Dover. As expected, he found life as a barracks soldier in England unbearable, and over the next few months applied, unsuccessfully, to join the British East Africa Company, the British South Africa Company, and the Bechuanaland Border Police. Finally, seeing no hope of action abroad unless he was posted to one of the 'best' regiments, Russell decided to resign his commission in the British Army and return to farming in New Zealand.

His grandfather, who had done so much to shape his character and ambitions, tried to dissuade him. He doubted whether Guy, accustomed to a privileged life in the army, would be mentally and physically tough enough to endure the primitive and lonely life of a colonial small farmer 'living on sour, heavy bread and often ill-cooked mutton'. His grandson would do better, he wrote, investing whatever capital he had in mortgages and 'living the life of a gentle-man'. Better still, he should stay in the army, where he would at least have 'a clean shirt every day, his boots blacked, and the prospect of one day commanding a regiment'. In similar vein, Guy's Uncle Arthur warned him that 'the bush on the West Coast abounds with young gentlemen, chiefly "Army failures", who get small sections, do their own cooking, and whom no one sees or wants to see'.

In June that year Guy Russell was appointed to the Indian staff corps and sent, as he had asked, back to Burma. What he had not asked for was garrison duty with the 25th Madras Infantry—clearly not one of the best regiments. Again, he felt cheated of the chance of active service and had nothing but contempt for the sepoys with whom he now had to serve. 'If I did not care overmuch for a British regiment,' he complained to his sister, 'this is 50 times worse.'

The end came in August the following year. Ordered to cut short his three months of leave with his family in Switzerland and rejoin his old regiment in Dover—effectively a return to barracks soldiering in England—Guy Russell resigned his commission 'in a diabolical fit of the blues' and sailed for home.

Chapter 4

Stranger in a Strange Land

'New Zealand is a good country enough to work in, but I cannot imagine living here after my working days are over . . . I don't believe I'm any more of a colonist than you were.'—Guy Russell writes to his father Ham in September 1897.

After five years in the British Army Guy Russell was a regular soldier no more, but the prospect of life as a sheep farmer in Hawke's Bay did not excite him. In the early months, he crossed the Tasman to Victoria and South Australia to assess the prospects of farming there, taking particular interest in the mallee country in northern Victoria, and the potential for investment in Queensland cattle stations. He found nothing to justify a shift of countries, and the Australians he had dealings with were uncouth. 'A miserable lot after Army men,' he wrote to his family. 'The clean shirt business I don't care one straw about, but I do like mixing with gentlemen as I understand the word.'

Guy now considered returning to England to qualify as a lawyer. He also investigated, unsuccessfully, the prospects of his being admitted to the bar in New Zealand—using his Sandhurst examination results as a foundation. In the end, family interests in New

Zealand, combined with a lack of capital, won out. With the agreement of his uncles William and Herbert, Guy would work for two years as a farm cadet on the Russell brothers' properties at Tunanui and Flaxmere, with a view to eventually managing his father's investment in the two runs.

The New Zealand to which Guy Russell had returned after 13 years abroad, however, was not the one he had left. The country was in the grip of a 'long depression' that would run from 1879 to 1896, and the political landscape had entirely changed. A new Liberal Party had swept into power in 1890 with a radical legislative programme that would establish New Zealand for a time as the social laboratory of the world, and would lay the foundations of the modern welfare state.

Unstable political coalitions dominated by big runholders like the Russells had given way to a party of small business, small-farming and working men. As historian Keith Sinclair put it: 'With their defeat in the 1890 election . . . the rule of the early colonial gentry, with their public school or university background, their Latin tags and cultivated English speech, their sheep-runs and their clubs, was done.'[12]

In 1882, the first shipment of frozen meat had been shipped to Britain, opening up an export trade in meat, butter and cheese, all of which could be produced efficiently on relatively small holdings. Living in poverty in the towns, unemployed men, many of them new immigrants, were desperate to exploit the opportunities that were now opening up. The new Liberal Government—first under John Ballance and then under 'King Dick' Seddon—was determined to give them the chance.

In 1892, and in the following years, the Liberals introduced a number of measures designed to encourage or compel big runholders like the Russells to sell undeveloped land to the Crown for subdivision. Among the measures were absentee and graduated land taxes—the first a penalty on absentee owners of property in New Zealand; the second a progressive tax on the unimproved value of land. Between

1892 and 1912, the Government bought over 200 estates totalling 520,000 hectares, on which it settled some 7000 farmers and their families.[13]

Meanwhile, Guy was being initiated by his Uncle Herbert, the manager of Tunanui, into the practicalities of back-country farming—mustering sheep and cattle, dagging, dipping, dosing and weaning. His reactions to this new life appear largely negative, driven no doubt by loneliness and the hard physical life he was now compelled to live. 'I grow country-like, rustic, day by day,' he wrote to his sister in March 1893, 'shaving at rare intervals and not wearing a tie for whole days at a time.'

He judged New Zealand as a good country to work in, but a poor country to live and play in. His work as a farmer he rated as 'intellectually inferior to that of a subaltern in a line regiment'. Society in Hawke's Bay—'a bore almost anywhere'—was intolerable. In short, Russell was feeling his isolation from the social and cultural life of Europe, his brother army officers, and even from a comparatively rough-edged colonial society: 'I no longer look down on the colonial born and bred,' he wrote, 'as I used to be half inclined to do once.'

But there were compensations. Guy spent his weekends setting up a local polo club to meet his need for company and the physical excitement of a sport he had played so vigorously in India. He tried to keep up his reading of serious books, despite the days of hard physical work. On the shelf, and obviously read, was John Stuart Mill's *A System of Logic, Ratiocinative and Inductive*. In spite of his isolation and criticisms of colonial life, however, Guy claimed to have no regrets over his decision to leave the British Army to go farming in New Zealand.

A diversion of sorts came in March 1893 with a visit to Flaxmere by the Governor-General, Lord Glasgow—probably at the invitation of Guy's uncle, William Russell, who had already served in the Atkinson administrations as Colonial Secretary, Minister of Defence and Minister of Justice. Glasgow, a 60-year-old former naval officer, was proving unsuccessful in the post, clashing frequently with his ministers over a range of issues, including defence. In 1874, he had been cleared by a court of inquiry after his ship was wrecked off Miquelon in the North Atlantic. Never overawed by people of high position, Guy saw him simply as 'an old gentleman of courteous manner, sound ideas and weak arguments'.

His Aunt Harriet (wife of William) was not so courteous towards Guy at a dinner in honour of the governor-general and his wife. When the younger Russell, eager for good conversation, attempted to join a discussion on the rights and wrongs of the women's suffrage movement, he was curtly dismissed by Harriet as being too young to know what he was talking about—a very public humiliation and one much resented. 'Harriet has been trying of late,' Guy recorded with commendable restraint. 'A cross-grained nature and one of little pleasure to her surroundings.'

Guy was not invited to the governor-general's garden party that followed, but his letter to sister Milly revealed a cynical appreciation of the aspirations of certain sections of colonial society. 'A garden party to which the common herd was invited en masse gave, I am told, heart-burnings to seekers after social recognition on account of non-introductions to people in high places, and consequent lost opportunities of making a meal off boot-licking.'

By this time, however, Guy was beginning to worry about the future after his cadetship on the two stations was over. In September 1893, he asked his father to declare his intentions: if the runs were sold, he would probably 'clear off' to a newer country; if not, was it worth his while to 'hang on for the management, which I presume you will give me. My meaning is, in plain English, what am I steering for?' A year later, nothing seemed to have changed. In a letter to his grandfather in August 1894, Guy expressed himself anxious to make an arrangement with his father that would put him on a more or less independent footing. 'I hate this sort of hanging on to other people's coat-tails.'

The early 1890s appear to have been particularly hard years for Guy—unenthusiastic about farm life, lonely, and largely in the dark about his father's plans for the two Hawke's Bay properties. There was also a nagging sense of potential unfulfilled. 'At 26,' he wrote to his sisters, 'one has pretty well found out that one is not more or less . . . than the average man. I often feel that I am not flying my kite high enough. But since I have left the service, I have hardly seen how to fly it.'

By 1894, he was unhappy enough to want to return to England and risk his father's displeasure. He appears to have been persuaded out of it by his Uncle Arthur, then farming a large tract of bush country at Ohingaiti on the other side of the Kaweka Range. Behind his decision to stay was also a sense of obligation to financially support his family of two sisters in England and his father in Switzerland. He would carry on with his cadetship, and seek solace in his books and playing polo when he could.

In 1895, two events gave Guy's life in New Zealand new focus and stability. By mutual agreement between Ham and William that year, the Russell brothers' partnership was amicably dissolved, each receiving about 4000 hectares of the original Tunanui and Flaxmere blocks under the terms of settlement. After assisting his father through the division process, Guy took over from Uncle Herbert as manager of Tunanui and the new Twyford station, which were Ham's share of the now subdivided Russell properties.

In this year also, Guy's lonely bachelor life came to an end. His liaison with Lili de Saugy had terminated in 1893 when Lili herself called off their engagement. This might have hurt his pride, but caused no permanent emotional damage. 'Am very glad,' he wrote in his diary, 'which shows how much protestations of eternal affection are worth in my case.' Over the next two years, he courted Gertrude Mary Beetham Williams, of Frimley, Hastings, the daughter of one of Hawke's Bay's most prominent landowning families and a young woman likely to contribute considerable assets to a marriage.

Gertrude, however, was in no hurry to succumb, and refused him more than once. At one point in the courtship Guy turned up at the Williams homestead and asked the maid if 'Miss Gertrude' was in residence and able to see him. Back came her reply: 'Tell Guy Russell he's a fool and is to go away!' On another occasion, Gertrude and Guy were to attend a local ball together. He asked that she wear a white rose if she accepted his offer of engagement and a red one if she did not. She wore a red one.

Persistence, and the services of Gertrude's sister 'Miss Elsie' as a go-between, finally brought success, and in January 1896 Guy wrote to his grandfather seeking his blessing for the union. The campaign for Gertrude's hand, he admitted, had been a long, hard one: 'I must plead guilty of having been on the warpath for some time, but could not succeed sooner in forcing the enemy to capitulate.'

In August 1896, Guy and Gertrude were married at St Matthew's in Hastings. The first of their five children, Katherine, was born the following year, and for the Russells it was a memorable beginning. Returning Gertrude to Twyford from confinement in Hastings involved a rough journey by horse-drawn wagon. The notorious 1897 flood had washed away the bridge at Fernhill, and mother and new baby were ferried across the Ngaruroro River by an old Maori in a canoe while Guy searched the river for a safe ford for the wagon. Soon after, he retired the 'sulky'—a one-person, two-wheeled, horse-drawn cart—as unsuitable for mother and baby, and bought a more roomy 'buggy and pair'.

Overall, the marriage appears to have been a happy one, but it was no meeting of minds. Guy was well read and widely travelled, and could speak several languages fluently. His wife had been educated in Hawke's Bay, had never been out of New Zealand, and her interests and experiences were limited.

What the Russells did share was a strong religious faith and commitment to family, and in the eyes of at least one of their five children, complementary strengths: 'My mother was an excellent partner for him, with her never-failing common sense, fairness and kindness, and was able to restrain him from possibly too quick judgments and decisions, whereas he gave her strength, courage, and devotion.' As later events would show, Gertrude Russell was also a shrewd investor and businesswoman.

Gertrude, however, was unable to break her new husband's addiction to polo. He was now playing regularly for the polo club he had founded, and with his usual aggressive and risk-taking style. In 1896—the year he was married—he smashed his jaw in two places in a horrific accident on the field. His head was bound up and he had to be fed through a tube until an operation could be done to remedy the damage. Five years later, another accident on the polo field would immobilise him for several weeks with a broken leg and dislocated ankle.

Accidents apart, Guy was now firmly settled on his future and could focus on increasing the productive capacity of his new domain. Fences were put in, trees planted and huge areas of land turned into pasture. Between 1896 and 1910, nearly two-thirds of the 9350-acre (3783-hectare) Tunanui block was cleared of scrub, ploughed and sown, most of it financed by bank overdrafts and loans. He was confident by now that he could generate an annual income for his father of 4000 pounds a year. If this could not be done, he wrote to his ageing parent, 'you must just get rid of me'.

From the start, however, there were tensions between owner-father and manager-son. On the one hand were Ham's expectations of a good income from his properties; on the other were the realities of frontier farming—low wool and fat-lamb prices, floods, droughts, caterpillar and grass-grub infestations, and the need for constant improvements. Guy wanted to invest more of his slim profits in the farms themselves and increase his overdraft with the banks. With large borrowings already on both properties, Ham was unwilling to increase his debt and was constantly urging restraint. Guy confessed at one point that reading his father's letters at the end of a hard day's work gave him 'the blues'.

While urging economy, Ham was also quite willing to charge some of his expenses to the station, including the debts of his free-spending younger son, Claude, who was now at Oxford studying law. Guy, much displeased, took a firm line with his father: 'I am sorry Claude's debts are so much, but you must not, as in the case of your original debt to Richardson of 2000 pounds odd, debit it to the station. It is not fair.' Necessity forced him to be exceptionally frugal at this time. His grandson, John Russell, the current owner of Tunanui, recalled that he kept incoming bills in two piles—those that offered a discount and those that did not. To those suppliers who complained about late payment, he would reply, presumably in writing: 'Well, which pile would you like to be in?'

Money worries apart, droughts and the flooding of the Tutaekuri and Ngaruroro rivers were to be recurring problems for the new manager, as they had been for his father and his Uncle William. During one bad drought Guy was forced to sell stock at rock-bottom prices rather than see the animals die from lack of feed. In April 1897, a severe storm dumped 20 inches of rain on Hawke's Bay in 20 hours, washing out roads and bridges, and drowning 120 of his hoggets. The storm also destroyed much new fencing, 50 hectares (123 acres) of new grass, nearly 20 hectares (49 acres) of barley, and deposited a heavy load of river silt on the flats at Twyford. On Tunanui, one dam burst and another silted up, temporarily wiping out the run's water supply.

Guy and his shepherds toiled for hours in driving rain to rescue flocks of sheep trapped in riverside paddocks as the waters of the Ngaruroro rapidly rose. One flock, driven by wind and rain onto the river bank, could not be coaxed to drier ground and had to be left to drown; and Guy himself had to swim his horse back to where a few minutes before there had been dry land. Overall, it could have been worse—several lives were lost in the flooding and one farmer in the district lost over 10,000 sheep.

The following year brought further trials at Tunanui. In April, the expected profit on the barley crop was wiped out when the biggest stack of the harvest was set on fire, possibly by a careless swagger. In August, 'a regular blizzard' carried off 40 or 50 of the breeding ewes Russell had bought just as lambing had begun. It then rained continuously for the following 10 days: 'Work at a standstill. Four teams and six scrubcutters all twiddling their thumbs and eating their heads off,' Guy wrote to his father. The ploughing contractors had given up the job, so he was doing the work himself, entailing a heavy outlay in horses and implements. In October, powerful westerly gales ruined most of the newly sown grass on the run and blew him off his horse at a high point on Tunanui known as The Flag.

Setbacks like these, three years of low wool prices, and lack of development capital fed Guy's nostalgia for the England of his youth and the army life that was now six years behind him. 'The war in South Africa seems a serious affair,' he wrote to his father in 1899. 'I see my old battalion is at the front and often wish I was with it.' He still looked on England as home, vowing that 'if ever some good fairy left me a fortune, I should pack up and say goodbye to this country. However, Gerty and I jog on very comfortably and happily, and if only things will pay well out here, shall feel that I haven't exiled myself in vain.'

Guy recognised early on that the 'virgin fertility' of Tunanui soils was steadily being exhausted by current farming methods and could no longer sustain the large-framed shorthorn cattle and Lincoln sheep with which he had stocked the run. The result was a switch to Hereford cattle and Romney sheep—smaller, lighter-boned animals that were capable of thriving on poorer pasture. Foreseeing also the role that Southdown sheep would play in the development of the fat-lamb industry, Guy established a stud of the breed.

He was also trying new methods and crops. In the pre-war years he experimented with turnips, kale and lucerne for stock feed, and grew large quantities of oats, wheat, barley and grass seed as cash crops. He introduced rotational grazing, a farming practice designed to 'rest' pasture from stock, which was then in its infancy in New

Zealand. In 1902, he began a series of topdressing experiments for the Agricultural Department that steadily increased the carrying capacity of Tunanui pasture. He also began applying lime to his paddocks—one of the first farmers in Hawke's Bay to do so.

By early 1898 Guy could report to his father that he was now running 21,000 sheep on the two properties. The overdraft had increased by 3000 pounds, but a new sheep station (Twyford) was up and running, and they had survived two years of low prices and a disastrous flood. He regretted that his father had not received a better return on his money so far, but felt confident of the future.

The shortage of development capital, however, continued to rankle. In 1900, he wrote to his father in exasperation: 'Owing to a constant and natural desire on your part not to increase the debt beyond its present limits, I am constantly trying to save money against my better judgement. Too often at Tunanui, ploughing, or rather working, is curtailed because of expense . . . It would have taken, say, 30 pounds to make the road properly down to the station, instead of which I spend 5 pounds annually in patching. A grain store would represent a large outlay in one year but would pay for itself in three or four . . . To be undercapitalised is ruinous—nothing more so, unless it be an extravagant manager.'

Guy complained regularly of not being given a free hand to manage Ham's investments in New Zealand as he saw fit. There were unsubtle hints that the old man should now accept a guaranteed income from his properties, 'take a well-earned rest' and no longer interfere: 'It seems to me that either you have confidence in me, or not. If you have, there can be no advantage in tying my hands.'

Staffing problems on the two runs were ongoing. At the end of 1902, Guy reported that his manager, Alick Shaw, and the couple employed as cooks on the station were not getting on, and that the latter were leaving, much to his regret. 'I find their successors extravagant,' he wrote to his father. 'I shall put in a contract-man cook. Not a comfortable arrangement: meaning as it does an exclusive [diet of] meat, bread and potatoes.'

The results of Guy's steady efforts to develop the Russell properties, however, were now beginning to show. In the 1904/1905 year, the two stations made a combined profit of 5670 pounds. Guy reported that Tunanui itself was 'paying well; is in first-rate order, stock, fences and land; and has, I believe, the reputation of being as well managed a hill farm as there is about'.

Now that the financial situation had improved, Guy wanted to increase his investment in the development of the run. He wrote to his no doubt reluctant father: 'I fear this will perhaps frighten you but the fact is that to do this land justice one must work, and to work one must pay, but I can guarantee proportionately higher returns . . . I consider Tunanui now in very fair paying order, but think a great deal more might be made of this place. That is why I am still hankering for ever more money.'

Early versions of the motorcar had the potential to save busy farmers time and physical effort. In April 1903, Guy asked his father in England what he had done about buying one, and if it was to be oil or steam-powered. 'I see that steam are regaining favour. They are great inventions. I wish I had one.' In 1904, Guy indulged his wish and bought a six-and-a-half horsepower two-seater Wolseley, saving him the daily 60-kilometre round trip from Tywford to Tunanui on horseback. 'It [the car] will add years to my life,' he noted, 'and hours to my day.'

In September 1905, Guy made his father an offer. He would lease the two Hawke's Bay properties from him, including livestock and plant, for an annual rental of 4000 pounds, rising to 5000 pounds per annum for the next three years. 'I am now 37,' he wrote, 'and should, I confess, like an opportunity to do something for my children. As it is, I live with one eye on the overdraft and the other on the undrained swamp and the sheep I lose, drowned in the drains. I am at my prime and must either go on, or go back. At any rate, I am prepared to take all risks.' A year later, Ham Russell went further. To reduce the absentee and graduated land taxes he was compelled to pay, he transferred the whole of Tunanui by deed to his son, keeping the much smaller Twyford run for himself.

But political winds were blowing, and by now the Russells were feeling the effects of government moves to encourage big runholders to sell land for resettlement. A Lands for Settlement Act had first been passed in 1892, giving the Government the power to acquire private land for this purpose. Subsequent amendments increased that power by allowing the compulsory purchase of land where the owner refused to sell or exchange.

'The Govt are going in largely for buying out people,' Guy wrote to his father in mid-1901. 'No doubt small settlement, if successful, is a good thing. The compulsory clause is a bad thing, however, and unnecessary. Many of the landowners here are trying to get up an agitation.'

In 1905, the Liberal Government toughened its land-purchasing policy with an amended Land for Settlement Bill. As introduced into Parliament, the Bill prevented anyone from owning land to the value of more than 50,000 pounds. It also prohibited sales of land to any purchaser who owned (including the land purchased) more than 640 acres (259 hectares) of first-class land, 2000 acres (809 hectares) of second-class land, or 3000 acres (1214 hectares) of third-class land.

Although the Russells had not yet been targeted, the owners of the nearby stations had been given formal notice of the Government's intention to take all or part of their runs by compulsory purchase. The proposed limitation on the value of land in private ownership raised Guy's hackles. He wrote to his father: 'So you would, if their proposals are carried, not have been able to transfer by gift or purchase, or will, Tunanui to myself. Hadn't we better get out of this country?'

By early 1906, Guy was in a more accepting frame of mind, and obviously prepared to sell if compelled to do so. Noting that Seddon would shortly be speaking in Hastings and would 'no doubt promise more land for the landless', he wrote: 'I think 2000 acres of Tunanui is all I shall have to worry over in a few years. I daresay it is all for the good of the country.'

In 1907, Guy sold off 3650 acres (1477 hectares) of Tunanui in two lots, reducing his holdings to around 5700 acres (2306 hectares) in total. The possibility that the bulk of the run might be taken by compulsory purchase appears to have been behind the sales. In Guy's mind it would have made sense to sell land while market prices were firm, rather than take the lower prices he might be offered by government purchasing agents. These early sales would also have given him a benchmark price with which to negotiate should the Government require more of the Russell lands.

However, Guy had long been keen to divest the Russells of the flood-prone Twyford run, and now hoped that the Government would buy it. 'Twyford is one of the worst investments I know,' he told his father. 'It pays, in my hands, little interest; does not appreciate in value anything like sound arable land or pasture lands; is located with a big risk in the shape of the river floods. There are many better investments to be had.'

In the end, the shadow passed. Guy kept the remainder of Tunanui, and Twyford was eventually sold. His approach to the taking of land for resettlement, however, would not have been typical of the big landowners of the time. While he was politically opposed to Seddon and the Liberals, and to compulsory purchase, he supported the principle of closer settlement and would lobby actively for it for the rest of his long life.

In 1909, Guy took over Ham's remaining land assets, stock and plant by taking his inheritance early and buying out his brother and sisters' shares by way of mortgages over the Hawke's Bay properties. He now had a good equity in the two runs and was at last his own master, freed from the need to produce a guaranteed income for his father in Switzerland and free at last to plough back his profits into developing the land.

Chapter 5

Facing Up to Fear

'Looking back, I realise what a wonderful friend as well as father
he was; sometimes talking to us, pointing out a lovely view or
sunset, and trying to make us appreciate anything of interest or
beauty—sometimes silent and full of thought, and sometimes
laughing at us (he was a terrific tease) but never unkindly.'

In Gertrude's mind, at least, the new independence of the New Zealand
Russells required a residence to match. In 1912, the old homestead
that had been transported piece by piece from its original site above
the Tutaekuri River was pulled down. In its place rose the magnificent three-storey, Natusch-designed homestead that now stands at
Tunanui, with its rimu-panelled halls, servants' quarters, plantings of
beautiful trees and gardens. It cost about 10,000 pounds to build—
a huge outlay in the currency of the time—and Guy Russell told
his grandson John in later years that the project nearly broke him.
Although he was happy to have pleased his wife by agreeing to it, he
would clearly have been content with something much more modest.

Meanwhile, there were the demands of family, and particularly
those of his five growing children—Katherine (Kath), Janet (Jan),

Subaltern Guy Russell passing out from Sandhurst with the sword of honour for best cadet officer of his year, December 1887.

Three generations of Russells. L to R: Guy, his father Ham, and his grandfather 'The Colonel', late 1880s.

The Russell brothers in 1895. Standing L to R: Arthur, William (later Sir William), Gerald (Rear Admiral, Royal Navy). Seated: (left) Herbert and (right) Guy's father Ham.

Katherine (Kate) Tinsley, Ham's wife and Guy's mother.

Above: Gertrude
Williams in her teens.
Right: Gertrude Russell
(nee Williams), 1896.

The first dwelling built at Tunanui by the Russell brothers—a two-roomed whare on the banks of the Tutaekuri River, 1860s.

Guy's sister Milly taking tea on the front lawn at Tunanui with Gertrude and Guy, about 1900.

The Russell family take tea at Tunanui, about 1912. L to R: Gertrude, John, Janet, Andy, Guy and Kath; Margot is in front.

The Russell family homestead at Tunanui in Hawke's Bay soon after it was built in 1912. Guy admitted that the expense nearly broke him financially.

Guy with three of his children, about 1912. L to R: John, Margot and Andy.

Guy and Gertrude's second son, Lieutenant-Colonel John Tinsley Russell DSO, killed in action in Libya, September 1942.

The Russell homestead at Tunanui in the early days (1920s–30s).

The funeral procession of Major-General Sir Andrew Russell leaving St Matthew's Church, Hastings, December 1960.

Andrew (Andy), John and Margot—all born between 1897 and 1906. Family records reveal a strict but affectionate father, requiring obedience, good manners and self-discipline of his offspring, including physical training before breakfast. From an early age the Russell children were taught to ride and shoot. Before lunch every Sunday, the family would gather for prayers.

Not unusually for the time, Guy believed in corporal punishment—for the girls as well as the boys. His daughters mostly got a stern lecture or a smack on the hand; if the boys had had a scrap, they were told to fight it out with staves or boxing gloves. Nor were there many idle moments—the Russells worked the station as a family, with the boys and girls all riding with their father to help muster sheep and cattle, helping in the yards, or burning the manuka left by the scrubcutters. Where chores on the farm had to be done, Guy would give the orders and expect them to be carried out to the letter; if not, the children would be sent back to finish the job.

Guy encouraged his children to both think for themselves and to face their fears. Fear, he told them, destroyed much of the enjoyment of life and had to be rooted out. Kath remembered him patiently helping her overcome her fear of jumping her pony, rock climbing, diving from heights and, later, flying. Margot remembered her father as 'always terrific fun out riding, urging us on to exploits of all sorts'.

Driving with their father was another risky experience for the young Russells. He always drove his cars as fast as possible along narrow country roads, and had many near-misses and several accidents. In later years, Kath recalled the impact of Guy's risk-taking on her mother: 'My dear and poor mother, who was also of a nervous disposition, must have and did suffer from my father's sometimes wild escapades—for he had no fear of anything—or if he did, never showed it.'

Guy and Gertrude were keen for their children to have the best education, and at that time the best was, arguably, still in Europe. They intended to send the two boys to Harrow, like their father had been, and the girls to a finishing school in Paris. In the meantime, the children were home-schooled by a succession of governesses, who stayed if they could stand up to the boisterous and assertive Russell brood. If they could not, they left—as did a good number of the domestic staff.

The Russells insisted on a good grounding in the arts and music, and so the drawing room at Tunanui became the classroom for their musical education. It included a trio consisting of Guy playing the cello, Kath the piano, Jan the violin, with their mother conducting. The ensemble was not a great success because Guy's timing was poor and Gertrude would eventually give up in despair. As Kath said later, 'It was the same with his dancing—he preferred a hard gallop.'

In the quiet times Guy would read to his children—mostly favourite stories from the classics or poetry—or entertain them with tales of his army days in India and Burma. Every summer, the family would go picnicking at Konini Creek or at the site of the old Tunanui homestead above the Tutaekuri River. There the children were taught to swim, catch small crayfish (koura) and eels and, when they were older, to swim their ponies across the river.

Their father's whimsical sense of humour and genuine interest in what young people thought made him a fine companion for his children. He also liked vigorous discussion and well thought-out opinions, even if they did not agree with his own. He became impatient if his offspring (or house guests) simply parroted the views of someone else, and he would sometimes change sides in a discussion 'just for the hell of it'. If Guy Russell had a fault, it was impatience with family members who showed fear, or whose mental processes— 'uptake' in the parlance of the time—were not as quick as his own.

The Russell children were all to inherit their father's prodigious energy, if not his seeming indifference to danger: Kath, short, plump, unsure of herself in the realm of vigorous physical activity but a talented organiser and perhaps the only one who was intellectually a match for their father; Jan, slim, athletic, impulsive, and 'brave as a lion'; Margot ('the little general'), impulsive too, but also immensely kind, and a skilful horsewoman; John, energetic, extroverted, physically courageous and a natural leader. In a family of extroverts, Andy—diffident, private and reserved by nature—stood out. Like his brother John he was not scholastically inclined, but was to make his mark in later years as a highly successful Gisborne farmer.

Farm and family dominated those early years, but Guy sought other outlets for his energy and leadership abilities. In 1899, he had helped form the 15,000-strong Farmers' Union, and in 1903 he was elected chairman of its Hawke's Bay branch. A prime union goal was the abolition of a protective tariff that compelled farmers to buy what they saw as expensive and shoddy locally made goods, and which, by creating jobs in 'unnecessary' industries, had caused a shortage of rural labour. The union also wanted to secure for farmers who held their land on lease-in-perpetuity the right to convert to freehold. 'It is solid,' Guy wrote of the new union, 'has sensible, shrewd views—a little self-seeking perhaps, but in no sense a tool of either [political] party.'

Guy's efforts to increase local membership of the union, however, were frustrated by apathy, and by what he saw as the bigger landholders' mistrust of small-farmers. At national level, he felt that the union lacked political clout: 'It is not productive to merely pass resolutions which Ministers receive politely and then shelve. What they want is a little fighting blood, but they are terribly anxious not to hurt anyone's feelings, or play the part of dictator, and consequently their influence is, so far, very little political.'

Guy Russell's public life did not end there. His interest in soldiering had revived and by now he was working to establish the first volunteer mounted rifles squadrons to be set up in Hawke's Bay since the South African War. He was also chairman of the local A&P (Agricultural & Pastoral) Association, chairman of directors of an agricultural implement factory, a director of the Frimley cannery (forerunner of the present-day Wattie's Canneries), and a director of the Hawke's Bay Farmers' Cooperative, a position he held for the next 52 years. 'I mean to retire as much as possible from public duties,' he wrote to his father. 'They interfere with business too much.'

It was not to happen. In 1905, he became deputy chairman of the Hawke's Bay branch of the Political Reform League. The league had its roots in the national associations formed by groups of business-men and farmers in the 1890s to promote conservative views and candidates for political office. In the early 1900s, it put its weight behind Reform Party leader Bill Massey, who campaigned on a policy of firmer resistance to the militant unions, an end to 'socialist' legis-lation, and support for the freehold policy of the Farmers' Union. In 1914, Russell would take his first step into national politics as vice-chairman of the party's Hawke's Bay branch.

As if the demands of family, large-scale farming and his exten-sive business, political and military interests were not enough, Guy became involved in the early 1900s in the management of another three large rural properties. In 1908, his youngest sister Evelyn mar-ried an aristocratic Englishman—Mowbray St John, the youngest son of the 16th Baron St John. Guy felt Australia offered good farm-ing prospects for the newlyweds, and combed the Australian outback by train and car for three weeks looking for a suitable property.

In the end, the hunt came to nothing and the couple was settled on the 2500-acre (1011-hectare) Dunmore run near Ngaruawahia. Despite Guy's tutelage, however, Mowbray was a failure as a farmer. In 1912 the family returned to England, leaving Guy to manage the property until it was sold, to his great relief and a small profit, in 1915.

The same year, Gertrude Russell bought the 6310-acre (2554 hec-tares) Mount View station in partnership with a Mrs Caccia Birch. Guy supervised its purchase and management (with the exception of the war years) until the property was converted into a private company in 1939. In 1914, he added to the family land holdings by buying, in partnership with his cousin Jim Dennistoun, the 4300-acre Craigdean estate at Mangamahu, but sold it at a loss in 1916.

In spite of his heavy commitments, Guy made time for other interests, this time of a quasi-religious kind. Although his beliefs were conservatively Christian, he became a member of the Order of the Table Round, 'a neo-Arthurian mystical and chivalric order' said to have been formed in Britain about 462 AD to bring Christian ideals into the social and political life of the time.

The order first put down roots in New Zealand in 1912 when its forty-first Grandmaster, Dr Robert Felkin, arrived from Britain with his family. Felkin was a man of varied and exotic background—a member of the Hermetic Order of the Golden Dawn, a medical missionary and explorer, a prolific author on Uganda and Central Africa, and an early anthropologist. Felkin's mission on settling in Hawke's Bay was to establish two secret schools. One would be a school of Christian spiritual wisdom and the other a school of Christian chivalry—the Order of the Table Round. Together they would work to spread Christian ideals throughout his adopted country.

Details of Felkin's subsequent activities and Guy's ongoing involvement with the order are sketchy, but on the former's premature death in 1914 Guy was installed as the second New Zealand Grandmaster after earlier initiation as a 'knight' of the order. That year, however, he was compelled to relinquish the title in anticipation of his departure overseas in command of the New Zealand Mounted Brigade. The new Jerusalem that Felkin had planned for the most distant of Britain's dominions would have to wait upon the exigencies of war.

Chapter 6

Return of the Soldier

'The Boer business is very interesting. I want to be off. Bother sheep, but I suppose someone must do the drudge.'—Guy Russell writes to his father in 1889 as a new imperial war threatens in South Africa.

In October 1899, simmering tensions between the British 'Uitlanders' and Boers in southern Africa came to a head and for the second time in 20 years Britain and the Boer republics of Transvaal and Orange Free State went to war. It was the first overseas conflict to involve New Zealand troops and by the time peace was concluded two and a half years later, 10 contingents of mounted rifles volunteers had seen action against the Boers.

Immediately hostilities began, Russell set about establishing the Wellington (East Coast) Mounted Rifles Regiment, with himself as its captain and first commanding officer. The regiment was made up of five squadrons, based separately in Gisborne, Wairoa, Hastings, Napier and Dannevike, and included a troop of Maori. The men provided their own horses and saddles; the Defence Department their rifles and other equipment.

Weekly parades were reinforced with weekend and annual camps at which a Regular Force sergeant-major and Russell worked to develop the keen young volunteers into a functional fighting unit. The raw material they had to work with could not have been bettered. Typically they were young farmers, shepherds and other country men—practical, resourceful men used to working with horses and thinking for themselves.[14]

Russell enjoyed his return to active military life immensely, particularly the fieldcraft exercises in open country. He wrote to his father: 'I had my corps camped out at Okawa for four days this Easter and had great fun on the hills, scouting, tracking and trying to do something practical, and I think I learn more from this sort of thing than ever we were taught on the barrack yard ... it is extraordinary how apt and keen the colonials are.'

Ham was co-opted into his training regimes without compunction. 'I want you to give 10 pounds to the smartest section (4 men) in HB Mounted Rifles of which I am captain,' Guy wrote in July 1900. 'I can't afford it, though I can give time. I think you might see your way to it. We as a family owe HM's [Her Majesty's] uniform some gratitude.'

In June 1901, Russell took his mounteds to Wellington to take part in the festivities arranged for the visit of the Duke and Duchess of York. It was a difficult experience for the 900 men involved, as their camp was 'very uncomfortable and woefully mismanaged ... It rained every day, the tents leaked, the ground was a mud hole ankle deep, and the food bad and only half cooked.' The mounted men paraded in front of the royals, but Russell avoided the reception at Government House and 'the empty honour of shaking hands with them'.

Because of his farming and family commitments, Russell had felt unable to volunteer for active service in South Africa, although he believed he could have gone with the second contingent of mounted rifles as a company commander. Once early problems with leadership, training and administration had been resolved, the 6500 mounted riflemen who did serve in South Africa did so with distinction.

After the South African War ended, the volunteer system went into steep decline—despite a Japanese victory in the Russo–Japanese War of 1904–05 and a German naval build-up that posed a possible threat to Britain's distant colonies. In the early 1900s, the volunteer force consisted of just 14 battalions of mounted rifles and 16 of infantry, along with a small number of artillery batteries, and a few engineer, field ambulance and signals units.

Russell himself was becoming disillusioned with a force based entirely on volunteers, and was contemplating resignation. 'Volunteering,' he wrote to his father, 'is an expensive farce, and merely an excuse for governments to do nothing except possibly laugh at citizen soldiers.' The army, he felt, was in poor condition and only conscription could revive it.

Russell stayed in the saddle but would wait another five years to get his wish. In 1909, an imperial defence conference found the armed forces of Britain's dominions poorly prepared to serve the military needs of the Empire should large-scale hostilities break out.[15] The result was an agreement by the governments of New Zealand, Canada, and Australia to develop properly trained and equipped expeditionary forces for use in overseas imperial emergencies.

That year also, a Defence Act brought in compulsory military training, providing for the establishment of a Territorial Force (TF) of 30,000 men. In 1910, Colonel Alexander Godley and a group of British Regular Army officers, warrant officers and NCOs came to New Zealand to reorganise the Dominion's armed forces. Godley's brief was to establish an effective national army out of the mass of independent squadrons, batteries and companies that made up the existing volunteer force.

By 1914, the country had a field army of two infantry divisions (one in each island) and two mounted rifles brigades, supported by artillery batteries, reserves and coastal defence units. Godley and his

British regulars had transformed the New Zealand Army, bringing local forces to a level of efficiency never before achieved and establishing a sound administrative structure to support them.[16]

Despite his disillusionment with the voluntary system, Russell had worked hard in the years following the South African War to keep his squadrons together and in fighting trim. He was rewarded with a steady rise up the chain of command. In 1907, he was promoted to major of the Wellington (East Coast) Mounted Rifles Regiment, to lieutenant-colonel in 1910, and to the command of the Wellington Mounted Rifles Brigade in 1911.

In 1910, Field Marshal Lord Kitchener, then Britain's most prominent soldier, came to New Zealand to report on the Dominion's defence forces to the Government and the War Office in London. 'Kitchener Camps' were set up in each of the new military districts and Russell was privileged to command his mounted regiment in manoeuvres before the great man in Wellington.

Kitchener's report targeted the inefficiency of the officer corps as the main problem, and Russell agreed unreservedly. Ten days of brigade training at Oringi in May had confirmed his belief that his squadrons lacked cohesion and any sense of instinctive discipline. One round of shrapnel in a real combat situation, Russell complained to his father, would have caused mass confusion and chaos in the ranks. A conference of senior officers the following June was hardly more satisfying 'owing to military etiquette which in itself precludes frank and outspoken criticism of what is'.

In September 1910, Russell delivered a lecture to the Hawke's Bay District Officers Club on a man he saw as an exemplar of military excellence—Lieutenant-General Sir John Moore, who fought in the Napoleonic Wars of the early nineteenth century. Moore, Russell told his audience, came to senior command at a time when discipline in the British Army was lax, drunkenness among both officers and men rife, professional pride rare, and professional knowledge more so.

A man of fierce personal integrity and reforming zeal, Moore made significant improvements to the discipline of the infantry, its dress, weaponry, tactics and particularly its training. Moore required of his officers that they be young, intelligent, active, practical and efficient, and that they have a real knowledge of their profession. At a time when the chief means of enforcing discipline was the lash or the gallows, they were also required to treat their men kindly. 'The whole system,' Russell told his audience, 'was one of developing, not repressing, intelligence, of enlisting the zeal of the private as much as the officer in perfecting the whole.'

In the Peninsula War of 1809, Moore achieved a major tactical success by avoiding open confrontation with Napoleon's 300,000-strong army. Instead he attacked its vulnerable lines of communication with his much smaller force and by a careful rearguard action drew it into the far northwest corner of Spain. Although Moore himself was killed at the Battle of Corunna, Russell had no doubt that this was the master stroke that began the downfall of Napoleon.

Moore's inspirational leadership, his training regimes and tactical skills, his essential humanity and moral courage, resonated strongly with Russell. He would apply many of the general's practices and principles to his own commands, starting with the undisciplined and inexperienced mounted men with whom he had to work in those early pre-war years.

In 1912, Russell spent six months in England on secondment to the British Army. Here he would have been exposed to Victorian doctrines that stressed the superiority of the offensive over the defensive in any kind of conflict. Young officers were taught that high casualties were the inevitable outcome of a technological war dominated by artillery and machine guns, but that these could be overcome by 'pluck' and fighting spirit. For this combination of old ideas with new weapons the British Army would pay a terrible price.[17]

A year later, Russell and his mounteds played a key role on the domestic front. In November 1913, they were called to Wellington to help the Massey Government deal with the so-called Great Strike, which centred on bitter industrial disputes with the miners' and watersiders' unions at Wellington and Huntly.

Judging that the police alone could not handle the situation, the Government mobilised a force of regular army troops, backed by the 'specials', most of them farmers and volunteer mounted riflemen. With stockwhip and long baton, 'Massey's Cossacks', as they were derisively called, broke up picket lines and street demonstrations, and evicted locked-out workers from their occupation of the wharves. Protected by naval and military escorts, the 'specials' and other strike-breaking labour worked the wharves and even manned the ships in the place of the seamen who had joined the strike.

In the course of the lockout, three MPs from the Opposition Liberal Party visited the wharves, only to be turned away by one of the more unruly of Russell's men, 'Wad' Starkey. Starkey was already in trouble for chasing a striker through a private house and pushing his head down the lavatory. Under pressure from the MPs, Russell sacked Starkey and undertook to improve the general discipline of his men.

The strike lasted a full two months and involved up to 16,000 workers across New Zealand. It was ended only when the United Federation of Labour (UFL) finally conceded defeat after its leaders, including future prime minister Peter Fraser, were rounded up and jailed. 'It was a class war of a brief but savage kind, fought, not with dynamite and bombs, but with stones and bludgeons. It could end only one way, with the complete rout of the unionist forces.'[18] For years afterwards, Russell kept at the end of his bed the long baton he had used as a leader of the strike-breakers.

In May 1914, Britain's Inspector-General of Forces, General Ian Hamilton—who later commanded the Mediterranean Expeditionary Force at Gallipoli—came to New Zealand, as Kitchener had done earlier, to report on the Dominion's fledgling territorial army. He described it as 'well-equipped and well-armed. The human material is second to none in the world; and it suffers as a fighting machine only from want of field work and want of an ingrained habit of discipline.'[19]

Hamilton had grounds for concern. While he was still in the country, territorial infantry units rioted at a divisional training camp at Takapau in Hawke's Bay, and the riot had to be forcibly subdued, fortunately without bloodshed, by the camp's mounted police and Russell's own mounted regiment. The roughhouse disgusted Russell: 'The infantry are without discipline, and their officers appear to have no control . . . The class of officer they have, tho' good enough fellows, are not up to handling men.'

Inclined to see things in black and white, Russell discounted the ill feeling generated by compulsory military training for men who had jobs to hold down, farms and businesses to run and families to support. Many of these saw little threat of a war and resented the loss of income the camps involved. Others appeared to have been driven by a general contempt for military discipline, taking pleasure in boasting about their riotous behaviour and what they thought of those in authority.

While the training went on, the threat of a major European war was steadily growing. On 28 June 1914, the fuse was lit when Archduke Franz Ferdinand, heir to the Austro-Hungarian throne, was assassinated by Serbian nationalists in Sarajevo. Backed by Germany, the Austro-Hungarians then declared war against Serbia, ostensibly in retaliation for the murder of the archduke.

Russia then mobilised its forces in support of its fellow Slavs, the Serbs. Germany saw this as a hostile act against its ally, Austro-Hungary, and immediately declared war on Russia. At the same time the Germans invaded neutral Belgium and northern France in an attempt to defeat the French before turning their armies against the Russians in the east. Britain was drawn into the conflict by its role as guarantor of the neutrality of Belgium.

The underlying causes of the Great War were complex, but included a stew of conflicting ambitions, rivalries and disputes involving two opposing alliances—the Triple Entente of Russia, France and Britain, and the Central Powers, Germany and Austria-Hungary. Germany, desiring an empire that would match its growing military and industrial power, had embarked on a massive naval shipbuilding programme. The British saw this as a threat to the supremacy of the Royal Navy at sea, and responded with a naval build-up of their own.

The French meanwhile nursed powerful grievances against Germany as a result of their defeat in the Franco-Prussian war of 1870–71 and the subsequent loss of the coal- and iron-rich region of Alsace-Lorraine. The Russians had ambitions of their own in the Balkans as champion of the Slav races then under control of the Austro-Hungarian Empire. Added to this was Germany's fear of encirclement by the three entente powers, and Britain's fear that German domination of the continent would threaten its security.

'In 1914,' wrote soldier and post-war pacifist Ormond Burton, 'the illusory splendour of European civilisation commenced to crumble under the storm of fire and steel.'[20] Nearly 10 million men of all nations would die in the four years of fighting that followed, or as a direct result of it, and nearly 6,300,000 were seriously wounded. The spiritual and material costs were incalculable.

No hint of such things yet troubled the Massey Government, and its response to the declaration of war on 4 August 1914 was swift. That day, it cabled London with the offer of an expeditionary force of one infantry brigade, a mounted rifles brigade, an artillery brigade and support units—the first such pledge from all of Britain's dominions. The offer was accepted on 12 August, and immediately the call went out for volunteers.

The response was instant and overwhelming, with 14,000 volunteering in the first week alone. Men from all trades and professions rushed to the recruiting offices to join up, and from there were dispatched to training camps in Auckland, Palmerston North, Wellington, Christchurch and Dunedin. Cargo and passenger ships were requisitioned for conversion into troopships, war funds were launched, and everywhere 'bands played, beer flowed, and hotel pianos tinkled as men drank and sang before going into camp ... A man would be a mug to miss out on this war.'[21]

That so many should answer the call to the colours is no surprise, for the currents of militarism and imperialism were running strong in pre-war New Zealand. Boy Scouts, school cadets and the Territorials had indoctrinated large numbers of young men in the values of patriotism and loyalty to the Empire; the popular press, the politicians and the Church had done the rest. As historian Paul Baker put it: 'It was no coincidence that the smallest and most isolated of the white dominions was also the most effusively loyal to Britain and the most determined to prove its worth to her.'[22]

The young men who joined up so willingly did so for a multiplicity of reasons—the serious-minded for God, King and country; others simply for 'the colonial love of a fight'. Most who volunteered probably did so for adventure and travel—the chance to escape the boredom and drudgery of life in post-Victorian New Zealand. Their combat skills were rudimentary, their drill and horsemanship rough and ready, but they were physically fit, confident and eager to prove themselves in action—if innocent of the real causes of the struggle to come and the horrors of death by machine-gun and shellfire.

New Zealand then was ready to fight, but for hard-headed security reasons as much as loyalty to Britain and her Empire. With the country heavily reliant on Britain for its independence and economic survival, the shield of British sea power was seen to be vital to a small, isolated South Pacific country facing a possible threat from European—and possibly Asian—nations with imperial ambitions of their own. An unwritten alliance, known as 'imperial defence', had been in place from the 1880s, and to ensure it remained so the Massey Government in 1914 was more than willing to send troops to stand by the mother country on the battlefields of Europe.

Massey suggested to the British Government that a New Zealand expeditionary force might be used in place of British regular troops in India or Egypt, elsewhere in the Empire, or on the European continent. After some debate in the British Cabinet, Prime Minister Asquith decided that New Zealand troops, along with Australian contingents, would be brought to Europe to fight the Germans alongside the British Expeditionary Force (BEF).

Russell's powers of command as a combat soldier were finally to be put to the test. His handling of troops on annual camp manoeuvres and the ruthless efficiency with which his Hawke's Bay mounteds had helped put down the Wellington strikers had impressed Godley as overall commander of New Zealand's military forces. Immediately war was declared, he offered Russell command of the New Zealand Mounted Rifles Brigade (NZMR) with the rank of Brigadier-General. Russell was immensely pleased by his appointment: 'It is quite the best command,' he wrote to his father, 'and many there are to envy me. This comes of helping things along.'

Russell's five years as a regular officer in the British Army would have counted strongly in his favour, as did his knowledge of military history and tactics, his familiarity with Europe, and his ability to speak both French and German. His administrative skills and ability to handle a brigade were also considered superior to those of the only other serious contender for the job, Lieutenant-Colonel Arthur Bauchop, commander of the Otago Mounted Rifles Regiment. As a territorial officer, however, Russell was an exception to the rule, as Godley firmly believed that only regular officers had the command and staff skills necessary to lead a brigade in the field.[23]

'I have had it out with him [Bauchop],' Godley wrote, 'and said to him distinctly that I did not think his qualifications were as good as Russell's and he now quite understands the position.'[24] Lieutenant-Colonels Mackesy, Meldrum and Findlay were appointed commanders of the Auckland, Wellington, and Canterbury regiments respectively.

There was much work to be done, however, if the mounteds Russell would command in the field were to meet his exacting standards. 'On arrival, went to the camp . . . inspected their lines. These I found in a filthy state, and a clear indication of what I feared. Bad discipline,' he noted in his diary. A night tactical exercise near Palmerston North was not up to scratch and Russell was quick to tell his subordinates so: 'The ground work of every squadron is very deficient . . . especially noticeable in squadron and troop leading. The men have not been got into the way of following and looking to troop leaders for instructions and orders; nor the troop leader to the squadron leader.'

Russell was particularly critical of the Wellington mounted regiment, which he judged to be undisciplined, badly organised, and not working nearly hard enough. 'However, peg away is the only game. I hope to be tolerably unpopular with some of them before I am done.'

The weeks before embarkation were busy as Russell inspected regimental training camps around the country, briefed his unit commanders, and attended senior commanders' conferences in Wellington. His drive to bring the mounted regiments to full battle-readiness, however, would have to wait. They had had basic training in drills, fieldcraft, rifle shooting, and general fitness; the gaps would have to be filled when they arrived in England, where it was planned to integrate them into a British or Australian formation.

On the home front, Guy felt he had little to worry about. A farm manager had been appointed, surplus stock had been profitably sold off, and wool prices were buoyant. 'So I leave with an easy mind on that score,' he wrote to his father, 'and feel that with a family of five, of which two are boys, the family name is secure.' At worst, he thought, the war would be over by August 1915 at the latest, which would mean a 10-month separation from Gertrude and his children—the oldest, Katherine, was then just 17.

It was not to be. Guy Russell would not see his wife and one of his daughters for over two years, and only after their ship had run the gauntlet of German submarines to reach England in December

1916. The other four, including his two sons, would not see their father for nearly five years, perhaps the most formative years of their childhood.

In early September 1914, the troops boarded their transports at Lyttelton and Wellington, but were almost immediately ordered ashore because of fears that the troopships might be intercepted in the Tasman by the German warships *Scharnhorst*, *Gneisenau*, and *Emden*, which were known to be operating somewhere in the Pacific and Indian oceans.

Eager to get away and into action, Russell felt that risks should have been taken (minor in his view) and the convoy dispatched without waiting for its escort of British and Japanese warships. 'It would be a terrible disappointment now to be out of it,' he wrote to his family, 'however much one might wish for the war to end tomorrow.'

On the morning of 16 October, 10 ships carrying the 8454 men and 3818 horses of the first New Zealand Expeditionary Force (NZEF) slipped anchor, and with their escort of four British and Japanese warships sailed slowly through the Wellington heads and out into the Tasman. Godley's force consisted of an infantry brigade, a mounted rifles brigade, a field artillery brigade, plus headquarters staff, engineers, signals, and other support units.

In command of the mounted rifles brigade was 46-year-old Brigadier-General Guy Russell, now the highest-ranked territorial soldier in the expeditionary force. Unlike many of his subordinates who had fought against the Boers in South Africa, however, he was totally untried in battle.

Chapter 7

The Road to Gallipoli

'A man with a growing family of youngsters may well be indifferent to the bubble reputation he may earn at the cannon's mouth, considering its risks. Personally, as a man with a wife and 5 children I don't feel in the least called on to display the same anxiety for adventures that I certainly felt 20 years ago.'—Guy Russell admits in 1915 to being a different man from the young subaltern who sailed for India in the 1880s.

The troops who sailed from Wellington under Godley's command presumed that they were bound for England and further training, and from there to the battlefields of Belgium and France. But while they waited for their naval escort to arrive, a rebellion broke out in South Africa, sparked by the opposition of Boer generals to plans by the South African Government to invade German Southwest Africa. The NZEF was ordered therefore to sail for Durban and put itself at the disposal of the South African Government.

In early November, and while the troops were still at sea, Turkey entered the war on the side of the Central Powers. Now allied with Germany, the Turks were seen to pose a threat to British control of the Suez Canal, and so the convoy carrying the New Zealanders, together with a division and two brigades of Australian troops, was diverted to Egypt. The plan was that the troops would be formed into a corps under the command of General Sir William Birdwood. They would then train together before going on to the Western Front in the spring of 1915.

Getting to their new destination, however, involved a seven-week voyage, first to Hobart, then on to King George Sound in Western Australia to link up with the troopships carrying the 20,000 troops and 7000 horses of the Australian Infantry Force (AIF). From there, the convoy would proceed via Ceylon (present-day Sri Lanka) to the Egyptian port of Alexandria.

The presence of German warships in the Pacific and Indian oceans made the voyage potentially hazardous, but for most it was simply uncomfortable. The mounted brigade's troopship, the 13,000-ton *Athenic*, was home to 1300 men and 380 horses, including six of Russell's own. The commander himself was quartered in a cabin and office converted from 'a ladies' "boudoir"'; his men were crammed into small cabins below decks.

The voyage began badly with blustery cold winds and a heavy swell, which made life miserable for men who had not yet gained their sea-legs—'many wishing no doubt that they had never been born or that the Kaiser hadn't'. But the weather soon improved and life aboard the crowded troopship settled into a daily round of drill, kit inspections, shooting practice, physical exercises and lectures—and, for the mounteds, the unrelenting work of caring for the horses.

Russell kept himself fit with a daily regime of skipping and fencing, and carefully watched his food intake in an effort to control the chronic rheumatism in the wrist and ankle he had broken in riding accidents some years before. At Godley's request, he began an essay on the tactical handling of mounted rifles.

On 21 October, the convoy reached Hobart, where the ships took on fresh water and the men were given a three-hour route march ashore. The population of Hobart thronged around the marching men, pressing on them gifts of Tasmanian apples, cigarettes and bunches of flowers. Russell was unimpressed: 'March discipline indifferent. Chief fault leaving ranks, loss of intervals. Otago Rgt especially bad.'

After a rendezvous with the Australians at Albany in King George Sound, the 36-ship convoy, escorted by the Australian light cruisers *Sydney* and *Melbourne*, the Royal Navy cruiser *Minotaur* and the Japanese cruiser *Ibuki*, headed on into the Indian Ocean and northwest towards Ceylon. Here the convoy missed by just two hours crossing paths with the German raider *Emden*, which was subsequently intercepted and destroyed at the Cocos Islands by the *Sydney*.

By November 1914, *Emden* had a formidable record as a raider. It had already sunk or captured 23 British merchant ships, sunk a Russian cruiser and a French destroyer, and bombarded an oil storage depot at the Indian port of Madras, igniting 50,000 tons of naval fuel oil. Had *Emden* made the interception at night, it might well have sunk several troopships with gunfire and torpedoes as the convoy's naval escorts could not have retaliated without hitting the transports.

Russell's diary commented laconically: 'She [the *Emden*] could hardly have failed to do great damage if she had got in amongst us . . . She is more than earning her tucker.' Given his earlier judgement that the risks of interception by German warships were low ('100 to 1 against'), this near-miss would have come as a rude shock.

On 3 December, the New Zealand troops came safely ashore at Alexandria and entrained for Zeitoun, a desert camp northwest of Cairo. Stretching away before them lay the city, with its forest of minarets and domes and its square-topped houses. Beyond it, far in the distance, were the familiar outlines of the great pyramids.

But the New Zealanders were not in Egypt as tourists, and there were practical matters to be seen to. The troops that arrived in Zeitoun were far from being a well-trained and effective fighting force. Their skills in drill, musketry and fieldcraft were rudimentary and standards of discipline highly variable—as, in Russell's opinion, was the calibre of the officer corps. The troops, he wrote to his father, were 'a magnificent lot of men, with ill-trained officers. Not their fault, but their misfortune'.

Under Godley's direction, Russell and fellow brigade commanders set to work to change all that. All day, they drilled, marched, practised musketry, tactical exercises, brigade and divisional manoeuvres, and under a hot sun and in choking dust drilled and marched again. Each infantryman carried over 25 kilograms of gear on the march—overcoat, blanket, waterproof sheet, water and rations, rifle and bayonet, and 150 rounds of ammunition. 'We were soon able to march 24 miles a day in full pack, bivouac, cook an evening meal and then dig trenches before sleeping behind the parados ready to man them at any hour in the darkness,' wrote Spencer Westmacott.[25]

The mounted troopers practised moving quickly across the desert, dismounting and advancing on foot under the cover of machine-gun and artillery fire. Mounted officers practised navigation, map-reading, fire control and giving orders. The experience of the practical Hawke's Bay farmer now came into play as Russell taught his squadrons how to swim their horses 'expeditiously and methodically' across the Nile. With his property bordered by two flood-prone rivers, he had several times been forced to do the same.

The tough training regime soon began to show results but Russell still saw room for improvement, especially among his junior officers: 'Troop training—many young officers as yet by no means understand how to lead—and many are ignorant of details they should have at their finger ends.' At a brigade conference on 17 March, Russell was blunt about the quality of training the previous day: 'Told them it was poor. Not enough interest taken.'

In spite of his demands, Russell appeared to be making a good impression on both the officers and the men under his command. Major A.A. Martin of the NZ Medical Corps wrote to Russell's wife Gertrude from Egypt: 'Everyone thinks the world of him here. The soldiers and officers equally. I have heard a lot about him since I came out and everyone are [sic] full of his praises and of his consideration and care of his men.'

Russell's tactical skills were also developing. In one exercise, Godley had arranged for his brigade to fight its way back to base and had turned out the whole division to oppose it. 'My plan turned out fairly well,' Russell wrote in his diary, 'and we got contact about 9.30 am, and were fighting intermittently until 5 pm. We caught quite a bag of the Australian Light Horse as prisoners.'

But the weeks of training in the relentless heat, wind and dust of the desert were beginning to tell: 'We are, to use a popular term, "fed up with it all", and not unnaturally, since we have, in one form or another, been constantly at it ever since the beginning of September, some longer still.' The men were getting stale and wanted a change of scene.

By this time Russell was having doubts about full-time soldiering. 'I think a year or so will be enough for me though,' he wrote to his father, 'and shall be glad if good luck is on my side to once again stand at the head of a drafting alley and run off the sheep for shearing. I should be sorry again to become a professional soldier, and run about from one end of the Empire to another at others' beck and call.'

In the meantime, Godley worried about the rate of venereal disease in the force, which in spite of the efforts of officers, doctors and chaplains, was still very bad; and about the effect on the troops of the drink freely available in the streets of Cairo. The NZEF, he thought, could lose up to 10 percent of its troops to venereal disease, let alone the losses to locally supplied booze. 'The filthy native liquor, diluted as it is with urine, makes anyone who drinks it quite mad,' he wrote to Defence Minister Sir James Allen. 'One can only be thankful that so few of our men do drink.'[26]

Russell was concerned about the lack of proper combat equipment, including artillery and ammunition for training—'the necessaries, to say nothing of the luxuries of war'—and that his mounted troopers, volunteers all, would in the end be condemned to garrison duties in Egypt until the war was over. His men had joined up to fight, he wrote to his father, not to do the Empire's 'watchdog work'.

Ironically, the enemy had already been met and beaten near Ismailia on the Suez Canal. In late January, 25,000 Turkish and Arab troops crossed the Sinai Desert with the aim of threatening the Suez Canal and provoking an anti-British uprising in Egypt. A Turkish and Arab force attempted to cross the canal on pontoon bridges but were beaten off with heavy casualties by Indian troops and men of the New Zealand Infantry Brigade (NZIB), assisted by the guns of an armoured train and British warships in the canal.

After four months of hard desert training, Godley was now satisfied that the New Zealand and Australian contingents had been transformed from an army of raw citizen-soldiers into a force of well-trained and disciplined fighting men. He told Defence Minister Allen: 'You have here a force of 11,000 well-trained men of splendid physique, nearly all fit, beautifully mounted, thoroughly well-equipped, and ready, and only too willing, to go and fight for the Empire.'[27]

Their chance was soon to come. At the War Office in London a campaign was being devised to break the military stalemate on the Western Front by opening a second front against Germany's ally Turkey in the east. Under this plan a combined British and French naval force would break through the Dardanelles Straits into the Sea of Marmara to threaten the Turkish capital Constantinople. Panicked by the arrival of so many enemy warships off its shores, the Turkish Government would then sue for peace and withdraw from its alliance with Germany and Austria-Hungary.

The capitulation of Turkey, it was hoped, would open a supply route through the Black Sea, allowing military supplies to reach the Russian armies fighting the Germans and Austrians in the east. Greece, Bulgaria and Romania would be encouraged by a successful campaign to join the Allied entente, and Russia, by a secret agreement with the British Government, would take control of Armenia and the Turkish capital Constantinople.

The detailed plan devised by the War Office envisaged that 16 old British and French battleships, supported by cruisers and destroyers, would steam up the Dardanelles Straits, bombarding and destroying the Turkish gun emplacements onshore while a flotilla of minesweepers cleared the water ahead of them. Once the fleet was through the Narrows, it would work its way through the Sea of Marmara and on to Constantinople.

In the end, nothing went according to plan. On 18 March, Turkish mines and shore gunfire put a third of the fleet out of action, sinking four of the battleships and drowning hundreds of British and French sailors. The navy had failed; the job would now have to be finished by the soldiers in a shore landing against now much-strengthened Turkish defences.

The first dominion troops sailed from Egypt for the Dardanelles on 10 April as the newly formed Australian and New Zealand Army Corps (Anzac), but horse soldiers were not needed in Gallipoli's rugged terrain and would miss the first landings on the peninsula. The mounteds cheered the infantry as they entrained for Alexandria and the ships that would take them to Gallipoli, but most were desperate not to miss the fight and some even talked of jumping the train and joining their mates.

Russell shared their frustration. His mounted brigade, he wrote to his father, contained 'some of the finest fighting material so far sent home from Australasia' and was eminently fit to fight as infantry. He need not have worried. In early May, Birdwood asked General Maxwell, the Commander-in-Chief Egypt, for reinforcements to build up the infantry battalions depleted by the heavy casualties of the initial landings on 25 April. Maxwell ordered the New Zealand Mounted Rifles Brigade, plus a brigade of Australian Light Horse under Colonel Harry Chauvel, to Gallipoli.

Captain H.T. Palmer probably spoke for most:

'At 2 o'clock we [the officers] had to parade before the Brigadier [Russell] to receive the usual criticism. He also informed us that we would be leaving for the front in a few days, which caused great excitement, but he further added that we would be going without our horses . . . Whilst we are delighted at getting to the front and showing what we are made of, we are keenly disappointed at leaving our dear old horses behind, for the trouble is we may never see them again.'[28]

On the night of 8 May, after a last parade, brigade headquarters, the three regiments of the NZMR, field and signalmen and the field ambulance left Zeitoun for their troopships at Alexandria. 'A rough crowd they looked, these amateur infantrymen, overloaded with awkward, extemporised gear. They stood silent, for thoughts ran deep now that they were at last on the brink of the real thing, a moment towards which they had looked so long.'[29]

As for all Allied forces engaged in that campaign, the road to the Dardanelles was by way of the Allied base at Mudros Harbour on the legendary Greek island of Lemnos, now servicing a huge fleet of British, French, and Russian warships and troop transports. Classically educated men like Russell would recall that it was here that Jason and the Argonauts made landfall in their quest for the Golden Fleece, and here that the Greeks mustered before launching their thousand ships at the shores of Troy. He and his mounteds were now part of a new armada, which would launch the largest—and perhaps worst prepared—amphibious landing in military history.

Chapter 8

The Making of a General

'It is a pretty tough business holding on here . . . The Turks are good enough fighters but have little heart to come to close quarters with the bayonet. We have an awful lot of dead ones, and some of our own, in front of us.'—Russell writes to his father in England after 42,000 Turkish troops attack the Anzac line at Gallipoli on 19 May.

By the time Russell's brigade arrived on Lemnos, the Gallipoli campaign was already into its third week. Birdwood's Anzacs had landed at Ari Burnu on the morning of 25 April after an error by the Royal Navy had put them ashore 1.5 kilometres too far to the north. Instead of facing what they believed would be lightly defended Turkish positions in relatively open country, 16,000 Australian and New Zealand troops were pinned down on two narrow ridges above the beachhead, fighting off fierce Turkish counter-attacks. Mixed groups of Australians and New Zealanders had thrust inland, only to be cut off and killed. Under murderous shrapnel and sniper fire, others had retreated to the beach or found shelter in steep gullies.

The Gallipoli Campaign: April–December 1915

RUSSIA

Vienna

Danube

Budapest

AUSTRIA

HUNGARY

Odessa

CROATIA

ROMANIA

Black Sea

Danube

MONTE NEGRO

SERBIA

ALBANIA

BULGARIA

Adrian Sea

ITALY

MACEDONIA

Salonika

Constantinople

OTTOMAN EMPIRE

Lemnos

GREECE

Aegean Sea

Gallipoli

Athens

Mediterranean Sea

Maximum Allied occupation August 1915

Aegean Sea

Suvla Bay→

GALLIPOLI

Anzac Cove

DARDANELLES

Chanak

Achi Baba

Krithia

Cape Helles

N

0   200

scale: kilometres

The attacking battalions were steadily forced back to a line of outposts that would form their front line for the next eight months—Courtney's Post, Quinn's Post, Steele's Post, Pope's Hill and Walker's Top. At Cape Helles, two Anzac brigades had been thrown into a series of hastily planned and badly coordinated attacks, inflicting 850 casualties on the NZ Infantry Brigade alone. An attempt by the Anzacs to seize the critical high point, Baby 700, on the night of 2 May had been beaten back with heavy losses. From Helles to Ari Burnu, the Allied advance had been held; the assault of 25 April had become a siege.

The morning that Russell and his 2000-strong brigade arrived off the Gallipoli peninsula was a relatively quiet one, broken only by the heavy guns of British warships as they pounded Turkish positions in the hills. To troopers accustomed for so long to the low, barren sand-dunes of Egypt, 'these high Gallipoli hills and islands, bathed in the glory of an Aegean evening, brought memories of other coastlines, Cook Strait maybe, or the Great Barrier'.[30] They crowded the rails trying to identify signs of battle ashore and the positions of the Anzac battalions that had landed on 25 April.

In the mid-afternoon their troopship, the *Grantully Castle*, anchored about 3 kilometres off Anzac Cove. Field guns could be seen firing ashore and shells bursting on high crests. Heavy shells from the German warship *Goeben* in the Dardanelles channel sent up great geysers of water near a four-funnelled British cruiser nearby. As darkness fell, destroyers and torpedo boats came alongside and took off the heavily laden troopers, transferring them to barges that would be towed by small boats once they were within 1500 metres of land.

On shore, the two mounted brigades were confronted with the harsh realities of the Gallipoli campaign—men, animals and supplies crowded into a narrow beachhead, machine-gun and rifle bullets whining overhead, freshly dug graves in a makeshift cemetery nearby. They spent an uncomfortable first night bivouacked on the slopes below Walker's Top, climbing the next day to the ridge where they were to take over two sections of the front line from the Royal

Marine Light Infantry and the Royal Naval Division. Walker's Top was vital to the security of the Anzac positions on Gallipoli. If the Turks captured it, they would overlook the Anzac rear areas along the beach and be able to fire into the backs of the defenders lining the edge of the ridge above Monash Gully.[31]

It was a stiff introduction for untried troops. Their new position was exposed on all sides to fire from the higher Turkish trenches, and any careless movement meant death. Every loophole had been targeted by snipers and at night the Turks sprayed the parapets with machine-gun fire, killing any sentries peering over them.[32] Out in no-man's-land lay the unburied bodies of many Turks and Anzacs, casualties of the previous two and a half weeks of fighting. Flies were everywhere and the stench was very bad.

Russell put his mounted riflemen quickly to work. The track bringing guns and supplies up to their position was widened and two 18-pounder guns were dragged up onto Walker's Top. The trenches, which were in a filthy state, were cleaned up and saps driven out into no-man's-land to give the troops a clear field of fire. Shelters were cut into the trench walls where the men could rest and sleep in safety, if not in comfort. Rolls of barbed wire were put in place to protect their positions against frontal attack, and wire-netting to protect against Turkish bombs and grenades. Sandbag barricades were built to shield tracks from Turkish snipers and pits were dug for home-made mortars. Counter-mining under Turkish trenches was begun.

Godley, ashore with the Anzacs since 25 April, noted approvingly: 'Russell's Mounted Rifles has [sic] arrived, taken over a section of the defences, and has [sic] already begun to do excellent work in the way of reconnaissance and sapping out towards the enemy.'[33]

In the following weeks, mounted patrols probed the foothills and plains to the north, giving Anzac commanders valuable intelligence about the state of the Turkish defences. They found the coastal hills were weakly held, with the ridges and valleys in between offering routes for infantry up onto the heights of the Sari Bair range. Their reconnaissance also revealed that the Sari Bair ridge north of Battle-ship Hill, including the heights of Chunuk Bair, Hill Q and 971, were undefended.

About this time the non-combatant Maori Pioneer contingent arrived directly from Malta. At first, Russell was unsure of how to use the force, as the men had not undergone the same hard battle training as the mounted riflemen in Egypt. In the end, he divided the contin-gent between his three mounted regiments, where they joined in the work of digging trenches, making roads, levelling terraces and drag-ging guns and water tanks into position. In the August attack on the foothills of Sari Bair, 100 pioneers would also fight as combat troops.

Russell could have chosen the comparative safety of the beach for his headquarters. Instead he sited his command dugout just 40 metres from the Turkish trenches, and there endured most of the dangers and discomforts of his troopers, including a diet of bully beef, biscuits, bacon and tea. The only concession to seniority and comfort was his sleeping quarters, a 'whare puni' built by the pio-neers, of the type usually made of raupo and manuka. 'It cannot claim to be in any sense bomb or bullet-proof,' Russell wrote to his family, 'but I have some sandbags round my bed and sleep peacefully. If a shell lands in it, well it's 'mafish' (finished!) as they say in Egypt.'

Insisting on seeing things for himself, Russell took big risks right from the start. Trooper W.B. Fitchett recalled finding his commander on hands and knees inspecting Turkish positions from a trench just 12 metres from the enemy's forward positions. On another occasion, Fitchett almost shot Russell dead as he returned from a foolhardy night reconnaissance in no-man's-land with sniper and machine gunner Captain Wallingford:

Hearing a suspicious noise, I challenged. No reply. Somebody fired into the scrub. Seeing something move, I aimed and was about to fire when the Sergeant-Major—a British Regular— alongside me suddenly shouted, "Put your hands up and stand up!" Two figures then rose from the scrub, hands upwards, while a cool voice (Russell's) that I can still hear to this day said, "Well, how long are you going to keep us out here?"[34]

The first real test of Russell's command abilities was soon to come. After repulsing the British attacks at Cape Helles in early May, the Turkish commander, General Liman von Sanders, was ordered to attack the Anzac positions at Ari Burnu and drive the invaders into the sea. On the night of 18/19 May, 42,000 Turks charged the entire Anzac front line, held at this time by 17,350 Australians and New Zealanders, supported by 43 guns.[35] The attack began at 5 pm with the heaviest shelling of Anzac trenches so far on Gallipoli. Three hours of heavy rifle and machine-gun fire followed at midnight, then at 3.30 am the Turkish troops attacked in waves, chanting 'Allah! Allah!' as they came.

Deployed in their trenches, outposts and saps, Russell's squadrons watched them come, the moonlight glinting on their bayonets:

> Closer and closer came the charge, but still fire was withheld . . . Not until the first line of Turks was 20 yards away was the order for rapid fire given. The troopers sprang to the parapet like greyhounds, and in a second they were pouring a devastating fire into the approaching ranks . . . There were no flares to throw out in front, and not even any jam tin bombs. It was a battle of bullet and steel.[36]

The Anzac machine guns did most of the killing that night, and after repeated attacks over 10,000 Turks lay dead or wounded between the lines. Some 630 Australians and New Zealanders had also been killed, among them 60 of Russell's troopers. The Turkish commanders had discovered what the Anzacs had learnt at such great cost at Helles—raw courage alone was no defence against strong entrenchments and well-sited machine guns.

In recognition of the brigade's stand on 19 May, Walker's Top was renamed Russell's Top—but it was not over yet. In broad daylight on 20 May, Godley ordered a counter-attack against Turkish trenches at the Nek, and 100 men under the command of Captain W.J. Hardham VC moved into position for the assault. Trooper Clutha Mackenzie was among those ordered forward for the attack, lying out under the hot sun waiting for the order to charge:

> Had we made the charge they consider that few of us, if any, would have come back, so terrific was the fire on account of which the attack was given up. Machine guns would have mown us down. Godley several times ordered us to move but our brigadier [Russell] refused.[37]

Meldrum and Mackesy, commanders respectively of the Wellington and Auckland regiments, had protested to Russell that the attack would achieve nothing and mean certain death for the 100 men who would make it. Russell agreed and told Godley he would not order it. Godley insisted that the attack go ahead, Russell again resisted, and Godley grudgingly gave in.[38] Another officer who resisted an order from his superior would not be so lucky. Lieutenant-Colonel Geddes, commanding officer of 1st Royal Munster Fusiliers, would be removed from command for refusing to attack at Helles on 6/7 August after judging the situation to be hopeless.

There is little doubt about what would have happened to the attacking force had Godley not backed down. The ground in front of Hardham's men was devoid of cover and could be raked by the Turks at will from numerous machine guns sited on strongpoints directly overlooking the Nek. Moreover, the Nek itself was so narrow that the New Zealanders would have had to bunch together as they crossed it: 'A mad fatal thing,' Lieutenant-Colonel William Malone—who was soon to die on Chunuk Bair—called it. During the August assault on Sari Bair, 450 men of two Australian Light Horse regiments charged the same Turkish positions in three separate attacks and were massacred; the heroic but tragically futile action was commemorated in the 1981 film *Gallipoli*.

Four days later, the two sides agreed to an armistice to bury the dead—Turks, Australians and New Zealanders. The corpses lay so thick in the scrub in front of the Anzac trenches that it was almost impossible to pass without treading on hideously swollen bodies, or avoid the stench that made men want to vomit. Russell, however, found himself increasingly unmoved by such sights: 'It is gruesome to find arms and legs sticking out of the sides of trenches,' he wrote to his father. 'But it is curious how absolutely callous one becomes to the sight of wounded and dead men. You treat it as a matter of course and go straight ahead.'

Nor did being under constant Turkish shelling, machine-gun and rifle fire seem to bother Russell much, and the moralist in him was never far distant:

> As to what one feels like under fire (nothing at all, practically). You think you are going to be hit, how lonesome it is being cut off from all you care for and about. Nor does human nature alter to any extent. Those who smoke too much still give way to this pernicious habit—the drunkard alone and the whoremonger are virtuous by necessity.

In letters to his family, Russell reported that his rheumatism was treating him well. He asked them, however, to send a few extra luxuries—potted meats, sardines, salmon, pâté de foie gras, raisins, pineapple chunks and a cake, along with glycerine suppositories and Kruschen salts. Clearly, army rations were by now having as dire an effect on his digestive system as they were on those of his men. But in spite of the constant danger and discomfort, he claimed to be happy and sleeping well: 'If heavy firing starts you only turn over and hope it doesn't mean an attack and your sleep cut short. I've a telephone connected with all my regiments, so can find out what's the matter without turning out.'

Turkish shelling made beach swimming a grave risk for men desperate to keep clean, but Russell assured Gertrude that he was able to walk the short distance from his dugout down to the beach and bathe every day in 'a moderately safe spot'. Privately, he could not help contrasting the dangers of his position right in the firing line with that of Hamilton and his headquarters staff 'comfortably and safely housed on a palatial liner' off the island of Imbros.

In spite of the hardships endured by his men, Russell faced few discipline problems on Gallipoli; and the one major incident that did occur, he handled with appropriate leniency. On 31 May, trooper Marshall was charged with the serious crime of sleeping while on sentry duty. He was found guilty and sentenced to 14 days' Field Punishment No. 2, most of which would have been served as hard labour.

By now, however, Russell's impatience with the static trench warfare of Gallipoli was beginning to show. 'It's time things were moving,' he wrote to his father. 'We don't want this to go on forever, even with wool at ¼d a pound, which I see the Tunanui wool fetched all round.' Meanwhile, he considered starting a garden of wildflowers outside his dugout, only to abandon it for lack of water and the risk that a Turkish shell would blow garden and gardener sky-high.

On 27 May, Russell and his mounteds watched as a German submarine sank the battleship *Triumph* in full view of the Anzac positions, and marvelled at the discipline of the British sailors lined up on her deck waiting for rescue. Admiral de Robeck, commander of the fleet covering the troops on the Gallipoli peninsula, decided to risk his ships no further and ordered them to sail for Egypt and Mudros Harbour. Two days later, *Majestic*, the one battleship still stationed off the coast, was torpedoed by the same submarine off Cape Helles. Apart from two destroyers, the Anzacs were now without naval support on the peninsula.

On 28 May, a squadron of the Canterbury regiment attacked and captured a Turkish trench about 300 metres inland from No. 2 Out-post and overlooked by Turkish positions on Table Top and Destroyer Hill. Enemy snipers in this new position, No. 3 Post, were 'making a nuisance of themselves' and Godley, perhaps at Russell's suggestion, wanted to clear them out.[39]

It was a mistake. The Turks counter-attacked the newly occupied post in force, and fresh squadrons of mounteds had to be sent under heavy fire to relieve the besieged defenders. Godley wanted the relief force to stay in the post, but Russell had already ordered it to be aban-doned once its defenders had been rescued. Godley countermanded Russell's order but was himself overruled by Birdwood. Russell admit-ted in a letter to Gertrude: 'I did not like the position at all and thought that it was too exposed, and finally got leave from GOC [Godley] to withdraw into another position—a consent very reluctantly given.'

Trooper Clutha Mackenzie blamed the debacle on Russell, who 'looked at things from a safe distance through his field glasses and desired the outpost to be held at all costs'. The decision to establish a weak and unsupported outpost, overlooked by the Turks on three sides and a long distance from the main New Zealand position, was 'a foolish error of judgment' that had cost the mounteds many of its best men.[40] NZMR historian Terry Kinloch is no less critical, blaming both commanders, but particularly Godley, for an ill-conceived attack that cost the lives of 23 mounted riflemen and wounded 57:

> Had Godley or Russell looked at the ground closely from No 2 Outpost before ordering the attack, they should have seen that No 3 Outpost could not have been retained while the Turks held the adjacent higher ground of Table Top and Destroyer Hill. Approving the attack was Godley's second serious tactical error to affect the mounteds after the 20 May counter-attack order.[41]

Meanwhile, Russell was blaming First Lord of the Admiralty, Winston Churchill. The concept of the Gallipoli campaign, he wrote to his father, had been a good one but its execution by the British fleet, without supporting ground troops, was foolishly premature. With a delay of three to four weeks and simultaneous cooperation between a landing force of say 40,000 men and the fleet, the goals of the campaign would have been readily achieved. Instead, the Turks had been given a breathing space of several weeks to prepare their defences, and the Anzacs now found themselves confronted by barbed wire and trenches where only rocks and scrub existed before.

Russell's opinions were obviously shared at the higher levels of command. After Churchill visited Gallipoli in July, Godley wrote to Ronald Graham, New Zealand's Minister of the Interior: '[Churchill] certainly is a plucky fellow, and I think he should be given a VC and then taken out and shot.'[42]

At 1.30 am on 30 June, the Turks launched their last assault on Anzac positions, the brunt of it falling on Chauvel's Australian Light Horse and a contingent of Russell's mounteds. In the moonlight, the Turkish regiments surged forward to the attack on No. 4 section: 'In the half light, the machine gunners found the range and mercilessly cut up the attacking waves. But they were not to be denied. On and on they pressed, right up to the parapets.'[43]

Russell's description of the attack was clinical and brief, recording only the 400 dead Turks left in front of his trenches, and his relief at the 'nominal' casualties incurred by his mounteds. Hamilton was once again more than satisfied, describing the action as 'the best business done at Anzac since May 19th ... Their defeat complete; very bloody. Nine fresh enemy battalions smashed to bits.'[44]

The casualties, however, cut both ways. By this time over 2600 New Zealanders had been killed and wounded on Gallipoli, and almost as many evacuated because of sickness. Over 700 of them were men of Russell's mounted brigade, which had fought tenaciously for six weeks to hold its section of the Anzac front line. The greatest tests of Russell's leadership, however, were still to come.

Chapter 9

Once on Sari Bair

'Heavy fighting has been going on since yesterday at the Dardanelles. The situation is obviously critical. Should the Dardanelles fall, the World War has been decided against us.'—Entry in the diary of Germany's Secretary of State for the Navy, Admiral von Tirpitz, as British, Australian and New Zealand troops assault the heights of Sari Bar in August 1915.

By the end of June 1915 it was clear to Allied commanders that they had now reached a stalemate on Gallipoli, no less real than the one on the Western Front. To break it, plans were drawn up for a new offensive that would smash through the Turkish defences on Gallipoli, as originally planned, and allow Allied warships through the Dardanelles into the Sea of Marmara and on to Constantinople.

From its early days on Gallipoli, Russell's mounted brigade had explored the hills and steep gullies to the north of Ari Burnu and had found what were thought to be safe routes for infantry up towards the dominating heights of Sari Bair. Birdwood initially planned to use this information for a June/July advance north through the foothills to seize Battleship Hill, Hill Q and Chunuk Bair, supported by

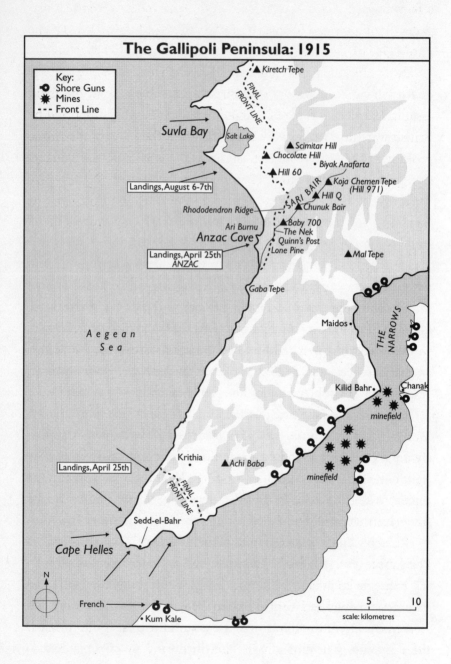

The Gallipoli Peninsula: 1915

Key:
- ⊙ Shore Guns
- ✳ Mines
- --- Front Line

▲ Kiretch Tepe

FINAL FRONT LINE

Suvla Bay

Salt Lake

▲ Scimitar Hill
▲ Chocolate Hill
• Biyak Anafarta
▲ Hill 60

Landings, August 6-7th

SARI BAIR

▲ Koja Chemen Tepe
(Hill 971)
▲ Hill Q
▲ Chunuk Bair

Rhododendron Ridge

Ari Burnu

Anzac Cove

▲ Baby 700
The Nek
Quinn's Post
Lone Pine

▲ Mal Tepe

Landings, April 25th
ANZAC

Gaba Tepe

Maidos •

THE NARROWS

Aegean
Sea

Kilid Bahr •

Chanak

minefield

Landings, April 25th

Krithia •

▲ Achi Baba

FINAL FRONT LINE

minefield

Sedd-el-Bahr

Cape Helles

N

French →

• Kum Kale

0   5   10

scale: kilometres

72

a feint towards Gaba Tepe in the south. It would involve three brigades of infantry and be spearheaded by the NZMR, which had some knowledge of the ground over which the attack would take place.

By late July elements of the plan had changed, including the role of Russell's mounteds, who would now be subsidiary to the main assault. Hamilton's force of 37,000 men and 72 guns, supported by British warships, would now burst out from the flank of the Anzac position at the same time as fresh British troops under Lieutenant-General Sir Frederick Stopford were landed at Suvla Bay. The whole force would then push on and capture the high points of the Sari Bair range—Chunuk Bair, Hill Q and Hill 971—before the Turks could bring up their reserves.

By gripping the waist of the peninsula, the British and Anzac forces would cut off the bulk of the Turkish army from land communication with Constantinople; Maidos and the Kilid Bahr range on the opposite coast would be captured, and the way to the Narrows would at last be open. With this key waterway secured, the British and French fleets could sail through the Sea of Marmara to threaten Constantinople, which would then surely fall.

The forces for the main Anzac attack on 6 August were divided into four columns, two of which were to act as covering forces to clear the Turkish posts on the lower ridges of the Sari Bair range. The right covering force consisted of the NZMR and a Maori contingent under Russell's command; the left covering force of two battalions of the British 40th Infantry Brigade under Brigadier-General Travers.

Russell's force was to capture Turkish positions at Old No. 3 Post, Table Top Hill, and Bauchop's Hill, allowing the two assaulting columns to advance unopposed up the deres to the main Sari Bair ridge. Speed and surprise were vital, as the foothills had to be cleared by 11 pm to give the main assault columns time to reach the ridgelines before dawn. To the north, the two British battalions under Travers would seize a lightly held valley known as the Damakjelik Bair.

Since its recapture by the Turks on 30 May, Old No. 3 Post had been converted to a strong redoubt protected by heavy wire entanglements laced with mines and strong overhead cover. Strongpoints covered the approaches, and several hundred Turkish troops were encamped on the far side of the position.

Connected to Old No. 3 Post by a razorback ridge, Table Top was a precipitous, flat-topped hill about 130 metres above sea level. Its approaches were steep, scrub-covered ridges and ravines, all of which were commanded by enemy trenches. The capture of the hill was essential before a further advance up a valley called the Chailak Dere to Rhododendron Spur could be made. The third objective, Bauchop's Hill, was, like Table Top, a mass of ridges and ravines, entrenched everywhere.

The task facing Russell's mounteds would test even the fittest and most determined troops. They would also have to advance in darkness, over steep, broken, mostly unreconnoitred country and against a Turkish garrison of unknown strength. As it was, the troops were already weakened by months of dysentery and enteric fever.

Russell, however, made sure his men were well prepared for their role that night, going through the operation in detail to make sure everyone—officers and men—knew their job. The enemy posts were to be attacked not by a single advance on a straight front, but by small detachments advancing on the Turkish positions from different directions. To ensure surprise, and to avoid his men firing on each other in the dark, the attack was to be delivered in complete silence, and with bomb and bayonet only.

The attack succeeded brilliantly—if at a cost. By 1 am on 7 August Russell's force was in occupation of Old No. 3 Post, Table Top and Bauchop's Hill, and Travers' left covering force had captured Damakjelik Bair. The whole operation—delayed from the start by a Turkish barricade at the mouth of the Chailak Dere—had taken two hours longer than anticipated, but the vital entrances to the Sazli,

Chailak and Aghyl deres were now in Allied hands and the way was cleared for the infantry to advance on Chunuk Bair.

In the words of Terry Kinloch, the mounteds had achieved something remarkable that night. Sick and emaciated men with empty rifle magazines and fixed bayonets had charged into concentrated rifle and machine-gun fire, and without firing a shot until their objectives had been secured. While they had the advantage of surprise and an element of luck, very few of them knew the country and they had to make their attacks in the dark, from different directions and to very tight deadlines.[45] Hamilton was effusive:

> The angle of Table Top's ascent is recognised as impracticable for infantry. But neither Turks nor angles of ascent were destined to stop Russell or his New Zealanders that night. There are moments during battle when life becomes intensified, when men become supermen, when the impossible becomes simple—and this was one of those moments.[46]

Remarkably, the operation had almost totally flouted the principles laid down in the British Army's Field Service Regulations, which stated that any night assault should be preceded by a 'complete reconnaissance'. If this was not done, the regulations warned, there was a high risk of elements of the attacking force losing touch, taking a wrong direction, and even firing on sections of their own side. That none of this occurred was due to a combination of luck and the planning skills of the force commander, Brigadier-General Andrew Russell. They were the same skills that he would apply later as a divisional commander on the Western Front.

The success of Russell's brigade, however, was not matched elsewhere that night, or in the following days. The mounteds had cleared the foothills two hours later than anticipated, and this and other delays meant that troops of the NZ Infantry Brigade did not reach their rendezvous below the heights of Sari Bair until dawn on

7 August. Chunuk Bair was still lightly defended, but the vacillation of Brigadier-General Earl Johnston allowed the Turks to reinforce their positions on the crest before the New Zealand infantry could arrive.

After a bloody and unsuccessful daylight attack by the Auckland battalion, Godley decided to attack Chunuk Bair again before dawn on 8 August. Russell allocated the Auckland and Wellington mounted regiments, supported by Maori pioneer troops, for his part of the operation, leaving the Otago and Canterbury regiments to guard the foothills.

Just after 4 am, Malone's Wellington infantry battalion, supported by the Auckland mounteds and a contingent of British troops, advanced on Chunuk Bair. They took it without firing a shot, as most of the Turks had been driven off the crest by the supporting artillery bombardment and down into an adjacent valley. From the heights they could now see the waters of the Narrows (the narrowest part of the Dardanelles) glinting in the distance.

It was not to last. For 36 hours these troops doggedly held their ground against repeated enemy counter-attacks, until their shattered remnants were relieved by the Otago infantry battalion and two squadrons of Wellington mounteds. Suffering extreme thirst and under heavy artillery and machine-gun fire, they held the crest for another 24 hours, fighting off Turkish bomb and bayonet attacks from shallow trenches choked with their own dead. It ended on the night of 9 August when they were relieved by two British battalions—the Loyal North Lancashires and the 5th Wiltshires. Chunuk Bair was lost early the next morning when these troops were overwhelmed by a massive Turkish counter-attack, personally led by Mustafa Kemal.

Soldier-historian Cecil Malthus later described the stand of the New Zealanders on Chunuk Bair as 'perhaps New Zealand's finest hour'. Its defence came at a high cost—to both sides. Three regiments of Turks were decimated in their attempt to push New Zealanders off the crest. Some 2400 men of the NZ Infantry Brigade and nearly

700 of Russell's mounteds were killed, wounded or missing. The Wellington battalion alone lost 690 of the 760 men who took—and so briefly held—the heights of Chunuk Bair. And in the end the assault had failed: the main ridge of Sari Bair was now completely in Turkish hands and would remain so until the end of the campaign.

Colonel John Monash, commander of the Australian 4th Brigade and a future Lieutenant-General, blamed the failure of the August offensive on 'insufficient troops, inadequate munitions, attempting more than was possible with the means available'. He targeted both Birdwood and Godley, whose command arrangements were 'hopelessly inadequate from the start'; and the poor quality of the 'New Army' troops who, in his view, had 'no grit, no gumption'.[47]

For military historian Chris Pugsley, the failure of 7 August was essentially one of leadership. Malone's achievements on Chunuk Bair offered enormous prospects, if they could have been exploited by the soldiers of the Empire struggling up the slopes of Sari Bair. 'It was the commanders,' he wrote, 'and Godley in particular, who failed to show the touch, the insight that marked a capable tactician. Not even brilliance was required; the bravery of their soldiers only needed a commander to show sound judgement at the right time.'[48]

In later years, Godley regretted that he had not gone forward and taken greater control of the battle instead of isolating himself at his headquarters. He conceded also that the objectives of the campaign had been too ambitious, considering the poor physical state of the troops under his command. Given the chance to assault Sari Bair again, he would have limited the attack to Chunuk Bair and Hill Q and given Russell the responsibility for capturing the critical ridge:

Had General Russell, who knew the ground better than anybody else, been given, in addition to his own New Zealand Mounted Rifles, the Australian Light Horse, whose attack on the Nek met with such disaster, I have no doubt that he would have gained the ridge on the first night without difficulty. The New Zealand, 4th Australian, and Indian Brigades could then have relieved him and established themselves on Chunuk Bair and Hill Q . . . But this is being wise after the event.[49]

Hamilton himself put much of the blame on Stopford's 9th Corps, which had remained immobile on the beach when it should have pushed forward across the Suvla Plain, captured the W Hills and linked up with the main assault on Chunuk Bair. He wrote to Russell in March 1917:

> I myself believe that if the 9th Corps had been on the heights between the Anafartas on the morning of the 7th as they should have been—that then the Turks would have been absolutely forced to throw against them at least half of the troops they actually employed against the Anzacs and 13th Division on Sari Bair.[50]

Then there are the 'what ifs'. What if Russell and his mounteds had been given the spearhead role in the attack as originally planned? What if Stopford's troops had been properly in position on the critical first day of the August offensive? What if Godley had taken greater control over the assault on Chunuk Bair instead of commanding from a telephone at the base of the ridge? What if Major-General Harold (Hooky) Walker—generally recognised to be the outstanding Allied commander on Gallipoli—had directed the Anzacs that day instead of Godley?

The failure to hold Chunuk Bair dealt a further blow to Britain's military reputation in the eyes of the Anzacs. The Royal Navy had put them ashore on the wrong beach on 25 April, and its supporting fleet had run for shelter in May after losing two battleships to German submarines. Now British forces had failed to support their assault with a strong thrust inland from Suvla, or to hold the positions on Chunuk Bair that the New Zealanders had struggled, at such huge cost, to take. Fairly or not, British commanders and their troops were blamed for both failures, and anti-British feelings amongst the Anzacs intensified.

Criticism of the failure of British units to hold Chunuk Bair is somewhat unfair: the New Zealanders would probably have put up a better fight, but would still have been wiped out by the final, overwhelming Turkish attack.[51] Russell, however, had been unimpressed with the British irregulars he had seen at Gallipoli. 'The poor fellows look as if they had been brought up "on the bucket", to use a farming expression, and hardly able to stand up to the lusty Turk,' he wrote to his father. 'There is so much hand-to-hand fighting nowadays that you want muscle and weight.'

His thoughts were echoed by Australian war correspondent Charles Bean, who scorned the 'puny narrow-chested little men' of Kitchener's New Army and claimed that the Australians and New Zealanders no longer had any trust in them. 'They have neither the nerve, the physique, nor the spirit and self-control to fit them for soldiers.'[52]

Some 50,000 British and Anzac troops were involved in the four-day battle for Chunuk Bair and Suvla Bay, of whom 2000 were killed and 10,000 wounded. Around 22,000 sick and wounded men were sent to hospitals in Egypt and Malta. Kitchener moved to replace the failed commanders at Gallipoli—but not all of them. Hamilton and the elderly Stopford were sent home; Hunter-Weston and Godley kept their jobs.

For the men of Anzac, however, there was more hard fighting to come. Two weeks after the Sari Bair offensive came the Scimitar Hill/W Hills/Hill 60 operation, the largest fought on the peninsula, and the next major test of Russell's command abilities. Birdwood believed that if the Turkish trenches on Hill 60 could be captured, the point of junction between the Anzac and Suvla fronts would be greatly strengthened. A bonus was that two extra wells would be added to the Allied water supply.

In conjunction with an attack on Hill 60, the British 9th Corps would again attempt to seize the Scimitar and W Hills from across the Suvla Plain—which under Stopford's inept leadership it had dismally failed to do on 6 August. The 29th Indian Brigade would attack Hill 60 on the left, the NZMR under Russell in the centre, and the 4th Australian Brigade on the right. In overall command of the operation would be Brigadier-General Cox.

The Allied commanders believed that the Turks had ringed the summit of Hill 60 with a single trench system. In fact, the whole hill had been turned into a strong redoubt, honeycombed with fire and communication trenches, and the Turks holding them were determined not to give ground. The troops that would undertake the attack were generally inexperienced new arrivals or tired and sick veterans of earlier fighting; and at a critical point in the attack there were problems with the artillery.

In full daylight on 21 August, the assault on Hill 60 began. Two depleted regiments of the NZMR, 500 men of the 4th Australian Infantry Brigade, and a battalion of Irish Connaught Rangers, all under Russell's direct command, attacked over open country and in full view of the Turkish trenches. It was a disaster. The artillery barrage, divided between two fronts—Russell's and the 9th Corps attacking from Suvla—was ineffectual, leaving the Turkish trenches intact but warning the Turkish machine gunners that an attack was imminent.

The Connaughts succeeded in seizing the wells, but the troops on Russell's flanks were cut down as they charged forward. The scrub caught fire, and wounded men were burnt to death or killed when their ammunition pouches exploded. Twice Russell urged the Australians to push on but was told it was impossible because of the strength of the Turkish fire. The surviving troops dug in where they were. At heavy cost, the Canterbury and Otago mounteds did better, seizing two lines of Turkish trenches in 'grotesque close-quarter trench battle . . . just brown grimy bodies, shaven-headed, walking skeletons fighting over bodies sprawled in the saps, with rifle butt, bayonet or bomb.'[53]

By nightfall, the New Zealanders had captured 120 metres of enemy trench and had a small foothold on the lower slopes of Hill 60. Russell knew that his exhausted men could do no more; if the rest of the hill was to be captured, it should be done before daylight, he told Cox, and with a fresh force. Cox agreed and asked Godley for reinforcements. Godley reluctantly gave him the raw and inexperienced 18th Battalion of the 5th Western Australian Infantry Brigade, newly arrived on Gallipoli.

At dawn on 22 August and without any preliminary reconnaissance, the Australians attacked the Turkish trenches, but were driven back after half their men were killed or wounded. The mounted riflemen, a few Connaught Rangers and the Australians now held about 200 metres of trench on the southern and western edges of Hill 60, well below the summit. On the plain to the north, the 9th Corps had been thrown back onto its start line with heavy casualties. Hamilton recorded in his diary: 'Suvla gone wrong again. Anzac right . . . The Indian brigade have seized the well at Kabak Kuyu and that fine soldier, Russell, fixed himself into Kaiajik Aghala and is holding on there tooth and nail.'[54]

Birdwood, however, was still set on taking the top of Hill 60, despite the fact that the Turks were now rapidly strengthening their defences. On 27 August, Russell renewed the assault with a force comprised of remnants of the NZMR, three Australian infantry battalions, and 250 Connaught Rangers—1000 men in all. Russell and the Australian commander Monash favoured a surprise attack in the dark with bomb and bayonet only—the type of operation in which colonial troops had already shown considerable skill. Cox overruled them. The attack would again take place in daylight, preceded by an hour-long artillery barrage.

The artillery was to bombard Hill 60 while the warships off Anzac and some of the land guns were to silence the enemy's batteries on the main range. To avoid the disaster of 21 August, Russell wanted the guns to concentrate on the trenches facing the Australians. This was not done, and again the attacking lines of troops were swept away by a storm of fire from the Turkish positions. Two-thirds of the men who made the attack and all the officers but one were killed or wounded.

The mounteds, however, pressed on, taking three lines of trenches as they struggled towards the crest. On their right and left the Australians and the Connaughts were either held up or could not hold what they had gained in the first rush. As night fell, the survivors were left alone to fight off Turkish counter-attacks, supported by heavy artillery, on their exposed position near the top of Hill 60.

Relief came the next night when the 10th Australian Light Horse launched a surprise attack on a section of trench that had been captured but then lost. The crest of Hill 60 was now at least partly in Allied hands—and it remained so until the evacuation of British forces from Gallipoli four months later. In sombre mood, Russell wrote to his sister: 'Four different attacks more or less successful, but not quite, as we have not got all the hill, tho' nearly so. Casualties as per usual. Poor fellows! it is a gruesome game.'

Russell's brigade had endured eight days and nights of the hardest fighting it would experience in the whole of the war. If success had been only partial, Hamilton's despatches acknowledged their epic struggle: 'The NZ Mounted Rifles refused to recognise that they were worsted. Nothing would shift them. All that night and all the next day, through bombing, bayonet charges, musketry, shrapnel, and heavy shell, they hung on to their 150 yards of trench.'

On 24 August, as the battle raged, Godley reported that both Johnston and, especially, Russell had proved themselves excellent brigadiers: 'Russell is really quite an exceptionally good man.'[55] After the fighting was over, Godley complimented Cox and Russell for the way in which the Hill 60 operations had been planned and carried out. 'Both these officers,' he wrote, 'have shown a capacity for the organisation and carrying out of offensive operations far beyond the ordinary.'[56]

In hindsight, these assessments cannot be taken at face value. The first problem is that Godley's appraisals of Cox and Russell were made on the understanding that Hill 60 had been entirely captured by the Allied force. It had not, and at least half the summit of the hill remained in Turkish hands until the end of the Gallipoli campaign.

Secondly, Godley's judgment that Johnston was an 'excellent' brigadier is highly questionable. Johnston has been widely criticised by historians of the Gallipoli campaign for his part in the failed attack on the heights of Sari Bair. At the time he was drinking heavily, sick with enteritis, and in no fit state to command troops in battle. His brigade major noted that during the battle for Chunuk Bair, Johnston 'was frequently barely coherent, and his judgment and mind were obviously clouded'.[57] Lieutenant-Colonel Aspinall-Oglander, author of a British official history of the Gallipoli campaign, wrote: 'It was nothing but a national calamity that he [Johnston] was allowed to continue in command.'[58]

Thirdly, despite Godley's accolades, the Hill 60 operation is judged to have been badly handled by its commanders, inflicting 2500 Allied casualties for minimal gains. Monash, whose troops played a key role in the attack, described the assault as 'a rotten, badly organised show'.[59] Robert Rhodes James is no less critical: 'For connoisseurs of military futility, valour, incompetence, and determination, the attacks on Hill 60 are in a class of their own.'[60]

Pugsley ascribes some blame to Russell, claiming that in committing the Western Australian Infantry Brigade to the attack on 22 August, he repeated the same errors that destroyed the Royal Marine Light Infantry below Baby 700 on 2 May.[61] Russell's error, if it was such, was to send inexperienced troops to do a job that veteran Anzac formations had failed to do the day before. Bean, though sympathetic to Russell, felt that the Western Australians' attack was compromised from the start by lack of proper reconnaissance, careful preparation and clear directions.[62]

Russell may well have made mistakes at Hill 60 as, like most of his fellow generals in 1915, he had no previous experience of trench warfare and had to learn its hard lessons on the job. In the words of Monash's biographer, all commanders at Anzac were inexperienced in every aspect of warfare, from operational staff work to administration and the particular problems of trench fighting. 'All of them were feeling their way; predictably, all made mistakes.'[63]

A key point, however, is that Russell was not in overall command of the assault, and the blame for its failure must therefore fall substantially on Cox, and particularly on Godley and Birdwood, whose staffs were responsible for planning the operation. The attack went ahead without a proper study of the Turkish positions, and without effective and properly coordinated artillery cover for the advancing infantry.

On 27 August, Russell and Monash had recommended a night attack without artillery. This would have had the advantage of surprise and, arguably, a greater chance of success. Cox wanted a daylight assault and prevailed, with predictably heavy casualties. Campaign historian John Laffin has no doubts where the principal blame should lie: 'He [Birdwood] was responsible for a bloody debacle at Hill 60, again (as in the attack on Hill 971) in failing to study the problem adequately.'[64]

Hill 60 marked the end of large-scale British offensives on the Gallipoli peninsula. On 13 September, after four months in the front line, Russell and the wasted survivors of his mounted rifles brigade were pulled back to their base on Lemnos to rest and reorganise— 'skeletons without energy, blasphemously fed up, ragged, lousy, and incapable of marching a mile in a soldierly fashion'.[65]

Three days later, they were inspected by a French admiral, who asked Russell if this was all that remained of his regiment, not at first realising that he was looking at the remnants of four regiments. 'When he did so, he turned round, looked at the men in wonder, gravely saluted, and rode off.'[66] As well he might. Of the 2000 troopers who landed at Gallipoli on 12 May, only 250 sick and emaciated men remained. Casualties and sickness had reduced the 4000-strong New Zealand Infantry Brigade to just over 1000, all ranks. Hamilton's 'beautiful battalions' had simply withered away.

On November 8, Russell was appointed Knight Commander of the Order of St Michael and St George (KCMG) for 'distinguished services in the field during operations at the Dardanelles'. Typically, he credited the honour to his mounted brigade rather than to anything he himself had achieved. 'I have not much use for these kinds of things,' he wrote to his family, 'being, as my schoolmasters used to say, devoid of ambition.' Godley was far less reticent, writing to Defence Minister Allen that Russell had richly deserved his knighthood 'as he stands out as a leader above all the rest'.[67]

Not every senior officer at Gallipoli was as pleased as Godley. The ambitious Monash, who was later to command the Australian Corps on the Western Front, felt the honour was undeserved because Russell was only a brigadier and much junior to himself. Also, Russell had not arrived on the peninsula until late May, and in his view had achieved 'nothing conspicuous'.[68]

Russell's superb mounted riflemen, however, were left out of the honours altogether. Almost half of the 4000 who served on Gallipoli between May and December had been killed or wounded, but Russell refused to recommend any of them for gallantry awards. Every man in his command, he argued, was worth a VC, and it was sufficient honour to belong to the brigade.

Chapter 10

A Poor Man's War

'I do not suppose any such landing as this, or combined naval and military operations on such a scale, have ever been attempted before in the history of the world, that is, landing on an open beach, in the face of the enemy, whose entrenchments and obstacles are absolutely down to the water's edge. If it comes off it will be one of the greatest feats of arms that has ever been done.'— Major-General Sir Alexander Godley, commander of the New Zealand and Australian Division at Gallipoli.[69]

The landing did not come off, and individual feats of arms could not compensate for a defeat made inevitable by splits within the British Cabinet over war strategy and monumental failures in campaign planning, support and battlefield leadership. They began with the unsuccessful attempt by a combined British and French fleet on 18 March to force the Narrows, unsupported by land forces. This not only resulted in four Allied battleships being sunk by Turkish mines, it also gave the Turks five weeks to build up their defences against a now expected Allied land attack.

Logistical failures compounded the blunder. The campaign on

the Western Front always took priority, and from the start Hamilton's army was starved of troops, reserves, artillery and munitions. The force engaged in the largest amphibious landing in history arrived on the Gallipoli peninsula short of heavy guns, shells, small arms ammunition, grenades and trench mortars; telephones and periscopes; barbed wire for trench defences; roofing iron for shelters and timber for shoring; and adequate medical facilities, including hospital ships, for the wounded.

Shortages in some areas would eventually be made good, but never adequately and never in time. As Pugsley put it: 'In every sense the greatest empire on earth embarked on a poor man's war where everything needed was in critically short supply.'[70] Bean damned the incompetence and lack of imagination of British staff officers and commented sourly: 'The British nation has not the brains to make war. It is much better at manufacturing socks.'[71]

New Zealand's Defence Minister, Sir James Allen was equally unimpressed, describing the Gallipoli campaign as one of the biggest blunders of the war: 'The successful forcing of the Straits would have required a large army supported by a powerful fleet, the two working in close cooperation, and with all the advantages of surprise.' Not one of those elements, he wrote to Godley, was present in the Gallipoli campaign.[72] New Zealand's High Commissioner in London, Sir Thomas Mackenzie, was sharply critical of the War Office's planning, which had resulted in 'the expenditure of lives instead of shells' at Helles and incompetent administration of the wounded.[73]

Diet and dysentery were additional problems. The troops had abundant food but always of the wrong sort for the fierce heat of a Mediterranean summer—bully beef, tinned cheese, jam and hard biscuits, when what was needed was fresh meat and vegetables, bread and milk. 'The tragedy of the commissariat at Gallipoli,' wrote O.E. Burton, 'was that it was controlled by a War Office mentality that could only think in standard terms. If a couple of experienced New Zealand housewives could have been made she-generals and placed in charge of a few boats to go shopping in, the results would have been very different.'[74]

Poor sanitation on Gallipoli caused thousands of cases of dysentery, diarrhoea and enteric fever, and the reasons were not hard to find. A hundred thousand British, Australian, New Zealand and Turkish troops were packed into 2 square kilometres of rough, steep country. Water was scarce and flies in their millions crawled over the unburied dead and the latrines, spreading diseases that weakened, and often killed, men who only months before had been strong and fit. The troops that fought on Chunuk Bair and Hill 60, including Russell himself, were for the most part sick men. The miracle was that they could fight at all.

The reasons for the Allied defeat were more complex, however. In the first place, senior Allied commanders consistently underestimated the strength of the opposition. The Turks were tough and courageous fighters, especially on the defensive, and for the most part were better led at the top levels of command than their British and French enemies. Hamilton, Birdwood, Hunter-Weston, Stopford and Godley were in the end no match for von Sanders, Kannengiesser, Mustafa Kemal (Ataturk), and Esat Pasa, who 'simply moved at a higher tempo'.[75]

Allied tactics were also a critical factor at Gallipoli. In 1915, most British commanders had been indoctrinated in late-Victorian concepts of military thinking that had not come to grips with what has been called 'the new firepower revolution'. Hamilton, Birdwood, Godley and Hunter-Weston had been exposed to doctrines that assumed superior morale and fighting spirit would invariably triumph over a weaker-willed enemy—the offensive over the defensive. Russell himself would no doubt have encountered such ideas during his six-month attachment to the British Army in 1912.

At Gallipoli, as on the Western Front, old ideas collided with the new technology. Quick-firing artillery, machine guns, trenches and barbed wire had shifted control of the battlefield from attackers to defenders, and British tactics and technical expertise had simply not caught up. At Gallipoli, wrote military historian Tim Travers, 'The Turkish defensive technology of artillery, machine guns, rifles and trenches was good enough to halt almost all offensive possibilities.'[76]

Training and experience were also a factor. For the duration of the campaign, Hamilton's mixed force of regulars and citizen soldiers, many with the 'barest veneer of military experience', faced a professional Turkish army, many of whom were veterans of the Balkan Wars of 1912–13.[77] In contrast to the Allies, the Turks were also well supplied by road with troops, munitions and other essential equipment, and had access to unlimited supplies of food and fresh water.

At both Helles and Anzac, the Turks were in control of the high ground, which allowed them to observe and fire down on their opponents on the beaches, plains, ridges and gullies below. To all of this must be added the generally high morale of the Turkish troops, who were motivated by a powerful combination of nationalism and religious belief to repel these infidel invaders from the West.

Yet with competent leadership, good planning and enough troops and heavy artillery to do the job, an Allied victory at Gallipoli was achievable. Russell's artillery brigade commander in France, Brigadier-General Napier Johnston, was convinced of it, as he wrote to Russell some years later:

Nothing will ever shake my belief that if we had had three ordinary common-sense men in London running the show, instead of the ambitious Churchill, the senile Kitchener, and the mad Fisher [First Lord of the Admiralty], we could have made a good show of it. A joint force landed at the correct time by surprise would have finished the job as far as the forts were concerned . . . and if they had only supplied us with howitzers and ammunition while they marked time in France, our three divisions, with the fine men we had, would undoubtedly have taken the whole Sari Bair Ridge.[78]

Meanwhile, Russell had been appointed an advisor to the British Territorial regiments on Gallipoli, a role that only reinforced his poor impression of the troops of Kitchener's Army. He found them not only difficult to motivate, but lacking in physique and fighting spirit: 'Babes in the matter of fighting. Too young and without sufficient red blood in their veins to really want to fight . . . They seem to care for nothing but eating, drinking, reading trashy papers and sleeping.' What was needed on Gallipoli, he wrote to his sisters, was 'an army of men, not half-fledged, ill-fed boys'. By contrast, the Anzacs had the essential will to fight, and their home countries could be proud of their performance on Gallipoli: 'My own brigade has never been put at a job which they have not succeeded in putting through—nor lost an inch of ground they have once won.'

With progress on Gallipoli at a standstill, Russell expected that the Allies were now facing a winter campaign. In mid-September he returned to Egypt for 10 days to visit the sick and wounded, collect 'stragglers', and inspect the reinforcements that had arrived from New Zealand to replace the heavy casualties from the August offensive.

Russell judged the reinforcements to be 'a fine looking lot', but once again found the new officers in need of much training to bring them up to combat standard. The high casualties on Gallipoli, however, had left him with few suitable veterans to help with this demanding task. 'Only about 80 left out of 2000 who landed on the peninsula last spring,' he wrote, 'and only one-third of the reinforcements who joined the brigade while there still going. Imagine then the work I have to get anything like a well-trained brigade.'

Russell wanted to commission experienced NCOs from the ranks to replace the many junior officers who had been killed or wounded on Sari Bair and Hill 60. Godley, however, insisted on using inexperienced reinforcement officers from New Zealand to fill the gaps, which angered veterans who had commanded platoons on Gallipoli and now expected to be promoted to commissioned rank.

Despite the threat of German submarines, Russell returned safely to Lemnos with his 1100 reinforcements, impatient to be back in action on the peninsula. There was no life on the island, he complained—no papers, no telegrams, nothing but bare hillsides and a harbour full of shipping, not even the chance to get a decent meal. The local peasantry were profiteering from the temporary occupation of their island, with eggs, fruit and vegetables all being sold at 'famine prices'.

Russell was angered by the reporting of the Sari Bair and Hill 60 attacks by influential British war correspondent Ashmead-Bartlett, who in both cases had credited successes to the Australians that Russell felt rightfully belonged to his New Zealanders. Russell was particularly incensed at the statement that the Australians had captured the foothills of Sari Bair on the night of 6/7 August when that had been done by his own mounted brigade 'without the help of a single Australian'. The successes at Hill 60 were mostly the work of his own brigade, he argued, although the Australians did play a significant part in that action. Ashmead-Bartlett's reports were labelled 'an absolute fabrication' and the man himself 'a fraud'.

With the news that his father was battling colon cancer, Russell's thoughts now turned to the past and happier times. 'Perhaps one remembers on the whole the pleasanter side of one's life,' he wrote to Ham. 'I know I look back on my childhood and boyhood, and recall the pleasant holidays and those tramps in Switzerland much more than, say, my inevitably bad reports at Harrow, and the grave face you assumed in firstly and very kindly pointing out the error of my ways. I wonder if I was really as bad as they made me out.'

After nearly two months on Lemnos, the rested, reorganised but still under-strength mounted brigade returned to Gallipoli. For Russell, it could not have come soon enough: 'I shall be very glad to get back to the firing line and have done with training,' he wrote to his family. 'It's no rest for me: and the only advantage is being safe. Sickness still rife.'

The political and strategic situation, however, had changed dramatically. All thoughts of further Allied offensives at Gallipoli had ceased, and Hamilton had been replaced as commander of the Mediterranean Expeditionary Force by General Sir Charles Monro. Bulgaria had allied itself with the Central Powers, allowing Germany to supply Turkey with artillery and ammunition directly by rail to Constantinople. The Allies would soon face the prospect of being blasted off Gallipoli by fresh Turkish batteries of heavy guns.

British leaders, both political and military, were increasingly convinced that the war would be decided on the Western Front, and that it made little sense to divert forces elsewhere. Pressure was mounting for the abandonment of the Gallipoli campaign before the approaching winter made the supply and reinforcement of the besieged force impossible. As Pugsley put it, 'Gallipoli was now an embarrassing backwater, expensive in men, material and effort and difficult to shrug off.'[79]

After consulting his senior commanders, Monro recommended that all Allied forces on the peninsula be withdrawn forthwith. Hamilton, however, had opposed any such move, telling his superiors in London that it would result in the loss of up to 45 percent of his force and most of his artillery and stores. To no avail. After a surprise visit to Gallipoli, Kitchener, now Secretary of State for War, made the final call, and planning began for the only successful British military operation on the peninsula—its evacuation.

Russell's role in the evacuation was a critical one. On the strength of his performance since arriving at Gallipoli in May he had been promoted to major-general and had replaced Godley as commander of the New Zealand and Australian Division when Godley moved up to overall command of the NZEF. By agreement between Birdwood and Godley, Russell was now to command the 20,000-strong rearguard that would protect the back of the retreating Anzac army.

Planned by Birdwood's talented Chief of Staff, Lieutenant-Colonel Brudenell White, the evacuation was to be a three-step process. All non-essential men and supplies would be sent away in early December, followed a week later by the evacuation of one regiment or battalion in each brigade to Lemnos, and finally by Russell's rearguard men on the nights of 19 and 20 December.

Heavy guns would be taken off the beach by night; surplus supplies, arms and ammunition would be dumped at sea, burnt in piles onshore or buried; and fires would be kept burning in deserted bivouacs. Self-firing rifles and booby-traps would be fixed in position and mines laid under the Turkish trenches at the Nek. Casualties that could not be easily moved would be left behind in dressing stations under the care of medical staff who had volunteered to stay behind and, if necessary, be taken prisoner.

If the Turks attacked during the critical stages of the evacuation, the rearguard—or whatever part of it remained—would be sealed off behind large, barbed-wire barriers and expected to fight, and if necessary die, where they stood. Like the Spartan rearguard that fought the Persians to the death at Thermopylae 2400 years before, the 'last-ditchers' were to be sacrificed for the army.

Russell's main worry was that the weather would deteriorate in the middle of the evacuation, whipping up rough seas and making it difficult to get troops off the beach. He was right to be concerned. The peninsula had been swept by gales as winter approached, wrecking piers, picket boats, barges and lighters, and there were already heavy casualties from frostbite at both Anzac Cove and Suvla. On 27 November, a fierce thunderstorm had flooded gullies on Gallipoli, drowning at least 100 British soldiers. Two days later, another 100 men died of exposure in a blizzard and driving snow.

In the event, the weather remained calm. The Turks held off, but strengthened their trench systems and put up more barbed wire— apparently in the belief that the growing number of transports lying off the beach signalled a fresh Anzac attack. The Turks were not entirely fooled, however: they had been expecting an Allied withdrawal from the peninsula; they were just not sure when it would happen. Had they known this, Russell and his rearguard would almost certainly have had to withdraw under heavy Turkish artillery, machine-gun and rifle fire.

By dawn on Sunday 19 December, there were just 10,000 of the rearguard, including 540 mounted riflemen, left at Anzac. That night—the last night of the evacuation—Russell divided them into three parties. The 4000-strong 'A' party would leave Anzac Cove at 6 pm. If all was quiet, 'B' party, also 4000 strong, would leave at 9 pm, and 'C', the last covering party of 2000 men, at 2 am the following morning. If necessary, 'C' party would stay and cover the evacuation of the remaining troops. Fifty machine guns would fire on Turkish positions in the hills around Chunuk Bair until the last moment. The men would then extract the bolts from the guns and head for the beach.

Although Turkish shells were now falling on the Anzac trenches, the final withdrawal went like clockwork. The A and B parties were embarked by 11.25 pm without incident. At 1.40 am the first men of C party filed quietly out of the trenches and down the Aghyl Dere to the beach, arming the booby-traps as they left and closing the big wire gates behind them. Commanders, staff officers and privates all packed onto the landing craft, which then headed for the transports and warships riding at anchor offshore. Scattered in the hills behind them, or buried in Gallipoli's hard clay, were the bodies of over 10,000 of their mates. Now they were to be abandoned, the detritus of a defeated army.

At 1.30 am on 20 December, Russell handed over command on shore to his subordinate, Colonel Paton, and joined Godley aboard the destroyer *Heliotrope*. He had given instructions that the mines at the Nek were to be fired when the entire garrison was clear. A few minutes before 2 am a shout rang out along the Turkish line, but no attack came. At 3.40 am, the mines that the rearguard had laid at the Nek blew up with a roar, killing some 70 Turks and pushing two huge red clouds high above their trenches.

Expecting an immediate attack, the Turks fired volley after volley into the Anzac lines, while their troops advanced cautiously against Quinn's Post and nearby positions. Meeting no resistance, they launched a general attack all along the Anzac line, pouring over the now empty trenches and down the hillsides to the sea. By mid-afternoon their heavy guns were still shelling the now silent Anzac positions, while their former enemies disembarked at their base on Lemnos, 100 kilometres away.

The outcome of the Allied withdrawal was better than anyone in the British military or political establishment could have foreseen. Meticulous planning by headquarters staff, clever deception, and good force discipline had seen the entire Anzac/Suvla force of 134,000 men, nearly 400 guns and 14,000 animals embarked for Lemnos under the eyes of 170,000 Turks, and almost without loss. It was, observed Monash, 'a most brilliant conception, brilliantly organised, and brilliantly executed'.[80]

Russell regretted that the Allies had failed to gain 'a real victory' over the Turks, but was pleased that his men were moving to a warmer and more comfortable winter climate. One experience of blizzard conditions on Gallipoli, he told his family, was enough for them not to want to repeat the experience.

Russell felt, however, that many of the key decisions made by the high command at Gallipoli were wrong. He did not make his feelings known at the time, he told his father, because 'junior and inexperienced officers don't care to give voice to their misgivings'. Privately, he had made his opinion about the Dardanelles campaign quite clear: the strategic concept behind it was good but its execution was abysmal, and the architect of the plan, Winston Churchill, was responsible for 'a stupid fiasco'.

Gallipoli was a fiasco—even if Churchill was not entirely to blame. In the end, the talent of a few individual commanders and the fighting qualities of the Anzac troops could not compensate for failures of leadership and administration at the top levels of command, or for the tragic error that put the Australians and New Zealanders ashore in the wrong place in the critical first hours of the landing. 'After Gallipoli,' wrote John North, 'the war was doomed to be a long war; it could only fight itself out to the last point of weariness and exhaustion. After Gallipoli, there was no other short route to victory.'[81]

Although the campaign was a defeat for the Allies, in the eyes of Hamilton, Birdwood and Godley, Russell had performed with distinction. Birdwood described him as 'an excellent commander' and 'a first-rate soldier, always ready to take anything on'.[82] The result was Russell's promotion to major-general, the first New Zealand-born soldier to reach that rank. He had become one of the few senior commanders to survive the Gallipoli campaign with his reputation enhanced, so why did he succeed where others—Birdwood and Godley among them—had largely failed?

Inevitably, Russell had made mistakes in his first experience of battlefield command. He had committed his mounteds to a foolhardy attack on No. 3 Post in May—although it is unclear whether the original plan to capture it was his or Godley's. If Bean and Pugsley are right, Russell also made mistakes in the struggle for Hill 60, although he probably had little choice about using the raw Western Australian battalion in the attack on 22 August. Russell's diary for 1915, which might have shed further light on both these matters, is missing.

Russell had also been lucky. He had missed the disastrous landing at Ari Burnu on 25 April, where other Anzac commanders had put their reputations on the line under the most testing conditions. He and his mounteds had missed the debacle of Helles in early May when the combat effectiveness of the New Zealand Infantry Division was decimated under the inept command of Major-General Hunter-Weston. And he was particularly fortunate in the calibre of his subordinate commanders and his mounted riflemen—described by Pugsley as 'perhaps the finest body of fighting men New Zealand has ever raised'.[83]

What mattered most to Russell's superiors, however, were the qualities he had shown as a field commander in the extreme conditions at Gallipoli. In his seven-month defence of a critical section of the Anzac front line, in the successful August attack on the foothills of Sari Bair in August, and in the 'brilliantly executed' evacuation of Anzac, Russell had proved himself a practical, determined commander and a skillful planner and tactician. Here he had demonstrated qualities that would make him an outstanding commander on the Western Front—moral and physical courage, intelligence and fighting spirit.

Leading from the front, Russell had shared many of the hardships and dangers of his men, rather than commanding from the comparative safety of the beach or a patrolling warship. This not only encouraged his mounted riflemen, but kept him in close touch with battlefield conditions and able to make quick decisions when the need arose. By selecting Russell as rearguard commander—a role critical to the safe evacuation of 48,000 Australian and New Zealand troops from Anzac—Birdwood had acknowledged his outstanding leadership abilities.

Russell had grown in the job—and so, too, had his men. The civilian soldiers who had been led to believe that they could never be as good as British 'regulars' had seen British incompetence and failure at first hand, and now had a healthy respect for their own abilities and those of their brother colonials, the Australians. They had endured eight months of fierce heat and cold, bad food, lice and disease, all under constant Turkish sniper, machine-gun and shell fire. They had experienced the brutal realities of hand-to-hand fighting, the loss of good mates, and the sheer monotony of war.

For the moment at least, the bitter fighting on Gallipoli had tempered their commander's appetite for war. 'What fools we are,' Russell wrote to his family after it was all over. 'The waste of money, men and material is enough to bring anyone to his senses. We must in future think more of 'humanity' and less of 'nationality'.

Chapter 11

Egypt to Armentières

The sector was known as the L'Espinet Salient and it was called 'The Nursery' unofficially because it was such a quiet place. The Huns and the British forces had sort of come to an arrangement not to hurt one another. It was the first place they put troops in to get the feeling of trench warfare. But we hadn't travelled 12,000 miles to sit on our backsides and wait for the Germans. So it wasn't long before the Rifle Brigade started to raid the German trenches . . . with the result that when we left to go to the Somme in '16, the French said that they would sooner have the Huns than those black-button bastards from New Zealand.'—Lieutenant-Colonel Curly Blyth, NZ Rifle Brigade, recalls the New Zealand Division's first months on the Western Front.

The eight-month campaign to wrest the Dardanelles from the Turks had cost the lives of 2721 New Zealanders and 7594 Australians but, for those who survived, the fighting was far from over. The failure of the campaign condemned the Anzacs to three more years of bloody trench fighting on the Western Front, until the German armies were finally beaten in the field.[84]

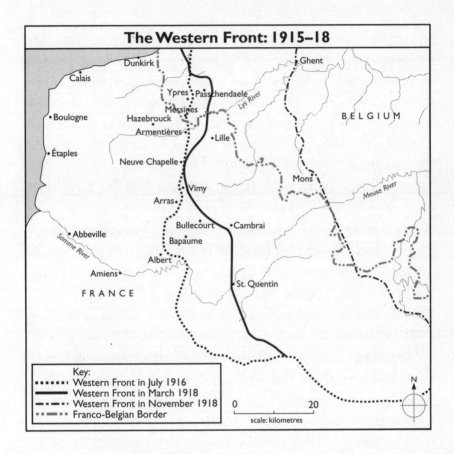

The Western Front: 1915–18

Key:
- Western Front in July 1916
- Western Front in March 1918
- Western Front in November 1918
- Franco-Belgian Border

0 — 20
scale: kilometres

In late December 1915, the skeletal remains of Russell's battalions—mounteds and infantry—were shipped back from Lemnos to camp at Moascar in Egypt where, just one year before, the New Zealand infantry had helped repulse a Turkish attack on the Suez Canal. For some, the rest from combat was shortlived. On 25 December, a battalion of the New Zealand Division took part in a desert action against a Turkish force near Matruh as part of the Western Frontier Force. Some 200 of the enemy were killed for the loss six Allied troops. Another action on 22 January, also near Matruh, resulted in the rout of the enemy force and the destruction of their camp.

While on Gallipoli Russell had thought that the New Zealanders' next deployment might be to Salonika, where British forces were confronting the Bulgarians in defence of Serbia—and that his troopers might at last use their horses in combat. Now it seemed more likely that his troops would remain in Egypt to help counter the threat of a German thrust through the Middle East towards the Suez Canal. The purpose of this would be to keep large numbers of Allied troops 'locked up' and unable to reinforce British forces on the Western Front.

Russell was almost right. His new division was first earmarked for the defence of a section of the Suez Canal, but was then told that it would go to France, after further training in Egypt. Brigadiers-General Earl Johnston and 'Bill' Braithwaite would command its 1st and 2nd infantry brigades respectively, Brigadier-General Harry Fulton the rifle brigade, and Brigadier-General Napier Johnston the divisional artillery. Included would be the 500-strong Pioneer (Maori) Battalion.

Russell was Defence Minister Allen's original choice to command the 20,000-strong New Zealand Expeditionary Force that would now go to France to fight the Germans. In the end, he settled on God-ley as overall commander of the NZEF and Russell as the divisional commander on the Western Front. Brigadier-General Chaytor would command the newly reinforced mounted rifles brigade that would go to fight the Turks in Palestine.

Russell seemed resigned, rather than enthusiastic, about his status as New Zealand's first divisional general, leading 'the first little Army' his country had produced. Growing Allied strength and the exhaustion of the Germans at Verdun had convinced him that the war would be over by the summer of 1916, which would give him no more than six months in the job. It was not to be. In the end, Russell commanded the New Zealanders on the Western Front for three unbroken years, and saw three of his brigade commanders and over 12,000 of his men killed in action.

But for now it was training and more training as Russell worked to toughen his new division and weld its mostly inexperienced officers,

NCOs and men into an efficient fighting force for the campaigns to come. There was much to be done, he told his sisters: 'Somehow the men have got awfully slack and will need a very great deal of brushing up before they are fit to go to France, as we hope to in the spring.'

As at Zeitoun before the Gallipoli landings, the training was rigorous—barrack-square drill, musketry training, live artillery firing and tactical manoeuvres—a gruelling 16-hour-a-day regime that included night operations in the desert to give the troops confidence to attack in the dark. A typical day exercise involved a long route march through heavy desert sand and in searing heat. 'Divisional training again and we fight and march over endless miles of burning sands,' wrote one of his junior officers. 'Lord! How sick I am of it all ... And the heat is cruel. Sometimes I feel the blood almost bursting from my nose under the high pressure. Can't last it much longer.'[85]

Russell shared the impatience of his men with the relentless training, and looked to the day when he and his troops would finally see action. 'I see the [German] mark is falling,' he wrote to his father, 'but we don't want to win that way. The men here want a good solid go, on even terms as far as the artillery, and then the devil take the hindmost. I wonder how the Germans are taking it, and if they are as anxious to cross bayonets as we are.' He was also feeling a growing sense of personal frustration: 'I am no longer a soldier,' he wrote to his sisters. 'I am a letter producer, a memo writer, a draftsman of orders, an administrator: anything you like but a soldier as one pictures him in battle harness. Perhaps if the Turks do come, I may yet don a revolver once more. I haven't fired a shot so far.'

By early February, however, the tough training regime was producing results. Officers and men, Russell noted, appeared generally alert, well disciplined and keen, even if some junior officers were not yet up to the job: 'Generally speaking the men are a fine lot, and if we do not compare favourably with the home-trained armies in matters of saluting, I believe we have other qualities equally useful.'

By March, Russell had changed his tune, admitting that there was still much to be done to improve the discipline and general turnout of his new division. Slackness in both areas, he felt, was the product of ingrained colonial attitudes: 'We in the colonies have lived so long in an atmosphere of "nothing matters" that the idea of self-discipline and self-respect is one that takes root with difficulty.' To his father he wrote: 'Discipline is my only worry at present. When shall we Anglo-Saxons learn the truth, and win the last and greatest victory of all—that of self.'

Monash, who was then in command of an Australian brigade, saw slackness in other areas of Russell's command and was not slow to blame him for it. Operations against the New Zealand Mounted Regiment on 17 February, he wrote, had resulted in much 'muddlement' and confusion. Overall, Russell's conduct of divisional manoeuvres had 'defied every fundamental principle of command and staff work and of ordinary common sense'.[86]

According to his biographer, Monash also disapproved of Russell's 'nonchalance' towards administration; he 'simply delegated these matters to staff and did not bother himself further'. Russell had given him 'an insight into the awful confusion, cross purposes, constant changes of plan and policy which characterise he higher command and get worse the higher you go'.[87]

If Russell was aware of Monash's complaints, there is no written record of it. In the meantime, he spelled his men when he could, giving them time off to swim in the deep waters of Lake Timsah, play football, and take part in athletics and mounted steeplechases over the desert dunes and canals. As in 1914, Alexandria and Cairo gave the troops much scope for 'unsavoury amusement', too, and inevitably there were cases of drunkenness and venereal disease. The chief problem, wrote their commander, was keeping his men 'in bounds and sober . . . It's not so surprising after all. If they have the spirit to attack well, the colonials naturally have the spirit for a bit of fun also.'

On 23 March, the Imperial General Staff in London ordered the New Zealand Division to follow the 1st and 2nd Australian divisions to France. On 3 April, the entire division paraded before General Murray, commander of the British forces in Egypt—the first time that an entirely New Zealand division had been on parade. Russell feared that his chronic back pain would make it hard for him to mount his horse, and that the event itself would be a test of endurance. His solution was to have his back massaged with a hot iron just before mounting his horse. He wrote to his sisters: 'The effect lasts for about 2 hours, and as the ceremony is not to be a long one, I hope it will just see me through.' It apparently did, and privately Murray had high praise for the smartness and discipline of Russell's new brigades.

Russell also knew, however, that after only six weeks in existence, the division now bound for the Western Front was still raw and relatively untrained, officers and men alike:

> In every way they reflected the standards and experience of the British divisions that deployed to France with them—generally superb material, keen, enthusiastic, but still largely amateur, committed to the most difficult operation of the war, that of driving a skilled enemy of equal mass out of carefully prepared defences.[88]

The responsibilities of command, however, meant that Russell could not attend to his now terminally ill father. 'I still hope I may get home in time,' he wrote to his sisters, 'if only fate spares him; but I don't want him to linger on unless he is reasonably comfortable . . . I rather hope from what you say that of actual pain father may have but little to suffer: of discomfort and weariness a great deal.' A month before his father died, Russell wrote that he wished he had been able to persuade Ham to return to New Zealand, 'so that I might have had the joy of taking you round Tunanui, and showing you all the improvements. But sometimes I almost regret the improvements, and the old wild look of the fern and manuka, so rapidly becoming a thing of the past.'

In early April, the New Zealand Division sailed from Alexandria for the French port of Marseilles. As enemy submarines were known to be active in the Mediterranean, the troops were ordered to wear lifebelts night and day. The threat was very real—a wireless message had been received saying that several ships had been torpedoed the day before the convoy sailed, including two just outside Marseilles. The *Arcadian*, a ship carrying 2400 men of the Rifle Brigade to France, was sunk by a German submarine on her return from Marseilles to Egypt.

The division, however, arrived at Marseilles without incident. On 13 April, it entrained for the village of Hazebrouck, near Armentières in northern France. Here it would be attached to the Second Army of General Sir Herbert Plumer, who would become one the most successful of the British commanders on the Western Front.

Each train carried a complete battalion, less transport—a Pullman car for the officers, third-class carriages for the men, and a few covered wagons for the cooks and stores. At the stations where the trains halted, French territorials and gendarmes plied the New Zealanders with urns of tea, sometimes laced with cognac. Whenever the trains stopped near a town, children begged for the money, biscuits and 'boully-bif' that the troops threw to them from the windows.

The change of scenery could not have been more dramatic. In place of the bleak, waterless hills and ravines of Gallipoli and Egypt's parched deserts were green fields, flowering orchards, woodlands, and small agricultural villages, each with its red-brick houses, its church spire, its manure heaps in farm courtyards.

Armentières itself was a dour little manufacturing town on the Franco-Belgian border. Only a few thousand of its inhabitants now remained, largely because all of its able-bodied men were in the French Army and most of the others had fled before the advance of the Germans in 1914. But it was now part of the front line and under constant bombardment by German heavy guns. As the Rifle Brigade marched in the dark to its billets in the ruined village of Houplines, bursts of machine-gun fire crackled down the streets, striking sparks off the cobblestones, and German shells crashed into the brick ruins nearby. The New Zealanders were in no doubt that they had at last arrived at the real war.

For the veterans of Gallipoli, the Western Front was in some ways familiar, but in other ways quite strange. The familiar things were the sentry duty at night, the stand-to at dawn, the sleeping in boots and clothes, the everlasting fight against lice and rats. There was the incessant work—mostly under cover of night—bringing up ammunition and rations; digging or improving trenches, dugouts and gun emplacements; building parapets and listening posts, and erecting wire entanglements while covering parties lay out in no-man's-land listening for German patrols.

Other things, though, were very different. Gallipoli's trenches had been dug from dry soil. Here they had to be excavated from water-sodden flats and protected by breastworks built up above ground level and reinforced with sandbags, wooden stakes and corrugated iron. Northern France was low-lying, the water table was high, and heavy shellfire tended to turn it into a morass of mud. When they were in the front line, the officers slept in sparsely appointed dugouts; the troops in 'damp, lousy, rat-infested' burrows excavated from the trench walls.

At Gallipoli, the Anzacs had been ravaged by diseases brought on by a hot Mediterranean climate, poor food and insanitary conditions. Dysentery, enteric fever and jaundice were arguably as much a factor in their eventual defeat as were the Turks themselves. Here there were occasional outbreaks of measles and mumps; but early in 1916 France was at least a healthier place to fight, and the food was a great deal better.

Twenty minutes' walk away, in Armentières, there were baths for the troops, shops and estaminets (taverns) where tired men might buy eggs and chips, coffee, wine and beer in a relaxed and cheerful environment. Russell's recreational pursuits took a different track— a hard evening gallop along the banks of the River Lys, after which he would often listen to classical music on his gramophone.

In April 1916, Russell's division was one of 57 British and Dominion divisions organised into four armies under the overall command of General Sir Douglas Haig. Together they were holding about 130 kilometres of the front line, extending from Ypres in Belgium down to the Somme region in northern France. Each army consisted of several infantry corps, and each corps three or four divisions. A typical division was a powerful and well-balanced force equipped with some 12,000 rifles, 24 machine guns, 40 trench mortars and 76 artillery pieces, along with some 5000 horses and 60 motor vehicles.

The New Zealand Division itself consisted of three infantry brigades and its support units of artillery, engineers, signals, ambulance and ordnance personnel. Supporting the combat division was a matching administrative organisation in England under Brigadier-General Richardson. Its primary role was to receive reinforcement drafts from New Zealand, train them at Sling Camp, and dispatch them from there to France. It also provided hospital and convalescent care for the wounded, and managed their eventual return, after retraining, to the front.

Because the division was both comparatively untried and lightly trained, Russell had hoped to arrange an extended period of training in France, but by May it was on combat duty in the trenches. On 9 May, after his first visit to the Australian and New Zealand divisions, Haig wrote to the King, confirming what Russell already knew well: 'They are undoubtedly a fine body of men, but their officers and leaders as a whole have a good deal to learn.'[89]

By the time the New Zealanders had arrived in France the war was 20 months old. On 4 August 1914, German forces had crossed the border into Belgium and northern France with the aim of swiftly defeating the French before turning their full force against Russia in the east. The Germans, however, were held by the French at the Battle of the Marne and after the First Battle of Ypres the two forces—Allied and German—were locked in a stalemate on what was now the Western Front.

Both armies had built opposing systems of trenches that stretched some 730 kilometres from the North Sea to the Swiss Alps. The German high command was resolved to stay on the defensive until some acceptable solution appeared—'a collapse of the Allied will to fight, a compromise peace or a sudden chance to gain victory'.[90]

The strategic situation, however, significantly favoured the enemy. German troops and their artillery were usually dug in on higher ground, from which their heavy guns could dominate just about every part of the British line. By the end of 1915, British attempts to break through this barrier of artillery, machine guns, barbed wire and concrete at Neuve Chapelle, Aubers Ridge, Festubert and Loos had cost their armies some 285,000 casualties. Added to this, the British and their allies had been defeated at Gallipoli, British troops were besieged in Mesopotamia, the Russians were retreating before the Germans and Austrians in the east, and the Italian offensives against Austria-Hungary were making little headway. For the moment, the strategic outlook for the Allies was bleak.

The British high command, however, had ambitious plans for 1916 in the form of a combined French and British offensive on the Somme in July. This, it was hoped, would break the stalemate on the Western Front and take the pressure off French forces at Verdun, where a massive German offensive under General von Falkenhayn was attempting to draw in and ultimately destroy the French Army.

Meanwhile, the New Zealand Division had orders to relieve the British 17th Division on a 6-kilometre section of the line in front of Armentières. There they would be opposed by troops of the German XIX Corps under General von Laffert, who had the reputation of being 'rather sluggish, but good fighters when aroused'.[91] The two forces would face each other across a no-man's-land no more than

200–300 metres wide, and in some places only 60 metres wide. The sector, which ran from just south of the Armentières railway to the River Lys, was a 'quiet' one where British troops were acclimatised to trench warfare before being committed to combat.

The New Zealanders soon changed all that. Russell put his troops on the offensive from the start and kept them there. Day and night the division's 18-pounders and howitzers hammered suspected enemy headquarters, artillery positions, ammunition dumps, billets, communication trenches and other 'tender spots'. By night, the New Zealand infantry patrolled no-man's-land, while Vickers and Lewis machine guns swept the German parapets and fired on their working parties. By day, snipers with telescopic sights and armour-piercing bullets duelled with their opposite numbers wherever they could find them. Russell's instruction to his men was to keep on making ground and clear no-man's-land of the enemy. After frequent fights with German patrols, his officers could report that command of no-man's-land had passed almost entirely to the New Zealand Division.

The aggressive approach of the New Zealanders came at a price, for the Germans retaliated by increasing their bombardment of Armentières, destroying the churches of St Roche and Notre Dame. Heavy and frequent German shelling of New Zealand trenches strained nerves and staying power to the limit. One such bombardment inflicted 36 casualties on the division in two days; many of the dead and wounded had to be dug out of collapsed bivouacs. On the night of 2 July, Armentières was heavily shelled and several buildings were set on fire, trapping a number of women and children in the cellars where they had taken refuge. Soldiers of the Rifle Brigade battled their way into the cellars to rescue the panic-stricken civilians from death by fire or suffocation.

There was chivalry, too. At the beginning of June New Zealand troops raised a billboard above their trenches to show the Germans the losses claimed for both sides at the naval Battle of Jutland in the North Sea. A dozen Germans stood up, fully exposed, to read it. The

New Zealanders held their fire and, after a decent interval, waved the Germans down, sending a couple of shots over their heads to make sure. Later the Germans put up a notice asking to be shown the table of losses again. Again the New Zealanders obliged.

The Armentières sector gave Russell's fledgling division time to become familiar with the terrain and conditions of northern France, and the tactics of their German adversaries, before they were committed to offensive operations. Most of all, it gave raw troops time to improve the skills they needed to fight and survive on the Western Front. There were classes for grenadiers, snipers, Lewis gunners, signallers, and senior and junior NCOs; and lectures and special instruction on the use of gas, bayonet fighting and trench warfare. Every afternoon all ranks were sent on a two-hour route march to make them hard and fit.

Russell was everywhere—inspecting his units daily in and out of the trenches, and berating inefficiency, slackness and inappropriate behaviour of any kind, including that of his senior officers. His 2nd Brigade commander, Brigadier-General Braithwaite, was reproved for standing his troops to arms all night, instead of spelling them after no more than four hours continuously in the line. Infantryman James Meek recalled Russell grilling the officer in charge during a frontline entrenching operation: 'Patrols been out there? You don't know what is actually out there? Never been out? Go out with your men tonight!'[92]

As usual, Russell was himself taking risks. Determined to personally resolve a case of desertion, he strode into the front line on a day when casualties from German shellfire were twice their normal rate and refused to take cover until his task was completed. On 22 June, he and his 1st Brigade commander, Brigadier-General Hart, went over the parapet into no-man's-land to inspect the German wire in preparation for an upcoming attack.

The same month—this time in front of his corps commander, General Birdwood—Russell was at it again, crawling along a shallow sap to a shell crater in the middle of no-man's-land and within bomb-throwing distance of the German front line. There he sat for a full 10 minutes, calmly discussing brigade defences with its worried commander, Brigadier-General Fulton, who had reluctantly gone with him.

Lindsay Inglis, a young brigade officer and future major-general in World War II, remembered the incident: 'That great man and leader had no thought of playing to the gallery. It was just natural for him to go anywhere and see anything, a practice not in favour with some other divisional commanders.'[93]

As at Gallipoli, the constant round of inspections kept Russell in close touch with his troops as they prepared for what was to come. Among the newer men he noted the same aggressive spirit the New Zealanders had shown before Gallipoli, but he was in no hurry to indulge it. 'We have a very large number who were not at Anzac and have therefore seen no fighting,' he wrote to his father. 'Their keenness to get to grips is great, and to their credit, but to my point of view quite illogical. I have lost any bloodthirsty tendencies, and am quite content to wait patiently until everything is ready.'

Maintaining the aggressive spirit of the troops was the task of Major Campbell, commandant of the GHQ Bayonet Fighting School. In August, he delivered one of his by now famous lectures on bayonet fighting to the assembled New Zealand troops. Titled 'Blood on the Bayonet' and supported with live demonstrations by his NCOs, it was an instruction on how to kill Germans, whether they resisted or not, and to take no prisoners. Russell's feelings about the presentation are unclear, but Inglis admitted that this type of bloodthirsty propaganda made him and most of his fellow soldiers acutely uncomfortable.[94]

Russell wanted his division to match the best in the British Army, both for combat performance and general smartness and discipline. The first week at the front had shown him he had a long way to go. General Plumer had been highly critical of his first view of Braithwaite's 2nd Infantry Brigade, and the other two brigades appeared to be not much better. On 17 April, Birdwood inspected Fulton and Earl Johnston's men. 'As yet they are very slovenly,' Russell noted in his diary, 'and make a bad figure amongst the more disciplined soldiers of Europe.' The result was a tersely worded instruction to all ranks on saluting and general bearing:

Men who fail to salute when they should, are untidy in dress, lounge about the streets, and fail to keep their eyes sufficiently open, and their wits sufficiently wide awake, to see when an officer is passing, may or may not be good fighters, but they certainly make a bad impression. To be smart and alert isn't servility. It is exactly the opposite. Every officer and man of the Division should walk about as if he had 10,000 pounds a year, and must be as jealous of our reputation as a woman of her honour.[95]

At this stage of the war, many of the division's officers and NCOs were inexperienced in handling large bodies of men, and Russell blamed this for most of the discipline problems. 'I never worry about the men,' he wrote to Gertrude. 'They are as their officers make them, and, I suppose it may be added, the officers are as I make them.' Russell urged his officers to study the character of the men under their command, and by 'advice, instruction etc ensure, as far as humanly possible that they do not offend to begin with'.[96]

Russell believed that his officers had a key role to play not only in ensuring the comfort and wellbeing of their men, but in explaining the need for restrictions on their behaviour.[97] The clear link between well-disciplined troops and their staying power in battle, he told them, needed to be explained and reinforced.

Russell's get-tough approach began to show results. A British officer noted at this time that 'the New Zealander is much more like the Englishman, more appreciative of appearances, he has a neater uniform, more brass and colour and cut about it—and less of a child of nature than the Australian, and more given to showing his respect for authority by saluting'.[98] The saluting, in most cases, was likely to have been perfunctory. While the British Army believed that saluting was important in recognising authority and so maintaining discipline, the New Zealanders, like the Australians, believed that it was servile to salute a man who had not earned respect by personality or performance in the field.

As with most divisions on the Western Front, crime was a persistent problem. Again Russell targeted his officers, alleging that in many cases they were not making sufficient efforts to prevent crime, or to properly deal with offenders. In units where the number of offences was large, he warned, the problem was invariably due to officers not being in proper control of their men and too inclined to excuse bad behaviour. He felt that his courts-martial were often too lenient with offenders: instead of trying to see justice done, they were wasting their energies in 'trying to find excuses for the prisoner'.

Russell and his brigade commanders were also unhappy with the large numbers of men sentenced to imprisonment and then released back to their units on suspended sentences. This practice frustrated his efforts to rid his division of 'incorrigibles'—the 10 percent of his division who were consistently in trouble—and led the offenders to believe that they had escaped punishment altogether.

In the pantheon of divisional crime, desertion was probably the most serious offence; but looting was also a serious offence, because it risked alienating the French population with whom the British Army was billeted. Russell forbade the theft of food, drink, household contents and animals from the local people, and any damage to buildings or crops. In June, a complaint from the mayor of Vieux Berquin that the grazing divisional horses were damaging his villagers' crops drew a threat of severe punishment for repeat offences. Another memorandum warned, with no hint of tongue in cheek, that bombing fish in the river—presumably the Lys—was illegal and was to cease at once.

But try as Russell might, men took from the locals whatever would make life at the front more comfortable—wine, foodstuffs and firewood, mattresses, crockery and furniture, and even timber from their billets. Despite a strict prohibition on such activities, men of the Canterbury battalion organised a 'drive' to flush out game across several kilometres of the countryside, supplementing its rations with the results.

With Russell taking a hard line, however, punishment rates started to climb. The courts-martial register of April–May 1916 records 82 convictions, 48 of them for drunkenness, the rest for a range of offences including theft, desertion, insubordination, striking a superior officer, and self-inflicted wounds. By August, the number of convictions had risen to 108, the highest number for the whole war. 'Russell wanted excellence, but his officers did not initially have the skills to produce it. A harsh discipline with too many courts-martial was the result.'[99]

Field punishment No. 2 was the most common penalty for misdemeanours of most kinds. It involved pack drill, loss of leave privileges, and being put on a roster for the most menial divisional tasks. The worst offenders, however, were dispatched to military prisons and divisional field punishment camps, where punishment was often brutal as the authorities attempted to bend serial deserters and other 'incorrigibles' to military law. A common punishment—prison with hard labour—consisted of being forced to work from 6 am in all weathers, including rain and snow. The prisoners were permanently cold and hungry, and were denied hot drinks and underclothes. Illness, especially diarrhoea, was common. If a prisoner continued to resist, there was solitary confinement, a bread-and-water diet, and the notorious Field Punishment No. 1—being spreadeagled against a gun wheel or (more commonly) tied to a post for two hours a day.

Twenty-eight New Zealanders were sentenced to death by firing squad on Russell's watch, and five of them were subsequently executed. Russell and his senior commanders had no doubts about the rightness of the death penalty for serious offences like desertion, mutiny, and sleeping on sentry duty: deserters and other persistent offenders were a threat to the integrity and efficiency of the division and their punishment needed to be harsh enough to deter others. After the execution of a soldier by firing squad in September 1916, Russell wrote to Allen: 'It is hoped its effect will prevent another being necessary . . . He has lost his life as an example to the rest, and to that extent has helped towards the desired victory.'[100]

Three of those executed, however—Sweeney, King and Spencer—were not division 'incorrigibles' who might have deserved the death penalty for persistent offending, but soldiers whose nerve had broken under the stresses of combat. Spencer, who was shot by firing squad for desertion, was a man 'numbed, concussed and in shock' from enemy bombardment.[101] Rummel, whose death sentence was commuted, was 'a victim of battle fatigue brought on by his youth, 33 months of active service, the lingering impact of his Gallipoli foot wound, the strains of the Somme, and the effects of the shelling in February 1917'.[102]

Today, these men would be diagnosed as suffering from post-traumatic stress disorder (PTSD), brought on by months of exposure to foul weather and the constant threat of death by shellfire, bomb or bullet. Like Sweeney, King and Spencer, many of the 300 soldiers of the British Army shot on the Western Front for desertion or cowardice were brave men who had simply cracked under the strain of life in the trenches. Their reserves of courage and physical endurance exhausted, they would do anything, including desertion, to avoid further service in the front line.

Pugsley observes that 'shell-shock', as it was then known, was treated with deep suspicion by the British high command. Haig directed that all such cases be kept in the army area until investigated, to see if disciplinary action by court martial was warranted. The fact that the endurance of soldiers in sustained battle conditions was limited cut little ice with Haig and his generals. Their overriding concern was that if threats of severe punishment were removed, the new citizen armies would melt away.

By the end of the war, genuine cases of shell-shock in the British Army—as opposed to temporary nervous disorders—had reached more than 70,000, requiring special centres to be set up for their diagnosis and treatment. Many of these soldiers were invalided out of the army altogether; the unlucky ones were treated and, after a period of rest, sent back to the front.

As for death sentences, Haig and his senior generals would usually confirm the recommendations of Russell and his brigadiers if they involved desertion in battle, repeated offences, or a long absence from duty. In other cases, sentences would be commuted to imprisonment, or even suspended altogether. As Pugsley put it: 'In the [New Zealand] division, the pressure to execute came from within and was not imposed on a reluctant dominion force by outside pressure from above.'[103]

If Russell's attitude to the death penalty seems harsh, it reflected the conservative society from which he came, and it was the common practice of the British Army during World War I. The Canadians and Australians also viewed the death penalty as essential to effective discipline, and both forces imposed it, although the Australian Defence Act prevented any of the offenders from actually being shot. In supporting capital punishment while failing to acknowledge the impact of sustained combat stress, Russell and his fellow generals were men of their time.

As the war progressed, however, the numbers of courts-martial fell, indicating a steady improvement in the discipline of the division. From a peak of 110 in 1916—including seven death sentences—the rate had dropped to less than ten by November 1918. The high number of disciplinary offences in 1916 reflected the stresses imposed on a raw division by four months in the trenches of Armentières, indifferent administration and inexperienced officers. A year later, combat experience and better administration had improved the figures significantly—as they had for the Canadian and Australian divisions, and for similar reasons.[104]

In July 1916, Private Nimot, a soldier of mixed Danish-German blood, deserted to the enemy. Russell's reaction was swift: he recommended to Godley that 96 men of German extraction then serving in the NZEF be withdrawn from the line and sent back to the divisional base camp at Etaples. The recommendation was accepted, but it deprived the division of a number of experienced soldiers and NCOs.

Russell's principal focus at this time, however, was on the New Zealand Division's supporting role in the coming Battle of the Somme. Drawing on the experience of General Sir Julian Byng's Canadian Corps, the division began the first of a series of raids on the German trenches opposite as part of a general British strategy to tie down German forces that might otherwise be shifted south to the Somme.

These short but bloody encounters had a number of other purposes, including identifying which German units were in the line, maintaining the offensive spirit of troops fighting a largely static trench war, and generally weakening enemy morale. 'The enemy was to be engaged so actively that he would regard it as unwise or unsafe to move any troops away to the south. No Man's Land was to be our land; our artillery was to be more active; the enemy's wire was to be cut; his parapets demolished; billets bombarded; frequent raids to be carried out and others threatened, and counter battery work engaged in.'[105] 'Useful in their way,' Russell observed cautiously, thinking perhaps of the potential loss of many good men. 'Inculcating the spirit of the offensive, I think they call it. No doubt it all helps, and in any case we want to know what is on the other side of No Man's Land.'

Both sides raided, and on both sides it was done with a high degree of preparation. Typically, the length of trench to be attacked would be first reconnoitred from both ground and air, and an exact replica constructed for the raiding party to practise on. On the night, the raiders removed all marks of identification, hands and faces were blackened, bayonets specially sharpened and their shine dulled. Revolvers, knives and clubs were the weapons of choice—the latter suspended from the wrist by a cord. Like players in a football team, each man had his job—'some kill, some take prisoners, others are told off especially for taking guns, others seeking documents, copying trenches, cutting wire, scouts, signaling, care of wounded etc'.[106]

Before the raid began, the enemy's front line, support and communication trenches would be heavily bombarded, during which the raiding party—loaded with personal weapons, bombs, wirecutters, torches, luminous tapes and flares—would crawl forward in the darkness over no-man's-land, enter the German trenches and inflict as many casualties as possible. Special signals were used to recall the raiders, and white tapes were set up to guide them back to the gaps in the New Zealand wire.

Russell stressed the need for 'vigorous scouting', both before and during raids. In this way, his men could intercept and engage enemy raiders in no-man's-land before they reached his division's trenches; and, if they did reach them, prevent their return. The strategy appears to have worked: divisional HQ reported in mid-July that after frequent fights with German patrols, command of no-man's-land had passed almost entirely to the New Zealanders.

On the night of 25 June a 73-strong party under Captain Powley raided the enemy trenches opposite the Pont Ballot salient. Over 30 Germans were killed and nine taken prisoner, along with a haul of rifles, gas helmets, letters and papers. Sappers attached to the party blew up a gas engine used for pumping, and destroyed the main dugout.

A raid led by Captain McColl on the night of 1 July—the fateful first day of the Somme—was another 'success' for the New

Zealanders. Many of the enemy had been killed by the preliminary bombardment and the few Germans who showed fight or tried to run were bayoneted or shot. Again, the raid produced a useful haul for the intelligence staff—helmets, shoulder straps, paybooks, messages, a pair of field glasses and a dozen fully packed valises.

As the Germans developed better defences, the raids became less effective. Now raiding parties not only had to deal with enemy patrols, but listening posts and strengthened barbed wire that proved impenetrable without heavy bombardment. On 8 July German troops attacked a position known as 'The Mushroom', garrisoned by 1st Canterbury Battalion. The raid was preceded by a 50-minute barrage which obliterated two New Zealand trenches, inflicting heavy casualties. The enemy attacked in the dark, forcing the Canterbury men to retreat down a communications trench; but the Germans were driven out half an hour later by a vigorous counter-attack. The battalion's casualties were 23 killed, 93 wounded, and three taken prisoner.

On 13 July came another tragic reverse when a party from 1st Otago Battalion was almost annihilated by German machine-gun and artillery fire as it lay in no-man's-land waiting for the bombardment to lift: 'Just before we reached the fire trench, hell broke loose. The communication trench, the front line, No Man's Land literally exploded with bursting shells and bombs—and all this laced through with streams of machine-gun fire. Wounded were stumbling in or being dragged or carried by their comrades—and then being hit again in our own line.'[107] Fifty-one officers and men were killed and over 100 wounded that night—an 80 percent casualty rate.

The Germans frequently intercepted New Zealand Division phone and buzzer messages by means of 'listening apparatus' sited close to the division's frontline trenches. As a result, they knew in advance of at least two New Zealand raids and were able to inflict heavy casualties. In this case they may well have been alerted by some unguarded talk over the telephone or in a local estaminet.

Godley, however, appeared fully satisfied with what had been achieved by the raids; he praised the excellent planning of Russell and his staff and the results achieved overall. 'The Division,' he wrote to Allen, 'has had a lot of fighting lately—most of it in the nature of raids on the Boche trenches—in which they have been very successful, having taken a good many prisoners and killed a lot of the enemy.'[108]

Judgements of the effectiveness of trench raids have been mixed. Military analyst Paddy Griffiths concluded that despite their unpopularity with the troops, trench raids made a substantial contribution to the BEF's tactical education.[109] The post-war Kirke Committee, set up to examine the British Army's handling of the conflict, took a different view. It concluded that trench raiding had no value as a morale raiser, and damned it for wasting the British Army's best leaders and men. Military historian John Terraine commented that raiding policy added tremendously to the strain upon the troops. It meant there were practically no 'quiet sectors' on the British front where divisions could actually be in the line but, in effect, resting. As well, German superiority in training and equipment for most of 1916 meant that the cost of small operations often far exceeded their value.[110]

Raids apart, snipers, machine guns and shellfire took a steady toll of New Zealand lives at Armentières. The worst was German shellfire—the kind that came before enemy raids, the retaliatory bombardment, the carefully targeted blitzing that destroyed parapets, blew in trenches and buried frightened men huddling on firesteps or in the darkness of their dugouts. Russell himself had a narrow escape in early July when his headquarters at Armentières was hit by German shellfire. He was slightly wounded and had to take refuge in a nearby cellar.

Life in the trenches at Armentières was lethal enough, but for the troops it lacked the visceral excitement of a major offensive. Russell felt it too, writing to his sisters: 'A big offensive would be inspiring.

War in these days is dull. We are too civilized. The days of the battle axe would be better.' And again:

> I really think I preferred Anzac. More romance about it, if more hardship. The blue Aegean Sea, with the islands dotted about it, the sun sinking behind Samothrace, the constant danger, all combined to give soldiering some zest. Here, as they say, either deadly dull or damnably dangerous, but mostly the former.

Damnably dangerous it was, if only in patches. In the New Zealand Division's first three months at Armentières, a so-called 'quiet' sector of the line, it had suffered 2500 casualties—mostly from German shellfire—and nearly 400 dead were left behind in the cemeteries of that shattered town.

It was just the beginning. On 14 August Russell handed over his sector to Lieuetenant-General George Harper's 51st Highland Division and began entraining his troops for the Somme. As the Scottish pipers played the marching New Zealanders out of town, Russell's diary grimly observed: 'Genl McKay commanding 5 Australian Division tells me the 1st Anzac Division lost 5000, and the 2nd Division 7000, at the Somme.'

Russell was about to get his inspiriting offensive.

Chapter 12

The Cauldron of Battle

'At 6.20 am the sky was a circle of vivid flame as the British barrage opened up. The German sky flamed in response as our men began slowly moving across the torn waste of No Man's Land. Looking backward it seemed the whole earth was full of the moving files of men. Coming up behind us in artillery formation were the battalions of the Rifle Brigade who were to sweep on through us to the village of Flers. About this movement was the most awesome sense of power.'[111]—The Auckland and Otago battalions begin their attack on the Somme, 16 September 1916.

The Somme is part of the ancient French province of Picardy, which had watched the march of foreign armies for 2000 years: Roman legions, the Vikings and the English armies of Edward III and Henry V in the Hundred Years War had all fought there. The Germans and French had fought on the Somme in 1870 during the Franco-Prussian War, and again in the opening months of World War I.

In 1916 it was to be the site of one of the greatest battles in military history. As devised by the Allied high commands, the purpose of this battle was to take the pressure off the embattled French at

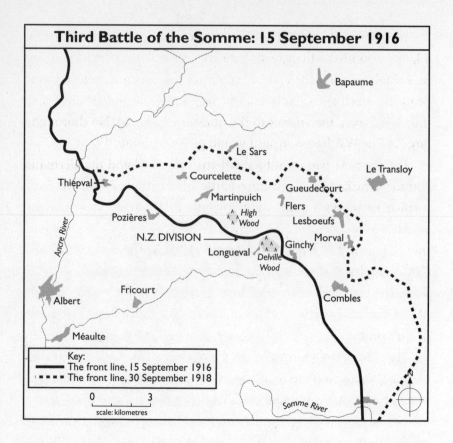

Third Battle of the Somme: 15 September 1916

Bapaume

Le Sars

Courcelette

Le Transloy

Thiépval

Gueudecourt

Martinpuich

Flers

High Wood

Poziéres

Lesboeufs

N.Z. DIVISION

Morval

Longueval

Ginchy

Delville Wood

Fricourt

Combles

Albert

Méaulte

Key:
The front line, 15 September 1916
The front line, 30 September 1918

0   3
scale: kilometres

Somme River

Verdun, to stop the Germans transferring forces to other theatres of war, and to generally wear down the strength of the German armies on the Western Front.

The great Somme offensive opened on 24 June with the heaviest Allied bombardment of the war so far—more than 1500 guns—designed to cut the enemy's barbed-wire defences, neutralise their artillery, and destroy their trenches and strongpoints. On the morning of 1 July, 11 British and three French divisions—over 150,000 men in all—climbed from their trenches and advanced on the German lines. The protective barrage, however, was lifted too soon and the guns had largely failed to destroy the wire. The German troops, sheltering for the most part unharmed in deep dugouts, were able to bring their machine guns quickly to bear.

By day's end, over 20,000 officers and men were dead and nearly 40,000 wounded—the greatest disaster to befall the British Army in a single day. 'By the end of the day,' wrote soldier-poet Edmund Blunden, 'both sides had seen, in a sad scrawl of broken earth and murdered men, the answer to the question. No road. No thorough-fare . . . The War had won, and would go on winning.'[112]

For the next two months the British attacked and the Germans counter-attacked in a grinding battle of attrition. Fresh divisions thrown in by both sides were consumed in bloody struggles for woods, valleys, ravines and villages. By the end of July, the line had moved hardly 5 kilometres, but over 200,000 British and French soldiers, and 160,000 Germans, had been killed or wounded. Now it was to be the turn of Russell's New Zealanders as part of XV Corps of Rawlinson's Fourth Army, in what was to be called the Third Battle of the Somme.

Haig believed—wrongly, as events were to prove—that the German Army was at breaking point and that one more thrust would break through its formidable defensive line into open country beyond. To achieve this, 11 infantry divisions, supported by 50 tanks—the new weapon of war—would attack over a 16-kilometre front from Thiepval on the left to Combles on the right.

To the north, the First and Third armies would seize Gommecourt, Moncy and Vimy Ridge to coincide with the advance of the Fourth Army from the south. The aim was to capture all three German lines of defence at a single blow, opening the way for a breakthrough by the five cavalry divisions that would be massed behind the front line. It was to be 'the climactic episode of the Somme campaign if not the entire war'.[113]

Despite Haig's grand plan, the struggle would inevitably be costly, just as it had been in all previous assaults on the Somme. The German defence system facing the British divisions was still essentially intact, and built to be as impregnable as military engineering could make it. The first line of defence alone consisted of a series of trenches protected by deep belts of barbed wire and dugouts deep enough to protect their garrisons from all but a direct hit by the heaviest artillery. Into this system, the Germans had integrated a number of defended villages, each able to shelter garrisons of troops and machine gunners and shielded by trench defences protected by barbed-wire entanglements. With good reason, Winston Churchill described the German defences on the Somme in 1916 as 'undoubtedly the strongest and most perfectly defended positions in the world'.

On 20 August, the New Zealanders entrained at Arques and St Omer for Abbeville, and in 'the delectable wooded valleys of the lower Somme' they began training in earnest. Russell had much to do in a very short time as his battalions were ill prepared for the demands being placed upon them by the coming Somme offensive. By this time, however, Russell and his fellow commanders were ready to apply the lessons of the British failures on the Somme in July 1916, along with those from the bloody attacks at Fromelles and Pozières where over 11,000 Australians had been killed, wounded or taken prisoner in their first action on the Western Front.

Under their commander's exacting eye the three infantry brigades practised the latest techniques for assaulting enemy positions. There were exercises in extended formation attacks, ground liaison with aircraft, fighting in woods and villages, and the consolidation of captured positions. The troops were trained to hug a creeping or rolling barrage—a protective curtain of shellfire that advanced in front of them, preventing the enemy from manning their machine guns—and to be ready to deliver their attack immediately it lifted. They were told that risking casualties from an occasional short burst from their own barrage was preferable to losing the barrage and being compelled to fight their way unsupported into the enemy trenches. Russell put it plainly: 'When we begin to lose a man or two from our own barrage, we are in the right place to go in with it when it lifts.'[114]

The men practised the manoeuvre repeatedly, advancing behind lines of flags representing the movement of the barrage. The leading waves kept within 60 or 70 metres of the barrage, kneeling while they waited for it to take another leap forward and then closing on it immediately. Following closely were small sections in single file to act as 'moppers up', systematically searching all trenches, dugouts and ground overrun by the leading waves and killing or capturing any of the enemy who remained.

On 1 September, Russell, along with 26 other generals and 72 commanding officers, was invited to Saint-Riquier for a demonstration of what Haig hoped would be a decisive weapon in the coming battle—the tank. What they saw were six machines resembling armoured traction engines, each weighing about 28 tons, armed with either cannons or machine guns, and capable of a breathtaking 2 miles per hour over reasonable country. The assembled officers were told that the Mark I version could crush barbed wire, climb parapets, cross trenches, and even go through thick woods. Russell appeared unexcited by the tactical possibilities of this 'new travelling fort', noting in his diary that its 'utility remains to be proved'.

On 2 September, the division began its march up the Somme River valley, billeting around various villages en route and rehearsing again and again the infantry tactics that would be used in the battle to come. By day, the rumble of distant guns fused gradually into a continuous roar; by night, the muzzle flashes of heavy artillery lit the sky like sheet lightning. On dusty, crowded roads, trucks and horse-drawn wagons moved steadily along, taking food, munitions, and troops into battle and tired and wounded men out—'feeding the furnace with fuel and carrying out the waste,' as Lindsay Inglis cynically put it.[115] From troops of the 51st Highland Division at Armentières, Russell's men had learned of the scale and brutality of the fighting on the Somme and knew what they were about to face.

By 10 September, the New Zealanders had reached their assembly positions between the villages of Mametz and Fricourt, both now no more than piles of bricks and splintered trees. The ground over which the division would advance was already much fought over. Eight weeks before, 3150 men of the South African Brigade had attacked German-occupied Delville Wood. Just 800 of them emerged from it a week later. High Wood, only half of which was in British hands, was a charnel house. Both sides had fought ferociously to take and hold it; both sides had shelled it until only a few trees and smoking stumps were left. All about lay swathes of dead, or parts of them—Germans and British; as well as broken rifles, machine guns, trench mortars, helmets, packs and other equipment, and shell parts of all calibres. The stench was overpowering.

The attack of XV Corps on 15 September had four objectives. The first was the German front line; the second comprised the defences covering the village of Flers; the third included Flers and the ground to the east and west of it. The final objective was the capture of the villages of Gueudecourt, Lesboeufs and Morval in order to establish a defensive flank for a cavalry thrust through the German lines into open country.

The specific task allocated to the New Zealand Division was the capture of three strong German trench systems—the Switch Line, the Flers Line and the Gird Line—that protected the village of Gueudecourt, an area of enemy territory 1 kilometre wide by about 3 kilometres deep. On the left and right flanks of the New Zealand-ers would be the British 47th and 41st divisions. The attack was to be preceded by a massive three-day artillery bombardment of the German positions. On 5 September, Russell recorded in his diary: 'GOC explained our task; a good one, and quite to my liking. We are lucky so far.'

The New Zealanders prepared early for the offensive to come. From their positions outside the village of Longueval saps were pushed forward into no-man's-land. Communication trenches were dug between assembly and frontline trenches by Maori troops of the Pioneer Battalion. Under Russell's direction, headquarters staff arranged for the transport of munitions, food and water, the evacuation of the wounded, the extension of roads, and the movement of troops and guns. Junior officers made themselves familiar with the ground over which their men would advance. Reserve 'B' teams, made up of selected officers and NCOs from each company, were set up to replace casualties sustained in the coming battle.

For the attack, Russell allocated his 2nd and 3rd brigades—about 6000 men in all—with 1st Brigade held in reserve. Their first objective was the Crest Trench followed by the formidable Switch Trench, 250 metres beyond it and up a long slope. Supporting the assault would be a creeping barrage from the New Zealand Field Artillery brigades, supported by the guns of the British 14th Division.

Hundred-metre-wide gaps would be left in the artillery barrage to allow the four tanks allocated to the division to advance safely in front of the infantry, crushing enemy barbed wire and dealing with their machine-gun nests and trench garrisons. The secret of the tank had been well kept, but by zero hour on 15 September most of the men in the trenches knew that a new weapon of war would be deployed that day.

The troops were kitted out in what was improbably described as 'light fighting order'. Along with rifle and bayonet, every man carried two gas helmets, 200 rounds of ammunition in pouches and bandoliers, two Mills bombs, sandbags for reinforcing captured trenches, a waterproof sheet, a water bottle, a day's rations and 'iron' ration, and every second man carried a shovel or pick—about 30 kilograms of gear in total. Each platoon carried a supply of smoke bombs to flush the enemy out of dugouts, and rockets and flares for signalling progress to patrolling aircraft. Each company was equipped with two Lewis light machine guns.

On 12 September, the guns allocated to XV Corps began their preliminary bombardment of the German lines. The following day Russell briefed his brigade commanders—Fulton, Earl Johnston and Braithwaite—in detail on the plan of attack. 'Everything is I think on a sound footing,' Russell wrote in his diary that night. Visiting the division just before the battle, Godley found the men 'all most eager and full of fight; their sick rate practically nil'.[116]

On the night of 14 September the division moved into its assembly trenches between High Wood and Delville Wood in preparation for the attack. The men settled into their positions and slept as best they could. By 6 am on the 15th the troops had finished their breakfast of bread, cold bully beef, water or rum. Their equipment was on, bayonets fixed, and they were ready to go.

At 6.20 am, the artillery opened up, bringing a firestorm of high explosive and shrapnel down on the German lines. The leading companies of Auckland and Otago infantry advanced in four waves, hugging the barrage that lifted 50 metres every minute ahead of them. Up the slope they passed the tanks, exhausts smoking and tracks churning uselessly in the mud. At the top of the slope, was a billowing wall of white smoke shot with shell flashes; in their ears was the scream and explosion of shells and the staccato chatter of German machine guns.

The first objective, the Crest Trench, was stormed and its garrison overwhelmed. Some Germans gave up easily; others fought doggedly. Either way, it did not matter—stretcher-bearers and wounded men were spared; the rest, including those who had surrendered, were shot or bayoneted. Men facing heavy machine-gun and rifle fire and seeing their mates fall around them were in no mood to spare the men who, seconds before, had been inflicting it.

Two hundred Germans turned and ran back towards the Switch Line, 250 metres away; many of them were cut down in the open by the Lewis guns of the Otago battalion. Just before the Switch, the leading waves of Auckland infantry, advancing too fast, overstepped the barrage and lost men to the fire of their own guns. On the left, 47th Division was held up outside High Wood, exposing the Otago left flank to enfilading machine-gun and sniper fire. The four tanks that were due to reach the Switch five minutes before the infantry were nowhere to be seen—out of action with mechanical problems or delayed by a muddy terrain cratered with shell holes.

As the barrage lifted, the surviving New Zealanders closed up and poured in one wave through the smashed wire and into the Switch Trench, now battered almost beyond recognition by artillery fire and filled with German dead. The ensuing fighting was brutal and short. Four German officers were the only prisoners taken. Of the 700 Aucklanders who went into action that morning, 324 had been killed, wounded, or were missing. The Otagos had lost 460, most of them from the enfilading fire from High Wood. Below them now lay the village of Flers and, 1 kilometre beyond, the village of Gueudecourt.

At his headquarters at Meaulte, 7 kilometres behind the front line, Russell waited anxiously for news of the attack. Despatch riders came and went, and badly shocked German prisoners arrived in a steady stream. 'Heavy fighting going on,' Russell wrote to his sisters as the battle progressed. 'It's difficult to see as much of this business as one would like: smoke, enemy fire, folds in the ground, etc, all make observation poor.'

At 8.20 am the Rifle Brigade battalions attacked the Flers trench system, but without artillery support and facing a barrier of uncut wire. The impasse was broken by a tank that had finally reached the forward New Zealand positions. Smashing through the wire, it destroyed the German machine guns, allowing the riflemen to attack and take the trench. One hundred Germans gave themselves up to the advancing New Zealanders.

Meanwhile, 2nd Battalion was meeting fierce resistance and losing many men to German machine gunners firing from the out-skirts of Flers village. Again, a tank played a critical role, crushing an enemy machine-gun post and forcing its garrison to run for their lives. From there to Abbey Road it was hard fighting all the way. The road was hidden in plantations and full of dugouts, and from there the Germans resisted stubbornly, but by 10 am the village of Flers had been secured.

The next objective, Grove Alley Trench, was taken by 1st Battalion, but again at heavy cost. German artillery and machine-gun fire swept the leading platoons from the front and right flank: 'The Boche kept his field artillery playing on us and opened a terrific fire from machine-guns,' wrote Lieutenant-Colonel Herbert Hart, 'but our men went straight through as bravely and steadily as if on parade, with heads down as though through a hailstorm. Right and left they fell until one third were out of action, then with a rush the remainder stormed the trench . . . It was magnificent but costly.'[117]

By noon, however, the remnants of 1st Battalion were far in advance of the supporting British units and in imminent danger of being cut off and annihilated by German counter-attacks. They were spared by a costly mistake: battalion officers, thinking that the movement of a platoon signalled a general withdrawal, ordered their men to abandon Grove Alley and pull back towards Flers.

By the end of the day, Russell's division had taken three out of its four objectives and established a defensive line around the village of Flers. The British 47th and 41st divisions, however, had failed to keep pace, leaving the New Zealanders in an exposed salient under heavy German shellfire. By nightfall of the next day they had secured the fourth objective and captured some 500 prisoners and 15 machine guns.

The price of success was high—over 600 men of the division had been killed and more than 1400 wounded. Russell's diary of 15 September noted drily: 'Zero at 6.20 am. We carried the first two objectives up to Flers line up to time—nearly 200 yards in depth— and the third which brought us in advance of Flers village some 3 hours later . . . Losses about 2500—a good many officers.'

Some of the British divisions had fared much worse. Against a final total of 2580 New Zealand casualties on 15 September, 14th Division had suffered an estimated 4500; the 47th 4000; the 56th just under 4500; and the Guards 4150. In total, nearly 30,000 British and Dominion troops were killed or wounded on the first day of battle alone.

Tactical deficiencies and mechanical problems were responsible for much of this. On 15 September, the troops went forward in the stereotyped 'wave' formation that had proved so disastrous on 1 July. The task of the tanks was to advance first, crushing the enemy wire and destroying the machine-gun posts before the infantry arrived to mop up the survivors. Rawlinson, however, decided that the tanks needed to be protected from the creeping barrage and so his planners created 100-metre-wide, artillery-free 'lanes' along which the lumbering machines could advance in safety. Many of the tanks were still far behind the front line when the attack began and when the whistles blew, large sections of the infantry, including troops of the New Zealand Division, were forced to advance without artillery cover. From strongpoints that were, for the most part, untouched by the barrage, the German machine gunners cut them down in swathes.

In spite of the heavy losses, however, Rawlinson appeared to be satisfied with the results of the first day's fighting. The villages of Gueudecourt, Lesboeufs and Morval were still in enemy hands, but other heavily fortified villages—Flers, Martinpuich, and Courcelette—had been captured, along with 4000 German prisoners. By nightfall on 16 September two main lines of German trench had been taken and an advance of 2 kilometres had been made over a front of 10 kilometres. The Fourth Army, Haig acknowledged, had made a larger advance in a single operation than any since the beginning of the Somme offensive in July. For its part, the New Zealand Division had taken all its objectives, earning it a commendation from Rawlinson for its 'fine fighting spirit and admirable energy and dash'.[118]

The three days from 19–21 September saw a fierce struggle for the vital junction of Flers and Flers Support trenches with Drop Alley and Goose Alley. The junction was finally taken after a night-time attack by a force of bombers from the British 1st Division and three companies of the Canterbury battalion under the inspired leadership of Captain Fred Starnes. 'No operation in which the division took part in the battle,' wrote Colonel Hugh Stewart, 'called for such tenacity and grim determination on the part of the individual soldier.'[119]

In the following days, the British 14th and 41st divisions were relieved. The New Zealanders stayed in the line, fighting in knee-deep mud, soaked by continuous rain and without greatcoats, blankets or hot food. Artillerymen and their horse teams struggled under ceaseless shellfire to reposition their guns. Stretcher-bearers carried seriously wounded men under fire to safety and medical help. Tired soldiers repaired roads, dug trenches and gun pits, carried essential supplies up the line, and buried the dead. 'The men,' wrote Byrne, 'were reduced to a state of deepest misery and exhaustion.'[120]

Russell, however, was more than satisfied with what the division had achieved so far, despite the exposed positions his men now held. His casualties had been heavy, but proportionately much less than those of the supporting British divisions. One factor was the success of the preliminary bombardments in destroying much of the Switch Trench system and its barbed-wire defences. When the attacking troops arrived at the Switch they found much of it had been demolished, and many of its defenders dead or wounded. A second factor was the speed of the New Zealanders' advance. Moving quickly behind a protective curtain of shellfire, as Russell had insisted, the troops caught many of the surviving German machine gunners still in their dugouts and unable to bring their weapons into action.

Diary entries at this time, however, reveal Russell's frustration with the slow progress of the British attack overall. This, he complained, was allowing the enemy to shore up their forward lines of defence, construct new ones further back, and so forestall any breakthrough by the cavalry. The sweeping opening attacks of the Third Battle of the Somme looked likely to degenerate into just another grim battle of attrition—'Grind forward yard by bloody yard,' as Malthus put it.[121]

Meanwhile, Russell applied himself to the problems of servicing his forward units. For the first four days of the offensive the only supply routes were over a wasteland of shell holes strewn with barbed wire, or via the road from Longueval, both of which were being shelled day and night. Heavy rain on 17 and 18 September had compounded the problem, turning the battlefield into a quagmire and making it impossible to get ammunition and supplies forward to the troops. After several inspections of the captured ground, Russell ordered the main communication trench, 'Turk Lane', pushed forward, trench duckboards laid, and a light railway constructed to get food, water, ammunition and other supplies to frontline positions around the village of Flers.

The division was involved in two other major attacks in the Third Battle of the Somme—the Battle of Morval on 25 September and the Battle of Transloy Ridges beginning on 1 October—but essentially in a supporting role to other divisions of the Fourth Army. On 25 September the New Zealanders were partnered by the British 21st and 55th divisions, and their objectives were those that Rawlinson had failed to reach on 15 and 16 September—the villages of Gueudecourt, Lesboeufs and Morval.

The attack by 1st Brigade on 25 September was a complete success. Aided again by careful preparation and good artillery support, the brigade took its objectives to the northwest of Gueudecourt with relative ease. The follow-up attack on 27 September was a disaster. The Otago regiment was cut to pieces in front of Gird Trench, the victim of rushed preparations and a weak artillery barrage that had failed to cut the German wire and destroy their machine-gun emplacements. Every officer and almost every man was either killed or wounded. It was, Byrne noted, the regiment's 'most bitter and costly experience on the Somme'.[122]

By 29 September the three villages and the German third line were in British hands, and 2nd Brigade was defending the Gird trench system with grim determination. Russell wrote to his sisters that day: 'We are still at it, hammer and tongs. I hope, however, that before long we shall get a rest, which the men have well earned . . . for apart from the danger, which I don't suppose worries them much, the discomfort, the physical weariness begins to tell. They have done well, and I hope that the good words the Corps and Army Commander have said for us have a solid foundation . . . I shall feel relieved for the men's sake when we quit.'

Russell contrasted his position some kilometres behind the front line with the dangers and discomforts endured by his troops. 'Personally I am as fit as a fiddle, live comfortably, and seldom find myself in the least danger; such is the ignoble share of a divisional commander. I do not altogether appreciate it. An admiral has a much better time; he at least shares equally the dangers of his men; and fortunately neither of them have the discomforts of the soldier in the trenches.' Russell was not being altogether honest. On the night of 16 September, the Germans had shelled the ground around his headquarters at Meaulte, forcing him and his staff to take shelter in their dugouts.

Encouraged by his successes, Haig and his staff now devised a new plan by which the two armies would again attempt to break through to Bapaume and then on to Cambrai, an advance of nearly 40 kilometres through the German lines. The role of the New Zealand Division was again to be a limited one. It would support an attack by the British 47th Division on the village of Eaucourt l'Abbaye by capturing the Goose Alley–Gird Trench junction.

On 1 October Russell noted in his diary: 'Made further attack—extending our line to the N.W. towards Eaucourt L'Abbaye—successful. It was not until this evening that the situation on our left was cleared up—the 47th division entrusted with the taking of Eaucourt L'Abbaye made a mess of it, and our flank was very much in the air.'

Once again, the cost of the attack was heavy—nearly 600 casualties, including over 100 killed. The brigade took about 250 prisoners, among them the headquarters staff of two battalions of a Bavarian reserve regiment. The village of Eaucourt L'Abbaye finally fell to British troops on 3 October after several days of hard fighting.

On 2 October Private John Joseph Sweeney was shot by firing squad in front of a dugout near Russell's headquarters at Meaulte. 'A deserter twice over and yet he went out to be shot without showing any fear,' wrote Sergeant Arthur Rhind, a clerk on Russell's staff.[123] Sweeney was one of more than 60 soldiers of Haig's armies to be executed for desertion or cowardice during the Battle of the Somme, and the second New Zealander.

On 3 October, the New Zealand Division ended its tour of duty on the Somme and pulled back to camps at Pommiers Redoubt and Fricourt. Many of them were laden with rings, watches, field glasses and other souvenirs of battle. All were wet and filthy from continuous exposure to bad weather and exhausted by lack of sleep and the strain of heavy fighting. Much of their clothing was in rags; many wore sandbags for leggings and waterlogged, mud-plastered German greatcoats. 'The only light all the way came from gun flashes blanketed by rain,' wrote Lindsay Inglis. 'The company arrived at last at a muddy archipelago where tarpaulin and ammunition-box shelters formed the islands. The men lay down in the slush. The rain beat down. It had taken us 7 and a quarter hours to come 6 miles.'[124]

In its first test of battle on the Western Front, Russell's division had done well. In atrocious conditions, it had stayed in the line for 23 days on end—the longest unbroken spell of any division on the Somme. The division had taken part in three major attacks and fought its way forward for over 3 kilometres. It had captured nearly 1000 German troops, many machine guns and other war material. On 15 September, the division had advanced further than any other division in a single day of the Third Battle of the Somme. It had also rendered timely assistance to British divisions on both flanks whose attacks had been temporarily held up.

The British high command was not slow to acknowledge the division's achievements during its three-week tour of duty. Godley reported to Defence Minister Allen that the performance of the New Zealanders had been unsurpassed by any British division on the Somme. General Sir Douglas Haig, a man not lavish with praise, cabled the New Zealand Government: 'The division has won universal confidence and admiration. No praise can be too high for such troops.'[125] Missing from Haig's dispatch was any acknowledgement of the appalling cost of the division's success on the Somme—nearly 8000 officers and men killed or wounded, equivalent to eight of its 12 battalions.

Whatever the feelings of the New Zealand Government about the division's blooding on the Somme, they obviously did not blunt its commitment to the imperial cause, or cause it to question the competency of the British high command. A month after the division was withdrawn from the line, Massey and Ward were assuring Haig in person that the Dominion had a reserve of 100,000 men to reinforce the division that New Zealand had already put in the field.[126]

Russell had reason to be pleased with his contribution to the division's first major offensive on the Western Front. His rigorous training and careful preparation had equipped his artillery and infantry well to deal with a range of battlefield situations. Junior officers and NCOs were able to assess situations quickly in the heat of battle and take over leaderless units when the chain of command broke down. As Malthus put it, 'The whole division was now well seasoned in the new type of fighting. Thanks to smooth coordination and plenty of initiative in meeting local obstacles, it won the highest praise.'[127]

The division, however, had endured its share of difficulties and near-disasters. There had been problems in getting food, ammunition and other supplies across a shellfire-swept battlefield and into the front line, and in bringing hundreds of seriously wounded men back under fire into overcrowded medical facilities. There had been difficulties in maintaining contact between Russell's headquarters and his forward units in key phases of the battle. There had been major problems also in ensuring adequate artillery support for the assaulting troops, as evidenced by the attack on the Flers Trench system on

15 September, and that on Gird Trench 12 days later. Inglis's battalion, for example, had to fight its way forward with exposed flanks, no creeping barrage and no tank support.

Russell's control over the battle was limited in its early phases by his isolation at division headquarters, 7 kilometres behind the front line. It was an archetypical situation: World War I commanders planned attacks with their staffs, issued orders to subordinates, then fretted at headquarters, sited for safety and tactical reasons well behind the front line. Once their troops had gone over the top, brigade or battalion commanders could send back information only by runner or telephone lines, both vulnerable to enemy fire.

The outstanding feature of the battles of 1914–18 was the almost total lack of control once the battle had started, and this was the case in the Third Battle of the Somme. Once the attack of 15 September was underway, control effectively passed from Russell and his brigadiers to the battalion commanders, junior officers and NCOs who went forward with their men. Progress reports from forward positions took an hour or more to reach divisional or brigade headquarters, by which time they had often been overtaken by events. On the first day of the battle it was 5 pm before Russell and his brigade commanders had a complete and accurate report from the front line.

To what extent Russell was responsible for the failed attack on the Gird Trench network on 27 September is difficult to determine. Plans for such operations would usually begin at corps or divisional headquarters, be passed through to brigade headquarters for refinement, then on to battalion commanders for action. In this case, the headquarters staff of XV Corps, Russell as divisional commander, and Johnston as brigade commander could all have had a hand in managing the assault. Given Russell's trademark attention to preparation and planning, it is difficult to conclude that he, rather than XV Corps staff or the sick and exhausted Earl Johnston, was responsible for the botched operation that day.

Arguably, the heavy casualties sustained by the New Zealanders on the Somme could have been much reduced had Russell asked for the division to be withdrawn and rested after the first four days of heavy fighting, in which nearly 1000 of his men had been killed.[128] There is no evidence that he did, and the division was kept in the front line when flanking British divisions were pulled back to be rested and reinforced. Because of its continuing success, the New Zealand Division was worked until it was exhausted.

Certainly, Rawlinson and his staff valued the willingness of the New Zealanders to stay in the line without complaint and without asking for relief. They particularly appreciated, according to Godley, the fact that once the division had received its orders, nothing more was heard from it until a report was sent back saying that it had achieved all its objectives.[129]

If the Somme campaign had exposed the division's lack of combat experience, senior British generals found little to criticise. Corps commander General Sir Henry Horne described Russell as 'a capable and determined commander, leading a division imbued with an excellent spirit'. 'Officers and men,' he wrote to Godley, 'were keen to attack and went in with the intention of winning, and consequently did succeed in every case whilst I remained commander of XV Corps . . . In short, I formed a very high opinion of the division.'[130]

Rawlinson praised the leadership of Russell and his brigade commanders for its skill and precision; and the division for not only taking every objective allotted to it, but securing and holding several enemy strong points beyond those objectives. The division's endurance and fighting spirit were beyond praise, he wrote, and its successes around the village of Flers would 'rank high amongst the best achievements of the British Army'.[131] It was on the Somme that the New Zealand Division would first earn its reputation in the eyes of the British high command as an outstanding fighting formation.

The British offensive on the Somme finally ground to a halt in mid-November, defeated by continuing foul weather and dogged

German resistance. Haig's armies had captured a piece of enemy-occupied territory just 32 kilometres wide by 10 kilometres deep. The price was over 600,000 killed and wounded on the Allied side alone, and the British armies were still 5 kilometres short of Bapaume, which Haig had aimed to capture in his opening attack on 1 July. The irony of it all was that all of the territory won so expensively would be recaptured in the first days of the Kaiserschlacht, the German counter-offensive of March 1918 that almost won them the war.

The Somme offensive failed to achieve its main aim: a break through German lines into open country that could be exploited by the cavalry. It did succeed in its crucial secondary aim: to break the force of the German attack on Verdun and give its French defenders a breathing space. It also prevented the Germans from transferring large numbers of troops from the Western Front to where they were badly needed on the Russian and Romanian fronts.

Haig's offensive had also inflicted huge losses on the German armies. In four and a half months of battle, between 437,000 and 680,000 German troops had been killed or wounded. Captain von Hentig of the German Guard Reserve Division would famously claim that 'the battlefields of the Somme were the muddy grave of the German field army, dug by British industry and its shells'.

German supreme commanders Hindenburg and Ludendorff were determined that their troops should at all costs be spared from another battle of the Somme. The result was a German withdrawal in February 1917 to the new and heavily fortified Hindenburg Line, some 40 kilometres east of the Somme battlefield. The Germans would now rest on the defensive in the west and attempt to knock Britain out of the alliance by unrestricted submarine warfare against both Allied and neutral shipping.

For now, however, Russell's men would live with their memories. They would remember the 'infernal roar' of the artillery as the New Zealand Division fixed bayonets for its opening attack on 15 September, and the massacre of 1st Brigade in front of Gird Trench because of hurried planning and the failure of the artillery to cut the German wire. They would recall the bloody struggle of the Canterbury battalion for Goose Alley under the inspired leadership of Captain Fred Starnes. They would remember the New Zealand wounded lying exposed to driving rain and shellfire, thirsty and in pain; the famished troops searching German bodies and haversacks for food and water.

On 6 October, the survivors of the Somme began their journey back north towards Armentières. In the village of Allery, many of the inhabitants dressed in their Sunday best and came out to meet the marching men. 'They had told us when we marched out to the Somme that we were "beaucoup bien aimé" (much-loved). Now they had come in great concern to see how we had fared. Shouts of joy when some popular lad was found to be safe and deep sympathy when Monsieur Jack or George was wounded. Many were weeping when they heard the long roll of the dead.'[132]

Chapter 13

Behind the Lines

'I have told the Brigadiers and Commanding Officers to forget all about the Germans for a few days and devote their minds and energies towards establishing a good system of interior economy, and improving the discipline of their units. It is no reflection on our men when I say we are weak in these matters. When one sees the waste and the unnecessary friction which is set up by want of administrative experience and knowledge, one realizes that it plays just as important a part in the success of the war as does the actual fighting.'—Russell writes to New Zealand Defence Minister Sir James Allen after the Third Battle of the Somme.[133]

On 12 October, the New Zealand Division became part of Godley's II Anzac Corps, taking over a quiet part of the line about 8 kilometres west of Armentières. In front of it, still occupied by the Germans, was the shattered village of Fromelles, a place of sinister memory for the Australian Infantry Corps. Here on 5 July 1916 some 5300 men of its 5th Division had been killed or wounded in a poorly mounted attack on German lines. New Zealand patrols were now collecting identity disks, paybooks, field glasses and all kinds of equipment from the hundreds of Australian dead that still littered no-man's-land.

Russell had much to do to rebuild his shattered division. Organisational and tactical weaknesses that had surfaced on the Somme needed to be addressed, reinforcements from England absorbed, and replacements found for the many officers and NCOs lost in the battles of September and October. NCOs and men from the ranks who had performed well on the Somme were now promoted; incompetent or unsuitable officers were weeded out and sent back to New Zealand.

'A good many officers who are returning to New Zealand are not wanted back,' Russell wrote to Allen. 'For various reasons, there are quite a few more who must go. They are in a few words not up to the job . . . Character first, health next, and experience last. If you can send us officers with a soldierly habit of mind and body, we can put on the finishing touches fairly easily.'[134]

By now 1st Brigade, manned mostly by Gallipoli veterans, was showing signs of exhaustion, as was its commander, Brigadier-General Earl Johnston. Russell dealt with the problem by reforming his 1st and 2nd brigades into separate North and South Island formations, keeping the 3rd (Rifle) Brigade intact and sending Earl Johnston away on sick leave. The brigade restructure was not a popular move with many of the veterans—as one of them wrote, 'No one but a number of the old Main Body and their subsequent reinforcements that fought on Gallipoli knew the sorrow that this caused amongst us—our old record was gone.'[135]

Russell's move to restore 1st Brigade's fighting effectiveness reflected an increasingly common problem on the Western Front— battle fatigue: 'Each brigade, as well as each man, could only stand so much combat before becoming exhausted, and each in turn needed to be rested . . . Good men became ineffective after months of combat and it was a command problem to recognise and deal with it.'[136]

Another problem to be faced at this time was the bad feeling generated by the preferment of officer reinforcements from New

Zealand over men who had earned their right to promotion by their performance in battle. It had surfaced in Egypt in early 1916, as Russell forged his Gallipoli veterans and reinforcements from New Zealand into the new division that would go to the Western Front. An increasing number of officers, however, were now being commissioned from the ranks. By the end of the war, they would account for nearly 50 percent of all officers serving with the division.

Meanwhile, there were important housekeeping issues to be dealt with. Up until now, Russell admitted, he and most of his officers had thought a great deal more about fighting than about efficient administration. Supplies and equipment were being wasted everywhere and the health and wellbeing of his men was being neglected, 'partly due to carelessness and partly to ignorance'. On 21 October, Russell's diary noted: 'Divisional Conference—Outlined policy—Men's comfort and safety first, the rest nowhere.'

Policy was now put into action, with the focus on improving the living conditions of the troops. Senior officers were instructed to devote at least half their time to the care and comfort of their men and to leave the more active operations, for the moment, to their seconds in command. Routine orders now required proper drainage and sanitation, the provision of hot meals in the trenches, and fresh vegetables in the divisional canteens. Trenches were drained, billets repaired, extra blankets issued and each man provided with dry socks daily. At platoon level, Russell required junior officers to attend to the wellbeing of their men 'exactly the same way as a mother does her boy of 10 . . . you cannot trust the ordinary mortal to darn his socks or look after his digestion'.[137]

Behind the lines, sports days and football competitions, concerts and films were organised to improve general fitness and morale, and a divisional rugby team was set up. Accompanied by his staff and subordinate commanders, Russell inspected trenches, billets, cookhouses and wagon lines daily to ensure that his new orders were being carried out. The welfare of the horses was not neglected. Russell's diary of

3 March 1917 noted severely: 'Napier Johnston and I went round the 11th Battery whose horses are a disgrace to the British Army.'

Russell's reforms had gained extra urgency because of the bitterly cold winter of 1916/17, which the French claimed was the worst in 50 years. By the beginning of February 1917, the ground had been covered in snow for a whole month. Frozen boots and socks crackled as they were put on; water spilled turned immediately to ice, and even the latrine seats were coated with a thin layer of ice after they were scrubbed. Most of the men washed only once or twice a week.

By now, however, the Young Men's Christian Association (YMCA) was also helping to improve the living conditions of the troops. As the New Zealand Division pulled out from its mauling on the Somme, Russell asked the YMCA's first director, Jim (later Sir James) Hay, to provide some basic services as the division returned to the north of France by train. The trip would take nearly three days, which meant that the men, huddled together in covered cattle wagons, would have nothing to eat or drink for the best part of 24 hours. Russell asked that YMCA staff meet each troop train at specific points en route and provide each man—nearly 20,000 of them—with hot cocoa and a packet of biscuits.

It was duly done, and afterwards Russell told Hay that he would make available whatever labour he required to set up YMCA facilities across the division. In less than a month the YMCA was providing the men with canteen, library and letter-writing facilities from a network of huts and marquees, as well as games, literary competitions and concerts. Lectures by well-known public speakers were also provided, for Russell was well aware of the stultifying effects that prolonged trench warfare could have on men's minds.

Venereal disease was an ongoing problem in the divisions. Russell took a tough, if somewhat puritanical line, recommending to Godley that officers who had caught VD be sent home to New Zealand for 'misconduct'. Godley agreed to this 'for the sake of example', though he conceded that the penalty might in some cases be a little harsh.

Russell dealt with drunkenness in the officer corps no less severely: the offenders were court-martialled, reprimanded and demoted.

In spite of Russell's pre-Somme efforts, discipline in the division was still not up to his exacting standards. During the battle, he had written to Allen: 'The discipline of the Division is fair, I can't say more. There are 70% first rate fellows, 20% weak and 10% who are born to give trouble. We should be a better fighting unit without the 10%. Bad characters do not make good soldiers. With our men we might well earn the title of being the best Division in France. That we shall not do so will be partly my fault, partly the fault of the 10%.'[138]

Russell wanted to send his 'incorrigibles' back to New Zealand to be dealt with by the military authorities there. Allen resisted this on the grounds that such men would only 'contaminate' the rest of the community and cause ongoing trouble. A better option, Allen felt, would be to give the troublemakers 'the post of honour' in the front line. 'It may be hard to say, but they are either better shot trying to do their duty at the front, or reformed if possible by the knowledge that they have been called upon to do the most dangerous jobs.'[139] Richardson, who commanded the NZEF in England, was equally pragmatic: 'When a man became a nuisance, I did not send him back to New Zealand, I put him to a place in the field where he could not miss.'[140]

In the end, Russell agreed that the division's persistent trouble-makers should not be sent home but put into the front line under firm military discipline. He had to admit, however, that on the Somme these men had, in general, fought just as well as the better-disciplined soldiers of his division. Among them was Private J.D. Stark of the Otago battalion, the anti-hero of Robyn Hyde's *Passport to Hell*. There were few 'incorrigibles' to match 'Starkie', who became a legend in the division for his run-ins with authority. In battle, he was 'like a berserk Norseman of old . . . completely oblivious of fear and driven to acts of bravado unmatched in the division'. Out of battle, he was equally uncontrollable.[141]

Russell's efforts to improve the administration of his division and return it battle-readiness after the heavy losses on the Somme eventually bore fruit. By February 1917, he felt that advances had been made in the discipline and 'interior economy' of the division since it had moved into its winter headquarters. By April, he could report to Allen that his division was now 'in first-class fighting trim. I have never seen the men look so well as they do today. The sick rate is low . . . Even venereal, for the time being, is a negligible quantity.'[142]

Russell had achieved all this by a combination of methods, including providing the necessary calibre of leadership at officer and NCO level, and giving proper attention to the care and welfare of his soldiers. With this went improved communication between the senior levels of command and the men, so that all ranks were kept regularly informed of what was happening and why.

By now Russell was confident that his New Zealanders were as good, or better, soldiers than any the British Army could field, and for much the same reasons that they were superior on Gallipoli. 'No doubt the overseas troops are better fighters than the Home article,' he wrote to his son Andy. 'This is not because they are better men really for we all come from the same stock, but because we are better fed, and in the case of men, as of sheep, half the breeding goes down the throat.'

Meanwhile, British fighting methods on the Western Front were being given a major shake-up. The Somme battles had shown up weaknesses at all levels, from tactics to command, and British Army commanders and their staffs were looking for solutions. Lieutenant-General Sir Ivor Maxse, commander of the British XVIII Corps, and Canadian Corps commander Lieutenant-General Sir Julian Byng were the main innovators. The result of their advocacy was a return to the small-group 'fire and movement' tactics that had been stand-ard in the British Army up until 1914.

In February 1917, Haig directed that these tactics be adopted army-wide, and Russell lost no time in introducing them to his division. The basic attacking unit was now to be the 40- or 50-man platoon divided into sections made up of specialist machine gunners, bombers, grenadiers and riflemen. Every man in the platoon would be expert in the use of all infantry weapons—rifle and bayonet, rifle grenade, machine gun and bomb.

In place of the mass 'wave' attacks of the Somme that were so vulnerable to German machine gunners, the troops would be trained to advance in sections and in short rushes, outflanking and destroying enemy positions as they encountered them. It was the beginning of a revolution in tactical doctrine that would play a large part in breaking the deadlock of trench warfare on the Western Front.

The pressures of command, however, were starting to put a strain on Russell's health. At the beginning of 1917 it was bad—a reaction to the heavy demands of the Somme campaign the previous September and the harsh winter that followed it. In January, he was admitted to a home for convalescent officers with bronchial pneumonia. After preliminary treatment there, he was sent to the south of France for two weeks to recover.

A month earlier, Gertrude and their daughter Jan had embarked for England for a reunification with their husband and father, and a visit to other members of the Russell family. Sometime before leaving New Zealand, Gertrude had written, rather ambiguously, to her husband: 'Don't forget to tell me about your lady friends, if you have any. I can't imagine you without. I shan't mind but don't treat them as a subject not to be mentioned between us.'

In fact, Russell had not gone without female company. On leave, he was paying regular visits to a Swiss countess at her chateau overlooking Lake Geneva. The nature of his relationship with Madame Lily de Condolle is not known, but Gertrude eventually found out about it and family sources confirm that, while it lasted, it caused considerable tension between them. Letters between husband and his wife that might have thrown some light on the matter were burnt on Guy Russell's orders after his death in 1960.

Chapter 14

A Tactical Triumph

'On the battered and blocked line of dirt, timber, wire-netting, concrete and dead, which was all that remained of the once splendid trenches of the front system, the whole attack had poured so swiftly that the Germans had no opportunity to resist. They were bombed in their dugouts or bayoneted within two yards of them.'—Colonel Hugh Stewart describes the New Zealanders' attack at Messines on 7 June 1917.[143]

By the opening months of 1917, the strategic outlook for the Allies had not improved. The Russians were now effectively out of the war and the Bolsheviks had seized power in Moscow. The Italians had been decisively beaten at Caporetto, and the Germans had declared a campaign of unrestricted submarine warfare against Allied shipping. By April 1917, 800,000 tons of shipping had been sunk and Britain now faced the prospect of defeat by starvation.

On the Western Front, morale in the French Army had collapsed after the failure of the Nivelle offensive, and mutinies had forced it temporarily out of the line. The Americans had entered the war, but it would be a year before their manpower and industrial strength

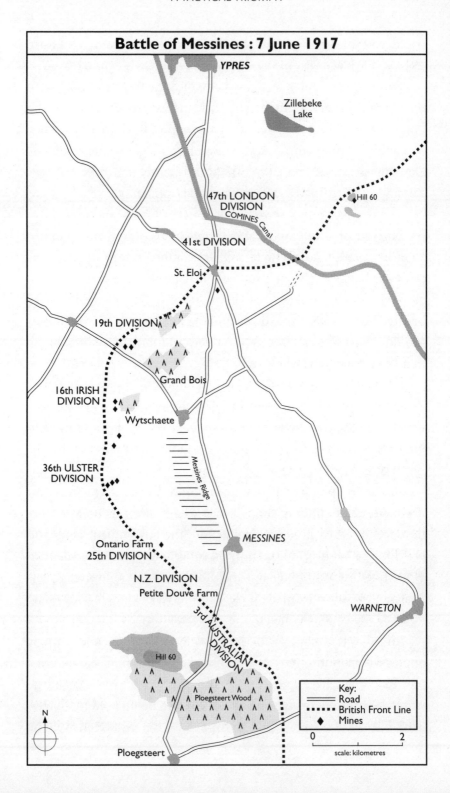

Battle of Messines : 7 June 1917

could be effectively mobilised. Historian John Terraine described 1917 as 'the black year of the war' for the Allies, with good reason.

For the New Zealanders based at Sailly, the trench warfare went on. On 21 February, a battalion of Aucklanders, preceded by a 98-gun bombardment, raided a section of the opposing German trenches, blowing up bomb stores, destroying machine guns, and taking 44 Germans prisoner. The 'stunt' was again a costly one: over 150 New Zealanders were listed as killed, wounded or missing.

The German response was chivalrous. Instead of shooting down the Aucklanders who were attempting to recover their wounded from no-man's-land, German soldiers climbed out of their trench, put their hands in the air, ordered a machine gun to cease fire, and allowed the men to recover their wounded. When all were in, they lowered their hands, stood down and the war went on. Ormond Burton described the incident as 'the finest and most chivalrous thing that I saw during the whole war'.[144]

Meanwhile, the War Council in London was pressuring New Zealand to provide a second division for service on the Western Front. The country, however, was growing war weary and increasingly unwilling to make more human and financial sacrifices for the imperial cause. Defence Minister Allen felt that New Zealand was sending more than its fair share of reinforcements, and it was now having difficulty finding enough men back home for food production and essential industry. In the end, the government agreed to provide another brigade, but only on condition that it be formed out of existing reserves in England and did not require reinforcing. New Zealand, Massey now made it clear to the War Council, could send no more than 100,000 men to the Western Front.

Russell was unhappy with the 4th Brigade proposal and strongly opposed it from the start. It would make his division 'the odd one out' in France, he argued. It would be difficult to billet, and he would be continually fighting to stop it from being used for 'navvy' work instead of being rested and trained for the next offensive. The choice, however, was ultimately not his, and he would now have to make the best of the situation. In March 1917, Brigadier-General Herbert Hart was appointed to command the new 5000-strong brigade, raised from troops in, or soon to arrive in, England. The four-brigade New Zealand Division now numbered 24,000 men, which made it numerically the strongest of the British divisions in France.

By March 1917 plans were well underway for a major thrust against the Germans in Flanders, in what came to be known as the Third Battle of Ypres. The plan had two major aims. The first aim was to drive the Germans off the ridges overlooking the Ypres salient, including the Messines–Wytschaete ridge and the Passchendaele Ridge further north. These ridges were strategically important as they gave the Germans a commanding view over the whole of the British lines around Ypres, and the ability to strike at the flank of any attack originating within the salient.

The broader and more ambitious objective was to clear the Germans out of Belgium altogether with a thrust out of the Ypres salient towards the English Channel, supported by a separate landing from the sea behind German lines. A key element of the plan was the capture of the German-occupied ports of Ostend and Zeebrugge, from which enemy submarines and other naval units were threatening British merchant shipping and troops and supplies moving across the Channel to France. By liberating the Belgian ports and driving the Germans back across the Belgian border, Haig was aiming for a major strategic victory.

The Flanders offensive would be divided into two distinct attacks, separated by seven weeks. The first of these, the capture of Messines–Wytschaete ridge, would be the first step in securing its southern flank in preparation for the main offensive at the end of July. Haig gave the job to the Second Army under General Sir Herbert Plumer. The attack would be carried out by Godley's II Anzac Corps and the British IX and X corps, supported by tanks, aircraft and artillery.

Their objectives were the German front line below the ridge, the fortified villages of Messines and Wytschaete, and the Oosttaverne Line some 1000–2000 metres behind them on the reverse slope. Plumer's attack would be preceded by a 17-day preparatory bombardment by 2266 howitzers and field guns—over 700 more than were in action at the Battle of the Somme.

During the first half of the year, British tunnelling companies had also been busy, driving 21 mine shafts packed with a million pounds of explosives deep under German lines on the crest. As in previous offensives by the Second Army, detailed preparations had been made for the attack—gun pits dug, cables laid, dugouts excavated for advanced brigade and battalion headquarters, regimental aid posts and dressing stations, dumps pushed forward and assembly trenches completed.

After two weeks in the warmer climate of southern France, Russell had recovered sufficiently to again take up the reins of command and prepare his division for the offensive to come. There were the usual inspections of frontline infantry positions, artillery batteries, signals, and transport units, with the general as always casting a critical eye over every operational detail.

Training for the forthcoming offensive began at the end of March, with every effort made to achieve realism. A large model was built of Messines Ridge and its defences, and every officer taking part was given the chance to study it. Replicas of trenches—both British and German—were dug and from these the troops, including the New Zealanders, rehearsed the attack by day and night. Russell and his commanders worked to ensure that every man was efficient in the full range of infantry weapons, and that junior leaders were proficient in the skills of fire and movement. 'No stone was left unturned to instruct every man in what he had to do,' wrote infantry officer Spencer Westmacott. 'The men spoke jokingly of all of this and of themselves as being "in the fattening paddock".'[145]

Russell was confident that the Messines offensive would give his New Zealanders the opportunity to show their abilities in open warfare to best advantage. His men, he wrote to Allen, could well have a better natural aptitude for this type of fighting 'than many of our people from the other side of the Channel'.[146] By mid-April, he seemed satisfied with what had been achieved in the training so far. His diary of 16 April noted: 'With Corps Cdr to Guelines to see the Rifle Bde put through an attack on marked positions to represent Messines. The Army Cdr was there also. We all thought the practice good. The men looked extraordinarily fit and ready to do anything . . .'

The task allocated to the New Zealand Division was a critical one—the capture of the dominating ground occupied by the village of Messines. Their success or failure would determine the outcome of Godley's corps plan, including the success of the supporting Australian 3rd Division. Russell realised early on that once it was captured, the village would be an obvious target for German artillery. His brigades would deal with the problem by outflanking Messines and establishing a defensive line beyond it. He would commit to the village, or its remnants, only the minimum number of troops needed to clear its cellars and bunkers before they took shelter from the inevitable retaliatory bombardment.

On 21 May, the British artillery began its preliminary bombardment of the Messines Ridge, everywhere cutting the enemy's wire defences, smashing in trench lines, and reducing Wytschaete and Messines villages to rubble. The same day, Haig began a round of visits to corps and divisional headquarters across the Second Army to check on planning for the coming battle. One general was sacked out of hand as a result of these interrogations. Russell's diary noted merely that Haig 'looked at our plans—discussed one or two details, spoke pleasantly of NZers work and departed'.

Haig, in fact, had been impressed with Russell's battle plan, but suggested a change to allow Messines village to be taken in three jumps to avoid creating 'an awkward salient', and to allow the artillery to do its job more effectively. A divisional commander faced with a 'suggestion' from the commander-in-chief would normally take it as an order to be followed, but Russell stuck to his original plan and there was no apparent fallout.[147] Haig's war diary observed only that Russell seemed 'a most capable soldier with considerable strength of character. His problem is a difficult one but he and his officers and men are all most confident of success.'[148] Overall, Haig rated the Messines attack as the most carefully prepared he had seen so far in the war on the Western Front.

On 5 June, Russell attended his last corps and divisional conferences before the attack, and visited his brigadiers and their men. 'All serene,' his diary of 6 June noted. 'Up the line for the last time . . . After dinner met several parties on their way up to the assembly trenches and wished them good luck—they are all very cheery and confident.'

At 3.10 am on 7 June, 19 great mines exploded with devastating force under the German lines on the ridge. Captain Lindsay Inglis was there:

> As the big guns opened, every near object showed clear cut in the light of their flashes. At the same moment six great fans of crimson flame slowly expanded upwards from the other side of the valley. The ground rocked beneath us in an earthquake . . . In less than a minute the whole face of the Messines Ridge was submerged in billowing clouds of dust and smoke.[149]

Russell's men now faced the toughest job of the day—'assaulting uphill into the heap of rubble that had been transformed into a fortress'.[150] The battle plan required two battalions to advance side by side to capture the first and second German trench systems. The following battalions would divide the village between them—half passing through the village to assault the outer ring of defences; half remaining in it to deal with the German garrison.

Following the creeping barrage closely, the New Zealanders caught two German divisions in the act of relieving one another. Spencer Westmacott described the result:

> Crowded together in front, support and communication trenches, the slaughter was terrific on the enemy side. So perfect was the timing of the artillery barrage and so close followed the infantry that the enemy could not use his machine guns, it being impossible to place and man them properly before being smashed by shellfire and the crews blown to pieces.[151]

The first phase of the battle—the capture of the German front line—was achieved relatively quickly. The detonation of the mines had destroyed most of the garrison, and the fire of German artillery against the advancing troops had little effect. In the second phase—the capture of the crest of the ridge—the New Zealanders encountered stiffer opposition, but not for long. The troops applied their by now well-practised tactics of fire and movement. Snipers held the attention of the machine gunners from shell holes while the other sections worked around the flanks of the positions, rushing them and destroying or capturing the crews. Pillbox garrisons that attempted to resist were outflanked and similarly captured or destroyed.

By 7 am the village of Messines was in New Zealand hands, along with 438 prisoners, 11 artillery pieces, 39 machine guns and 13 trench mortars. Russell's description of the assault was brief: 'Attacked at dawn after a successful assembly, with no disturbance or shelling to speak of. All our objectives were gained up to time. Messines gave slight resistance. Later on a brigade of Australian 4 Divn went through and established themselves on a line further east.'

New Zealand casualties were so far light, but it was not to last. The ridge was now crowded with troops and German shellfire throughout the day took a rising toll of killed and wounded. Russell wanted to protect his men by withdrawing one of his two brigades, evacuating Messines itself and relying on a combination of artillery and machine guns to break up German counter-attacks.

Army headquarters would not allow it—the front line, he was told, would be held in strength and both brigades would stay on the ridge. Despite this, Russell was able to withdraw his men from the 'shell-trap' of Messines and position them around the village. Visiting New Zealand Division headquarters on 9 June, Haig noted that Russell was holding Messines with machine guns in great depth, and that all his men were positioned around and outside the village to avoid shellfire.

For Plumer and his Second Army, Messines was a triumph. The Germans had been forced off the southern arc of the high ground that dominated Ypres and the countryside nearby, and the front had been pushed back 3 kilometres at its furthest point. The British now held the Messines Ridge from the Douve River to Mount Sorrel: 'Behind was a ploughed-up wilderness, ahead a green and unspoilt countryside with the towns and woods of the Lys Valley visible in the far distance.'[152]

Godley described the capture of Messines as 'quite the greatest success of the war so far, all of it achieved with much lighter casualties than those incurred on the Somme'. 'I cannot tell you,' he wrote to Allen, 'how proud I am to have had command of the NZ Division, and to still have it with me. You may tell the people of New Zealand with authority that there is no Division in the British Armies in France which has a higher reputation.'[153] Messines, noted divisional historian Colonel Hugh Stewart, was a classic example of battle undertaken with limited objectives, combining outstanding leadership at officer and NCO level with fine fighting spirit.[154]

German losses from the offensive were severe. Some 10,000 soldiers were killed by the mine explosions alone, and over 7300 were taken prisoner. General von Kuhl, chief of staff to Crown Prince Rupprecht, described the battle as 'one of the worst tragedies of the world war'. The British and Dominion forces, however, had also suffered. Total casualties from the attack were 25,000—half of them incurred by the Anzac divisions and largely because of overcrowding on top of Messines Ridge. The final cost to the New Zealand Division was nearly 3700 killed, wounded or missing.

As at the Somme, Russell emerged from Messines with his reputation significantly enhanced. His careful planning and tactical grasp had impressed Haig in the days before the attack. His subsequent performance in securing and holding the village had marked him out as a man to watch. 'At Messines,' wrote Pugsley, 'Russell showed that he learnt the lessons of the Somme, using a combination of all-arms tactics, trained infantry, artillery, machine guns and tanks in support, backed by engineer effort and logistic preparations.'[155]

Russell, however, was adamant that the New Zealanders' success could have been achieved at much less cost. As he put it to Allen: 'Had we been allowed—as I proposed—to reduce the garrison, our losses would have been considerably smaller with the same result.'[156] Without naming names, Russell made clear his feeling that lack of tactical common sense had caused his division unnecessary casualties. Army commanders, Russell told Allen, needed to think more carefully about how to conserve men's lives, and about the conditions under which they compelled men to fight.

Could a practical, non-professional soldier like himself be better at the business of fighting than a career officer in the British Army? Russell's letter seemed to hint as much: 'I do sometimes think that a non-professional mind takes a more detached view of the operations than those who have given their whole lives to the study of these problems.'

Russell sent Allen a full description of the Messines offensive, which Allen then read to an approving House of Representatives. 'The battle in a few words,' Russell wrote, 'was won through the weight of metal thrown onto the enemy positions, and the mettle of the men who advanced to attack them. Everything went like clockwork. The actual positions were carried at very light expense. Our losses began to mount up after we had reached our different objectives.'[157]

What Russell did not tell Allen was his narrow escape from death on 8 June when he and Brigadier-General Brown went up to the front line to inspect his division's positions. A shrapnel shell burst over the party, killing Brown instantly and wounding another senior divisional officer. Russell escaped without a scratch. On 10 June, he confessed to being nearly 'bagged by a sniper' when he and another senior officer were on an inspection of the New Zealand front line. The bullet went clean through his helmet, this time inflicting a minor scalp wound.

Shortly after, a deputation of senior officers confronted Russell in his quarters and bluntly, if kindly, told him to take fewer risks. Allen reinforced the message in a following letter: 'Napier Johnston [divisional artillery commander] tells me that you yourself run too many risks. I hope you will not do this in future.'[158] Two months later, 2nd Brigade commander Earl Johnston was shot dead as he inspected his trenches early one morning. Russell's diary of 7 August noted: 'Poor Earl Johnston was killed by a sniper up at Steingnaast Farm at 6 in the morning—a very sad affair.'

The Battle of Messines was over, but the fighting went on. The weather was continuously wet, the German bombardment of New Zealand positions was severe, and night bombing raids by enemy aircraft were frequent. Casualties in the division now averaged 50 per day. On the night of 26 July, Russell dispatched troops of the 2nd Wellington Regiment to attack the village of La Basse Ville. The fighting was hand to hand and typically grim: bombs thrown into a large cellar at a sugar refinery destroyed the entire 40-man German garrison. A platoon fighting its way up the main street against fierce opposition succeeded in capturing the village, but was forced out of it by a counter-attack the next morning.

But now came an unwelcome distraction from the business of fighting. It appeared in the form of 14 conscientious objectors (COs) sent over from New Zealand and into Godley's care as II Anzac Corps commander. By mid-1917, government policy, as determined by Defence Minister Allen, was that conscientious objectors would serve a prison term in New Zealand, after which they would be transported to Europe and there treated as normal soldiers. If they refused non-combatant duties, they would suffer the standard military punishments, including courts-martial and execution by firing squad. The official belief, however, was that the reality of frontline warfare, strict discipline and the example of men already conscripted to fight would soon pull them into line.

In July 1917, 14 of the most obdurate of the COs were secretly loaded aboard a troopship and shipped to England. They arrived at Sling Camp in September after enduring considerable mistreatment en route. The NZEF commander in England, General George Richardson, took a tough line with the objectors from the start, ordering immediate detention and field punishment. After this, they were dispatched to frontline units in France.

Russell and the commandant of the New Zealand base at Etaples in France, Lieutenant-Colonel Mitchell, supported this policy but were initially overruled by Godley, who felt that sending the COs into the trenches would inevitably result in disobedience or desertion, a firing squad and martyrdom—to his mind, the worst of all possible outcomes.

At Etaples, where for the time being they remained, the objectors suffered more mistreatment, ranging from threats of courts-martial and execution to beatings and imprisonment with hard labour. Most of them eventually succumbed, agreeing to non-combatant duties as stretcher-bearers, but three of them—Kirwin, Briggs and Baxter—held out and still refused to serve.

At this point, Russell visited the divisional field punishment camp and sought Briggs out personally. Briggs was told quite bluntly that if he was in Germany, he would have been shot, but that the military authorities had come to the conclusion that he was 'honest and sincere' in his attitude and that he would be treated differently. 'You know Briggs,' Russell is quoted as saying, 'you are fighting for freedom; so am I.

But I use different methods from you. Your methods may be right or they may be wrong. Mine may be right or they may be wrong. I didn't hold the same ideas when I was your age that I hold today.'[159]

Russell sent Briggs to work for a month in the divisional stores depot at Cape Belles, at the end of which he would ascertain whether there had been a change of mind. On the face of it, it was a humane gesture from a commander to a man who had already suffered much for his beliefs; but whatever Russell's motives, they had little effect— Briggs told his captors that he would go on resisting any attempts to break him to the end.

Godley now changed tack and decided to send all three into the trenches in the hope that being under fire with fellow New Zealanders would finally reform them. Here they were deliberately exposed to shellfire and, in the case of Baxter and Kirwin, given Field Punishment No. 1 and starved and beaten by the division's military police. A wire cable was put under Briggs's arms and he was dragged over rough ground and duckboards, which ripped off his clothes, lacerated his body and tore a hole in his thigh. In spite of being the worst treated, Baxter and Briggs held out. Baxter was eventually hospitalised, found 'insane' and sent home in August 1918. Briggs was invalided back to New Zealand six months later.

The extent of Russell's involvement in the harsh treatment of the 14 objectors is unclear, but it appears that both he and Godley, fully preoccupied elsewhere, were prepared to leave responsibility for their management in the hands of Richardson and Mitchell. It was Mitchell who implemented Richardson's policy of isolation and punishment, and it was the brutal treatment handed out by his military police that finally broke the resistance of all but two of the objectors.

Ormond Burton, however, believed that Russell's involvement in the issue was essentially benign. Arriving at a divisional details camp, he noticed a group of COs under guard. 'They had apparently been given a very bad time by the military police of the Army Corps. Evidently there was a considerable deal of sympathy for them. Some said General Russell had rescued them from the detested "Red Caps" [military police]. This I think was probably true for the General was a very humane man.'[160]

The New Zealanders were not the only ones to treat conscientious objectors harshly. Some 16,000 British citizens objected to military service on grounds of conscience during World War I. A government tribunal found some 4000 of these to have a genuine case for conscientious objection and offered them alternatives to frontline military service, including agricultural and medical work. Those who refused were generally sentenced to prison, in many cases with hard labour, and many were brutally treated. Thirty-four British COs were sentenced to death, although all of these sentences were commuted.

There were more unwelcome distractions to come for Russell in the wake of Messines. In August 1917, Lieutenant-General Godley came under attack in the New Zealand Parliament from the MP for Eden, Christopher Parr. Parr had made a personal visit to the Western Front that year and had spoken to many officers and men of the division. His subsequent comments to the House were as scathing of Godley as they were complimentary of Russell and Richardson. He credited Russell and Richardson with 'the excellent efficiency and morale' of the division in England and France; Godley, on the other hand, was immensely unpopular and bitterly disliked by all ranks. Parr suggested to the House that Godley be replaced with the 'beloved' General Birdwood, then in command of the Australians on the Western Front.[161]

Russell felt that the criticisms of his superior were undeserved, and reiterated this in a letter to Allen three months later: 'Popularity, or otherwise, is not the test of a soldier's virtue. Well-intentioned of course they are, but many criticisms levelled against the conduct of the NZEF are unfounded.'[162] The cautious use of 'many' rather than 'all' criticisms may be significant, given that Russell's comment was made just a month after the Battle of Passchendaele, in which Godley, as II Anzac Corps commander, had played an undistinguished role.

Chapter 15

The Guns of October

'At length our barrage lifted we all once more formed up and made a rush for the village. What was our dismay upon reaching almost to the top of the ridge to find a long line of practically undamaged German concrete machine-gun emplacements with barbed wire entanglements in front of them fully 50 yards deep. The wire had been cut in a few places by our artillery but only sufficient to allow a few men through at a time. Even then what was left of us made an attempt to get through the wire and a few actually penetrated up to his emplacements only to be shot down before their surviving comrades' eyes. It was now broad daylight and what was left of us realised that the day was lost . . . We had lost nearly 80 percent of our strength and gained about 300 yards of ground. This 300 yards was useless to us for the Germans still held and dominated the ridge.'—Corporal Len Hart describes the New Zealanders' attack at Passchendaele on 12 October 1917.[163]

By September 1917, the combined casualties of the Somme and Messines offensives and the steady drain on manpower were worrying the New Zealand Government. There was a feeling within the

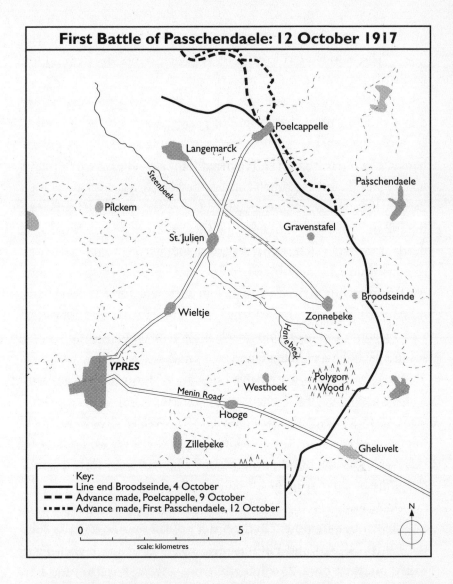

First Battle of Passchendaele: 12 October 1917

Key:
— Line end Broodseinde, 4 October
– – – Advance made, Poelcappelle, 9 October
·–·–· Advance made, First Passchendaele, 12 October

0   5

scale: kilometres

country, Allen wrote to Godley, that New Zealand was being 'bled to death' while Australia and Canada were not making a fair contribution to the war effort.[164] Godley rejected the suggestion, arguing that Australian troops in France had been more regularly employed and had seen harder fighting than those of the New Zealand Division. By September 1917, he wrote, the New Zealanders had been used only twice in offensive operations—on the Somme and at Messines. At all other times they had been deployed in a quiet and easy part of the line.[165] The bloody sacrifice of Passchendaele a month later and the costly battles of 1918 would soon remedy that.

In 1917, Passchendaele was a small, nondescript village astride a low ridge in northwest Belgium, near France's northern border. By September that year it was a pile of rubble and still in German hands. The offensive that had reduced it to that state would not have taken place if British Prime Minister Lloyd George had had his way. Despite the success at Messines, Lloyd George was haunted by the rising toll of British casualties on the Western Front—already 250,000 dead—for what he felt were paltry strategic gains. His preference was to conserve manpower by postponing any further offensives until American troops arrived in France in sufficient force to swing the military balance of power against Germany. In the end, however, Lloyd George and his Cabinet gave Haig reluctant approval for the second part of his planned Flanders offensive.

Haig's task was a formidable one. Since Messines, the Germans had strengthened their defences on the ridge and their positions were again some of the strongest on the Western Front. To reach the German positions the attacking British divisions would have to traverse low-lying, flood-prone ground that had been turned into a quagmire by three years of constant shelling.

On 22 July 1917, the Third Battle of Ypres opened with the greatest artillery bombardment in the history of land warfare. On 31 July, the British Second and Fifth armies, and part of the French First Army, attacked on a 25-kilometre front—their objective, the low ridge on which stood the remains of Passchendaele village. By the end of the first day of the offensive Gough's Fifth Army alone had lost more than a third of its strength in killed, wounded and missing. Haig assured the War Cabinet in London that the results were 'highly satisfactory and the losses slight for so great a battle'.[166]

On 4 September, Haig was summoned to London to justify a campaign in which 18,000 British troops had now been killed or were missing, and 50,000 wounded. Lloyd George wanted the offensive stopped immediately, arguing that with Russia now out of the war and a mutiny in the French Army seriously undermining France's ability to carry on, British forces should stay on the defensive until American troops arrived in force the following year.

Haig and Chief of General Staff Sir William Robertson took the opposite view, arguing that it was precisely because the Allies were now so weak that the offensive should continue. Again the soldiers' case prevailed. As military historian John Keegan put it: 'However ill-judged his [Haig's] strategy and harmful its effects on his long-suffering army, it was to be continued for want of a better man or plan.'[167]

By the first week of October, Allied casualties in the Third Battle of Ypres had reached nearly 163,000. Alarmed at the high cost for so little gain, Haig's two senior generals, Gough and Plumer, urged him to halt the offensive. Haig, however, would not be moved. There were solid reasons still for carrying on, he argued—securing the positions already won, robbing the enemy of observation over the British line, and assisting the forthcoming French offensive on the Aisne. Enemy losses so far had also been severe and their morale was assumed to be low. One more blow might do the trick.

It was at this point that the New Zealand Division joined the Third Battle of Ypres as part of Godley's II Anzac Corps. The bloody fields of the Somme were a year behind it, and three months earlier it had achieved a brilliant, if costly, success at Messines. Now it was to play a key role in what subsequently became known as the Battle of Broodseinde, scheduled for 4 October.

Birdwood, now in command of I Anzac Corps, wrote to Allen of his pleasure in having the 'magnificent New Zealand Division' fighting once again beside him. 'I know it will do as well as it has always done, and that is saying a great deal, for I am not flattering when I say that no Division in France has a higher reputation than yours.'[168]

The main attack on 4 October was to be carried out by I and II Anzac corps, and 44th and 66th divisions of the British Fifth Army. The task of the attacking forces was to seize the low ridge in front of Passchendaele village as preliminary to capturing the village itself. For the first time on the Western Front four Anzac divisions would advance side by side in the centre of the battle line. Three Australian divisions were to take Broodseinde Ridge and the village of Zonnebecke while the New Zealanders would capture the Abraham Heights and Gravenstafel Spur. To ensure surprise, there would be no preliminary bombardment until zero hour.

Unknown to the Anzacs and their supporting divisions, the Germans were massing for an attack of their own, timed to begin at almost the same time. Packed densely in their assembly trenches, the German infantry were slaughtered by the opening barrage, which fell on them just as they were about to advance. On the front of 1st Auckland Battalion alone, 500 of a German Guards division lay dead, and every shell hole contained several corpses.

By 11 am, however, the New Zealanders had gained all their objectives and taken over 1100 prisoners, 60 machine guns and a large quantity of war material. Ten German counter-attacks were successfully beaten off. If victory this time was relatively easy, it was again costly— over 1650 killed and wounded, mostly from machine-gun fire from German pillboxes and shellfire on the bare slopes of Abraham Heights.

From his headquarters on the Ypres Canal, Russell observed that the enemy infantry did not put up much resistance on the day, 'the mud being a worse enemy than the Germans'. The division's casualties were 'not so heavy as at Messines, nor nearly as heavy as at the Somme, which was the biggest battle, and the heaviest fighting that we shall ever see I hope. These long casualty lists, with all they mean, do not lose their effect through familiarity. It seems so futile, though one knows it isn't.'[169]

The Battle of Broodseinde cost the British forces over 20,000 casualties, but took the line about 1000 metres closer to the Passchendaele

Ridge. Over 5000 Germans had been captured. Plumer was ecstatic, describing Broodseinde as 'the greatest victory since the Marne'. Godley was convinced that the Germans were now quite demoralised. He wrote to Allen:

> Units were chucked into the attack anyhow, obviously without proper preparation, or method, or orders, and on our front line alone we took prisoners of a very large number of German divisions. Their artillery retaliation, though severe, was very desultory and unmethodical and irregular . . . The whole of the battlefield of our successive advances is covered with dead Huns.[170]

The excitement of Plumer and Godley was premature. On 5 October, the rain set in, turning the cratered battlefield into a lake and preventing artillery and essential supplies, including ammunition, from getting forward. Anxious to exploit the successes of 4 October, Haig instructed his commanders to continue with the offensive, at least until the Passchendaele Ridge was secured. 'We are practically through the enemy's defences,' he told a meeting of war correspondents on 9 October. 'The enemy has only flesh and blood against us.'[171]

The attack that day—the so-called Battle of Poelcappelle—was a dismal failure. Preparations had been rushed, the weather was bad, and many of the attacking troops were exhausted before the assault even began. Failure to get enough heavy guns forward resulted in a feeble supporting barrage, which left the dense wire entanglements intact. As a result, none of the attackers' objectives were reached, and little or no ground was taken. The cost was again severe: the British 49th Division suffered over 2500 casualties; the 66th over 3000; and the supporting Australians over 1200.

Haig and Plumer were undeterred. The attack would be renewed and extended in spite of the foul weather and evidence that no useful gains had been made. Anxious to atone for the failure on 9 October,

Godley told Haig that his corps was determined to take Passchendaele in this attack and would plant the Australian flag on it.

For the attack of 12 October, the 3rd Australian and New Zealand divisions would be used in tandem, supported by the 9th Division of Gough's Fifth Army. The aim of the attack was to strengthen the British hold on the ridge by capturing the village of Passchendaele and the Bellevue Spur to the north. The New Zealanders would take the spur; the Australians the village of Passchendaele itself. The Australian advance, however, would largely be determined by the speed with which the New Zealanders secured Bellevue Spur.

The task facing the Anzac divisions was formidable. The distance set for their final objective was some 1000 metres deeper than had been achieved in any of Plumer's three previous advances. Moreover, all of these attacks had been carried out after a preparation time of between 6 and 21 days. That had now been squeezed into just 20 hours, and the weather was abysmal. The war diary of the Pioneer Battalion noted 'a steady fight with mud . . . guns and horses are bogged down everywhere. We have pulled many guns out and into position but the road is in a fearful condition . . . rain every day.'[172]

Bad weather and limited visibility meant that there had been no effective counter-battery fire to neutralise the German guns. Since 9 October the Germans had strengthened their barbed-wire defences, especially around strongpoints and pillboxes. The élite Jäger troops opposing II Anzac Corps had also been equipped with twice the usual number of machine guns—177 per regiment. Added to all of this, the New Zealand troops were tired, particularly the men of the 3rd (Rifle) Brigade who had just spent a month burying cables and building roads, mostly at night and often under fire. Badly in need of rest and time to train for this attack, they were given neither.

The New Zealanders relieved the British 49th Division in the St Jean sector at 10 am on the morning of 11 October, with Russell's headquarters on the Ypres Canal. Before them lay the evidence of the failed British attack of 9 October—scores of wounded men abandoned in no-man's-land without protection from the weather or enemy shellfire. In the short time available, every effort was made to recover these men, but many were still there when the New Zealanders attacked the following morning.

On the night of 10 October, a patrol led by Sergeant Dick Travers had brought Russell bad news: no-man's-land was covered with water-filled shell holes, strewn with broken wire and overlooked by lines of pillboxes surrounded by thick barbed-wire entanglements. The reconnaissance revealed that, in spite of a preliminary bombardment, the pillboxes were intact and the wire was uncut.

On the morning of the 11th, Plumer was advised of the formidable wire entanglements facing the New Zealand Division and the supporting 3rd Australian Division. He was told that that these could not possibly be cut by shellfire within the 20 hours left before the attack, and that something also had to be done about the hundreds of wounded men still stranded in the mud between the lines. 'Sir Herbert was non-committal; he turned his face aside; the attack would go on.'[173]

About midday, a worried Brigadier-General Napier Johnston, commander of the divisional artillery, called on Russell at his headquarters. Russell noted in his diary: 'Napier Johnston came to see me after lunch: the guns are all forward, but he evidently feels uneasy about the attack—says preparations inadequate.'

As events were to prove, Johnston was right about the lack of preparations but wrong about the guns. Congested roads torn by shellfire and often submerged in mud had made it almost impossible to get all the guns forward for the attack, and many of them had bogged down in the mire. Artillery batteries that should have had thousands of rounds of ammunition at their disposal had in most cases only a few hundred.

Sometime in the afternoon, Major Bob Wilson, a New Zealander in command of a supporting battery of British artillery and an old polo-playing friend of Russell's, also called in to divisional headquarters. He told Russell that the attack could not succeed under such 'awful' conditions and should be immediately called off. Russell told Wilson that he had already tried to have the attack postponed, but that his attempt had failed. The army commander (Plumer) had made it clear that this was an 'army' attack and that it was too late to delay it, he told Wilson. Their information was that with one more push the enemy would collapse, so nothing could be done.[174]

Monash, in command of the Australians, had also attempted to get the attack postponed, but the message was essentially the same: 'The chief [Plumer] decided that every hour's postponement gave the enemy breathing time.'[175] Concerned about the Anzacs' chances of success in the dreadful conditions, General Gough phoned Plumer that night to add his voice to the opposition. Plumer was again unmoved—the attack would go ahead as planned.

The start line for Russell's 2nd and 3rd brigades was Waterloo Farm on the Gravenstafel Road. The march up the night before in high winds and rain had been a nightmare, with men sinking up to their knees in mud. Soaked and exhausted, they dug foxholes in the slush and waited in the dark and rain for zero hour. Facing them on the high ground across no-man's-land was their objective—dark rows of concrete bunkers and many concealed machine-gun nests, all protected by thick belts of barbed wire. Around them still lay scores of badly wounded men, unattended and unprotected from the weather, evidence of the disastrous attack of 9 October.

The German positions on Bellevue Spur had been bombarded by the division's artillery from 9 October to the afternoon of the 12th, but with little damage to either strongpoints or their protecting wire. At zero hour, 5.30 am, the artillery opened up again, but the creeping barrage was weak and patchy. With no stable platforms on which to rest, the guns tilted and sank into the mud as they fired and shells fell short, killing and wounding troops still in their assembly positions. Many of the shells landing on the spur buried themselves in the mud and failed to explode, or sent up harmless geysers of mud and water.

Unmolested by the artillery, the German machine gunners and snipers now had a free hand.

Under a hail of machine-gun and sniper fire, the leading waves went forward to the attack. Many were cut down almost as soon as they left their trenches; the remainder came up against great belts of uncut wire and pillboxes surrounded by their own wire entanglements. The wire had been cut in places but only enough to allow a few men through at a time. Some reached the pillboxes, only to be shot down before they could use their bombs; others found a break in the wire where the sunken Gravenstafel road ran up the slope. They made a dash for the gap but soon discovered it was a trap, swept from all points by enemy machine guns. In the water-filled shell holes that covered the ground dozens of wounded men slipped back and drowned.

At 10 am both brigades reported that they were being held up by machine guns and uncut wire; the barrage had been lost and they were digging in on the line gained. On their flank, the Australians had been stopped by 'the same withering blasts of fire, the same tremendous difficulties of uncut wire and enemy blockhouses'.[176]

Believing that that the Australians had secured their objectives and now had a dangerously exposed left flank, Godley ordered that the attack be resumed at 3 pm. The commander of the 2nd Brigade, Brigadier 'Bill' Braithwaite, was adamant that it should not. He told Russell that his brigade could not go on without suffering further heavy casualties, and could not be reorganised in daylight because of heavy German sniper and machine-gun fire. Further bombardment of the pillboxes was also out of the question because his men were too closely dug in under the enemy wire. Braithwaite's protests were at first ignored, but the order was finally cancelled once it became clear that the Australian brigades and elements of the 9th Division had either made little progress against the German defences or had been forced to withdraw.

By now, over 850 men of the New Zealand Division had been killed and about the same number wounded—making 12 October the worst single day in New Zealand's military history. Monash's 3rd Australian Division was also badly mauled, with 3200 casualties. The supporting British 9th Division had fared no better—its troops were massacred by German machine guns while trapped in swampy ground to the left of the Anzacs.

The area captured by the New Zealanders was minimal: 500 metres on the left of the planned 2500-metre advance, but no ground on the right. Russell's diary entry that day was brief but poignant: 'Attacked this morning at daybreak. We and indeed all other divisions were held up from the start by MG [machine-gun] fire . . . the artillery preparation was insufficient, the barrage poor, and it goes to show the weakness of haste. Our casualties are heavy . . . I am very sad.'

Phase two of the tragedy now began—the recovery of hundreds of badly wounded men lying out in no-man's-land, including the last survivors of the British attack on 9 October. For the rest of that day and throughout the night, stretcher-bearers toiled in deep mud to clear the wounded from the battlefield—a 6-kilometre carry under fire from enemy artillery, machine guns and snipers. On 13 October, an informal armistice was agreed with the Germans. More than 3000 extra troops, including 1600 New Zealanders, worked to get the remaining wounded to casualty clearing stations behind the front line, unmolested now by enemy snipers or machine-gun fire.

Atrocious weather, rushed preparations, weak artillery support and uncut wire had defeated the best efforts of the attacking divisions in what came to be known as the First Battle of Passchendaele. From a deserter, the Germans had known on the night of 11 October that they would be attacked early the following morning. All units had been alerted and the New Zealand troops walked into a trap. Burton had no doubt about the causes of the failure on 12 October: 'Mud, uncut wire, an ineffective barrage, and an attack that gambled on a German loss of nerve. Instead they had taken heart of grace, stood to their machine guns, and the helpless infantry went down in hundreds in the black slough.'[177]

Reporting to Defence Minister Allen, Russell's assessment was blunt:

> We were brought in on the 11th to renew the attack on the morning of the 12th. This, though not an entire failure, was very nearly so. Uncut wire was the cause of our failure. It is true that the artillery barrage was quite inadequate, owing to the difficulties in getting guns forward, so reducing the number available. With no stable platform from which to shoot, their registration was also faulty and they were frequently out of action owing to the trails or wheels sinking in the mud and soft ground.[178]

Godley glossed over the disaster of 12 October, describing the battle as 'a very good day's work' that had gained the division an advance of 500 metres and nearly 600 prisoners. The casualties from the two October attacks, he told Allen, were 'not unduly heavy'. Godley quoted with approval the comment of a captured German officer that in such conditions no troops in the world would have attempted to advance—choosing to see this as a tribute to the fighting qualities of his men instead of the statement of disbelief it probably was. He concluded evasively: 'There is no doubt, however, that these repeated blows are having their effect in wearing the Boche out. One of his few remaining good Divisions [a Jäger division] was entirely knocked out by the NZ Division in the last fight.'[179]

In contrast to his superior, Russell took full responsibility for the debacle on 12 October, and particularly for his failure to check the state of the wire before his men went over the top. 'Whatever then the obstacles might have been on our front,' he wrote to Allen, 'it was too late to deal with them by artillery preparation. We, as a Divisional staff, assumed that the wire had been cut. Assumption in war is radically wrong if by any means in your power you can eliminate the uncertain. This, of course, is pure theory, but we made a mistake.'[180]

Had the wire been cut, Russell was convinced that the attack would have been successful despite the weak creeping barrage and the heavy fire from the German pillboxes: 'You cannot fight machine guns, plus wire, with human bodies. Without the wire to check them the men would have tackled machine guns in spite of their losses. As it was, they tried heroically to tackle both. This was humanly impossible.'[181]

The pressures Russell and his staff were under on the afternoon of 11 October made errors of some kind almost inevitable. They were dealing with the myriad details of an attack into which the division was being rushed at very short notice and in appalling conditions. Brigade and battalion headquarters had to be selected and medical stations set up, planked roadways and duckboard tracks laid, streams and swamps bridged, approach routes for the troops taped, and detailed instructions issued to unit commanders. Harried by deadlines and coping with the effects of a severe cold or bronchitis, Russell failed to do what he customarily did—go forward and see the conditions for himself, or ensure that a member of his staff did so.

While admitting his error, Russell also identified its underlying cause—a rushed attack that gave the commanders responsible for it insufficient time to prepare: 'Want of careful preparation, due probably to the hope that the Boche was played out and prepared to run, covers the whole question,' he wrote to the president of the Board of Agriculture, Sir James Wilson. 'These risks no doubt have to be taken occasionally in war if you are ever to secure a big success, but I am very sorry for the sake of the men and all the poor fellows whom we shall leave behind that it was the lot of the NZ Division to be in the line at that particular juncture.'[182]

Would it have made any difference if Russell had checked the wire, found it uncut, and again asked for a postponement? Probably not; Plumer had already made it clear that the attack would not be held up because of the particular difficulties of the two Anzac divisions, and this had been reiterated to Monash and to Russell the day before the attack.

Russell himself believed this was the case. On 24 October, he told his senior officers that even if the strength of the German defences had been known earlier, it was unlikely that 'the non-success of one division' would have caused the programme already set for the two attacking armies to be changed in any way.[183] As Stewart put it: 'The decision did not rest with the Division or with the Corps. The Army's orders had been issued and the divisions were but pawns in the tremendous game played over these Flanders swamps and ridges.'[184]

Russell's subsequent letter to Allen made no reference to an attempt to secure a postponement the day before the attack on Bellevue Spur. He indicated only that responsibility for the disaster should be his alone, if any questions were asked in Parliament. It was a rare example, wrote Pugsley, of a military commander's willingness to accept responsibility for failure in war.[185]

The political fallout Russell expected did not immediately occur. No comments were made or questions asked when Allen revealed the casualty figures in the House on 1 November 1917.[186] By January 1918, however, the events of 12 October were creating unease on the home front. Allen wrote to Russell:

> Rumours have been circulating through parts of New Zealand that the situation was not properly appreciated, and that it was known to some senior officers, at any rate, that it would be impossible for the Artillery to clear up the wire and to preserve the barrages as they have done in previous attacks. I quite understand your position, namely, that you and your Divisional staff assumed the wire had been cut, and I lay no blame on you, nor indeed do I blame anybody, but there is a feeling of unrest and I have it myself. There is no use denying it.[187]

The principal responsibility for the failure of the New Zealanders' attack on 12 October, however, lay not with Russell but with Haig and his senior generals. Against the advice of his peers, Haig had chosen this part of Flanders to launch his next major offensive in 1917. The Passchendaele Ridge was one of the most strongly fortified parts of the German line, and the plains in front of it were prone to severe flooding, even in summer.

Once embarked on the offensive, Haig consistently refused to call it off, despite atrocious conditions, heavy casualties and minimal gains. He and his senior commanders nursed the delusion that significant progress had been made on 9 October. The Germans, they felt sure, were on the brink of defeat, and one more push would take the British Army through their defences and onto higher, drier ground for the winter.

The second of the architects of failure on 12 October was Plumer himself. Godley's II Anzac Corps was given only six days to march from its training area at Lumbres to Ypres and plan and execute an attack on a front quite unknown to the corps and its divisions. More seriously, the 20 hours' notice Plumer gave Godley for the attack of 12 October was impossibly short. Under pressure to meet Haig's expectations, Plumer then ignored the difficulties faced by the two Anzac divisions and brushed aside requests for a postponement.

The causes of failure on the 12th, however, were more fundamental, and again Plumer and his staff were mostly responsible. No attempt had been made to ensure that the road forward to the front line was fit for heavy traffic before II Anzac Corps took over its section of the front on 11 October. There were no light railway tracks or tramlines forward of Wieltje, 4 kilometres behind the front line, and the few tracks in place ceased altogether 3 kilometres short of the line. In the opinion of the commander of the Pioneer Battalion, the failure to ensure that proper road and rail links were in place when the weather was fine—that is, before 5 October—was the direct cause of failure of Godley's corps on both 9 and 12 October.[188]

The future major-general, Lindsay Inglis, felt that the tragedy of 12 October had its roots in the failure of the British commanders to exploit their gains at Broodseinde eight days earlier:

The tragedy of the attack [at Broodseinde] was that we were tied down strictly to limited objectives, for we could have walked on to Passchendaele almost unopposed that morning . . . At the time we cursed the inelastic British tactical methods, but were more bitter still when the attempt to do a week later what could so easily have been achieved on the 4th failed in atrocious weather at the expense of thousands of casualties in our 2nd and 3rd brigades.[189]

Heavy rain and mud compelled Haig to cancel the offensive the day after the failed Anzac assault, but the Canadian Corps under General Sir Arthur Currie was then ordered to finish the job. Currie was determined not to repeat the mistakes that had doomed the attacks of 9 and 12 October. He insisted on sufficient time for planning and preparation, enough guns and ammunition to support his infantry, and proper tracks to move and supply his troops. His careful planning paid off. On 26 October, 'the wild bull charged against the iron wall' and the remains of Passchendaele village finally fell to the Canadians on 6 November at a cost of another 16,000 casualties.

Haig brought the Third Battle of Ypres to an end six days later. The deepest penetration made by his forces was just over 10 kilometres, and they had yet to fully accomplish the first of the objectives laid down in July. Less than half the ridge was now in British hands, and Haig's ambitious plan to capture the Channel ports of Ostend and Zeebrugge had been abandoned. The decision to press on with the attacks when all the factors were against it, wrote military historian Trevor Wilson, was 'the most lamentable decision of his [Haig's] lengthy and sometimes distinguished command'.[190]

Army and corps commanders rarely visited the front line and were ignorant of the appalling conditions under which their men were fighting. On 7 November, General Sir Lawrence Kiggell, Haig's second in command, paid his first visit to Passchendaele since the battle had begun nearly four months before. 'Good God', he exclaimed, 'did we really send men to fight in that?'[191]

They did indeed. Some 70,000 British and Dominion soldiers were killed in the Third Battle of Ypres and over 200,000 wounded, for no significant gain in territory. With total German casualties at about 200,000, General von Kuhl, the chief of staff of German forces in Flanders, had good reason to describe the battles that culminated in Passchendaele as 'the greatest martyrdom of the World War'.

The Third Battle of Ypres weakened the German Army's ability to continue the war, but in the end it was all for nothing. The ground so grimly fought over for four months was lost in three days when the great German counter-offensive was launched in March 1918. The 10 or 12 British divisions squandered at Passchendaele were the reserve that could have halted the German advance a great deal sooner and at less cost, so sparing the Allies 'the gravest crisis of the war'.[192]

Burton wrote:

> At the end of the battle we were left sitting in the mud while the Germans had merely dropped back into comfortable unbroken country. The Russians were out [of the war] and we did not know that the tide was beginning to turn against the German sub-marines. Fortunately, nothing was known of the mutiny in the French Army. The Tommies had just about had it. Some deeply moving songs were going round among them about the useless slaughter at Passchendaele.[193]

Lieutenant-Colonels King and Winter-Evans were killed at Pass-chendaele on 12 October. So too was the legendary captain of the 1905 All Blacks, Dave Gallaher, the two Stewart brothers—Jock and Harold—and all three of the Newlove brothers—Edwin, Leonard, and Leslie. George King was buried by the men of his Pioneer Battal-ion to the poignant words of the Maori lament for a fallen chief. The others are listed on the Memorial to the Missing at the beautiful Tyne Cot cemetery just below the village. With them are the names of hun-dreds of other New Zealand soldiers whose bodies were never found.

Chapter 16

The Road to Recovery

'We were to spend the next five months in the Ypres Salient—
a field of squalid horror . . . Shell-hole touched shell-hole, no
blade of grass was anywhere to be seen, the trees were splintered
stumps, the villages heaps of rubble scarcely to be distinguished
in the brown waste of churned earth. The small streams that had
wound about the gentle valleys were now horrible bogs. The
debris of battle was everywhere—broken guns, smashed vehicles,
tangled heaps of twisted rusty wire, empty shell cases, rusty tins,
riven helmets, smashed duckboards and ruined trenches.'[194]

By the end of 1917 morale in the British Army had fallen to dangerously low levels, largely due to its heavy losses in the Third Battle of
Ypres and a sense that the war would never end. A malaise had begun
to infect all Allied armies—'a crisis of spirit, ground down by bitter
memories of muddle and waste, a distrust of high-level strategy'.[195]

On the night of 14 October, Russell's brigades moved back to positions in front of the ruined town of Ypres. There they would spend
the harsh winter of 1917/18 in damp, frozen trenches while their
commander worked once more to rebuild his shattered division. He

had much to be concerned about. Sickness rates soared and morale plummeted as the failure at Passchendaele and the grim winter conditions hit home. For the first time, the New Zealand brigades had completely failed, and the taste of defeat was bitter.

Russell's first response was to call a meeting of the so-called Soldiers' and Workmen's Council, composed of senior officers and representatives of the rank and file. The solution, the meeting decided, was to improve the living conditions of the men and to help them to better understand the causes they were fighting for. Russell discussed the matter with YMCA director Jim Hay, who had previously discussed it with Ormond Burton.

Burton, then a mere corporal, was summoned to see Russell at his headquarters. 'When I arrived he was in bed with a mild attack of flu. I was shown in and told to sit down on the edge of his cot. General Russell looked like an ugly, but kindly, king who was also somebody's father. We had a good long talk. He was very interested. Probably they knew a good deal at Divisional Headquarters and were very concerned.'[196]

The sequel was a conference of Russell and his brigade officers, including both Hay and Burton. Brigadier-General Young argued that low morale in the division was due to the recent heavy losses at Passchendaele, the depressing environment of the salient, and the winter conditions. It would improve, he said, once the division was moved elsewhere. Taking Oliver Cromwell as his text, Burton insisted that soldiers' morale could only be high if they 'knew what they were fighting for and loved what they knew'. He emerged from the meeting with 'a profound admiration' for General Russell—'for his directness, a certain simplicity and sincerity, and a very real humility, with a devotion to what he saw as his duty'.[197]

With the talking over, a programme for the division's recovery was now put in place. Its ingredients were much the same as those in the months after the Somme—dry accommodation, clean bedding, hot food, sports days, leave to England and Paris, and better communication with the troops.

By now, however, Russell was also looking ahead to demobilisation and how he might help his men readjust to civilian life back in New Zealand. An educational programme was initiated with lectures on such weighty subjects as German and Allied war aims, and the relationship between Britain and her dominions. Books that might stimulate men with intellectual interests were provided in the huts. Those who would benefit most from his programme, Russell surmised, would be men whose university education had been interrupted by war, older men whose intellects had grown 'stiff with disuse', and those who would gain from technical training.

But with the Battle of Passchendaele now over, Russell wanted to give his division a break from the misery and filth of Flanders, and add a new dimension to their experience. The result was a request to the War Office in London that his division accompany the British troops that were being sent to Italy in late 1917. On 30 October, Russell was told that his request had been refused. 'Unfortunately,' his diary noted, 'we must make the best of Flanders and its mud.'

Russell was also keen to spell his veterans, some of whom had been serving in the front line since late 1914 and were badly in need of rest. Initially, he secured an agreement by which every month 250 men who had completed three years' active service with the NZEF would be given six months' leave in New Zealand. The War Office, however, opposed the scheme, fearing that it would have the same effect as similar schemes had previously on the much-depleted Australian and Canadian divisions.

Russell and Godley protested vigorously to Massey and Ward, who were in England at this time. The result was a more modest scheme under which 50 men a month would return to New Zealand, and 100 selected NCOs and other ranks would be sent to England for duties with reserve units. The veterans selected would be given a month's leave at home, and in most cases would return to the Western Front as NCOs with a reinforcement.

The position of the 4th Brigade again became an issue. Russell had never wanted the extra brigade, and now wanted to break it up to recoup the losses of Passchendaele. It would be better, he argued, to create two or three extra Pioneer battalions solely for work, rather than retain a brigade that was 'fighting today and working tomorrow'. However, it was not until the following year that the 4th Brigade was finally disbanded and the men not absorbed into the division formed into a divisional entrenching group.

Meanwhile, the day-to-day work went on. Russell's headquarters was sited in a medieval castle with its own tower, moat and portcullis. His staff declared the tower to be haunted because of the shrieking of the wind on the stairs from a dungeon in which prisoners had once been chained to cold stone walls. If Russell was disturbed by this, there is no record of it: his focus, as always, was on the task at hand. Captain Tom Seddon MP, Russell's aide-de-camp at this time, recalled a typical day during that grim winter outside Ypres:

> The work of the Major-General began before dawn. In a lamp-lit dining hut the General with his aide ate a hasty breakfast. An alert chauffeur drove us through the ruins of Ypres and then a little distance further to a point beyond which no military vehicle was permitted to pass. Nimbly out of the car the General alighted and then with a swinging stride he strode on the duckboard route humming all the while 'The Cock of the North'.[198]

After delegating specific projects and activities to his battalion commanders, Russell would insist on personally inspecting the work being done, while anxious aides wondered how they could devise some excuse to get him back to a safer distance from the front line. Officers of the division had ordered Seddon not to let his general take unnecessary risks, but he found himself powerless to deter a determined commander who insisted on 'seeing for himself'.

As a relief from the pressures of work, Russell would saddle his Irish-imported hunter ('a perfect jumper') and ride the back country behind the lines with Colonel 'Jumbo' Wilson, a member of his staff seconded from the British Army who also loved horses. Russell would often read far into the night on topics that held his particular interest, among them the works of Shakespeare. Seddon recalled Russell's staff sitting 'entranced' as he and a young officer and Rhodes scholar discussed the bard's plays and poetry over a mess dinner.[199]

By now, however, the strains of rebuilding his division in the wake of the First Battle of Passchendaele and the severe winter of 1917/18 were affecting Russell's health. British doctors diagnosed a recurrence of bronchitis and Godley again ordered him to the south of France, where it was hoped that a complete rest in the company of his daughter Jan would restore him to full health.

On 3 December, Braithwaite's 2nd Brigade attacked German positions at Polderhoek Chateau in an attempt to pinch off a salient that was protruding into the New Zealand line. It was a costly failure, with close to 50 percent casualties in the attacking force. The main causes were identified as the lack of a preliminary bombardment to clear the enemy wire; intense enemy machine-gun fire from strong points and pillboxes; and the inexperience of the attacking force, many of whom were recent reinforcements. Braithwaite's report noted that when experienced officers and other ranks became casualties, the new troops 'failed to show the necessary qualities of dash, determination, and readiness for self-sacrifice which were indispensible factors for success in this operation'.[200]

Russell had made his usual careful preparations for the attack, supervising the training of units selected for the operation, and had watched it being rehearsed. Unusually, he appears to have had no influence on the tactics used on the day, possibly because they were devised when he was still on sick leave. 'The casualties at Polderhoek appear excessive for ground gained,' he noted in his diary. 'Failure due I gather to untrained men not following the officers boldly.

Think it was a mistake to attack frontally—prefer my idea of coming in on a flank—pillboxes too well sited.'

Meanwhile, the heavy losses of the division in recent attacks were fuelling the debate in New Zealand on whether it was doing more than its fair share of fighting on the Western Front. Allen obviously felt it was, but Godley again assured him that the Australian and Canadian divisions had been more consistently used overall, and had seen harder fighting than the New Zealanders.

'The NZ Division has done splendidly,' he wrote, 'but does not want to be given credit for having done more than other people.'[201] Allen responded by sending Godley a table of Allied casualties to 1 December 1917, showing the proportion of Australians to New Zealanders killed, wounded and missing at about 3:1. The point he seemed to be making was that casualties for the New Zealand Division were disproportionately high, given that New Zealand had only one division on the Western Front while the Australians had five.

Allen was also becoming increasingly uneasy about the quality of British generalship and the resultant cost in New Zealand lives. Although reluctant to criticise the handling of specific offensives, he wrote to Godley:

> You ought to know that there is a very uncomfortable feeling spreading throughout New Zealand that men's lives have been sacrificed unnecessarily, not only at Gallipoli but on the Western Front also. You cannot help communications coming to NZ from men who have been in certain campaigns at the West, and latterly there have been some disquieting remarks about the want of artillery preparation in one of the recent attacks . . .

Expecting some domestic criticism of the generals' handling of the failed Passchendaele offensive, Allen asked Godley for more detail about conditions on the night of 12 October, and particularly about the uncut wire.[202]

Meanwhile, the future of Russell's command was being discussed at senior levels of the British Army. Two weeks before the New Zealand Division's attack at Passchendaele, Birdwood had suggested to Allen that Russell be asked to take command of the NZEF in Europe if there was 'any further anxiety' in New Zealand about the performance of Godley, the incumbent commander. 'I originally doubted if Russell could do this,' he wrote, 'but after three years on service he has learnt much and would I think do it well . . . He is much liked and trusted.'[203]

In November, Godley himself raised the possibility that Russell might succeed him in command of the NZEF, while still commanding the division in France. He concluded, however, that Russell could not do both jobs effectively, and added: 'It would be a great pity if the Division lost Russell's services as its commander (as he commands it very well and would be difficult to replace) if, as is very likely, he found it necessary to devote himself chiefly, or perhaps entirely, to the higher command.'[204]

While these issues were being debated, Russell was making a steady recovery from sickness and exhaustion in the south of France. But events had taken a turn that would soon require his presence back with the division. The Germans were by now in the thick of preparations for the 'Kaiserschlacht' (Kaiser's Battle), their last great offensive on the Western Front. In its opening weeks, the New Zealanders would perform what one historian has described as a 'magnificent feat of arms, perhaps their finest of the war'.[205]

Chapter 17

Closing the Gap

'At the moment we did not know the exact details but we did know that the Germans were racing to get through. They had in fact only about two more miles to make—roughly to the crest of the big ridge rising above us. If they could take and hold this they had command of the Amiens railway. Amiens and Doullens would fall and the British line would crumple up. Two miles! Almost at once our leading battalions swung out—1/Auckland and 2/NZRB. Morale was at its highest. The British had broken but we were New Zealand going into the breach. Challenge and response! What the Turks could not do at Chunuk the Germans would not do on the Somme.'[206]

By the end of 1917, the Germans were in a stronger position to achieve victory on the Western Front than at any time in the past two years. Russia had signed an armistice with Germany in December, and the German high command could now transfer nearly 50 divisions of infantry to the west for a final, war-winning offensive.

Hindenburg and Ludendorff planned to exploit this superiority by launching an all-or-nothing offensive in the west in February

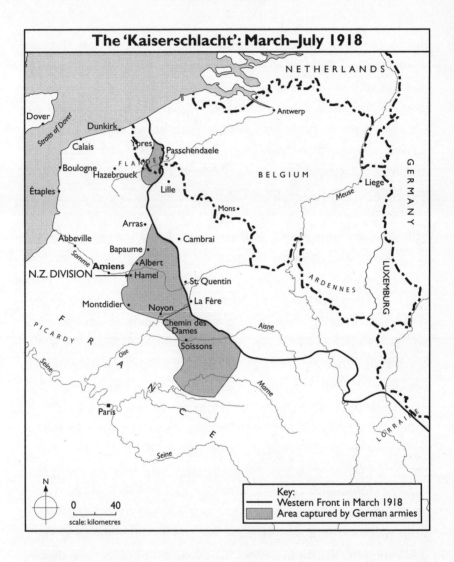

The 'Kaiserschlacht': March–July 1918

or March 1918. Its success, it was hoped, would allow Germany to negotiate a peace settlement with the Allies from a position of strength. At a minimum, Germany aimed to secure its borders, retain control of the industrial capability of occupied Belgium, and incorporate French coal and iron resources into its Ruhr industrial region.

Ludendorff's plan for the Kaiserschlacht was to smash through the British front line on the Somme then swing north and drive the

British Army back on the Channel ports, the vital lifeline through which troops, their weapons, ammunition, food and other supplies moved between England and France. Britain and a militarily exhausted France, the reasoning went, would then be forced to sue separately for peace on German terms before American troops arrived in strength on the Western Front. It was the last throw of the dice for the German armies, and Ludendorff was well aware that it would either win or lose them the war.

The British high command was aware of what was to come, but not where and in what force. Haig believed that the main thrust of the German assault would be against the fronts of his First, Second or Third armies, the guardians of the Channel ports, and had built up his reserves behind the northernmost Third Army. He was cleverly and deliberately deceived. The German assault would come not against the obvious fronts, but against Gough's Fifth Army, the weakest of Haig's four armies and still recovering from the holocaust of Passchendaele four months before.

The German offensive began at 5 am on 21 March 1918 as nearly 6500 guns and over 3500 trench mortars opened up on British lines in the most intensive artillery barrage of the war. Artillery positions, machine-gun posts, telephone exchanges, road junctions and brigade headquarters were obliterated, ammunition dumps destroyed and whole garrisons annihilated. Five hours later, 76 German divisions attacked through thick morning mist on a 65-kilometre front, infiltrating the British front line, bypassing strongpoints and thrusting deep into enemy territory. The 'Michael offensive'—the greatest German onslaught since 1914 and arguably the decisive battle of the war—had begun.

By nightfall on 21 March the Germans had penetrated the British forward and battle zones to a depth of 13 kilometres, inflicted over 38,000 casualties—including 21,000 prisoners of war—captured 500 guns, and taken nearly 260 square kilometres of territory. Two British armies—the Third and the Fifth—fell back, and over the next six days would retreat some 60 kilometres before the rapidly advancing Germans. Although 10,000 of the attackers had been killed and 29,000 wounded, the British Army had suffered its first real defeat since trench warfare had begun three and a half years earlier.

On 24 March, the Germans crossed the Somme and broke through between the French and British armies, capturing Bapaume and Noyon. The British high command feared that if the Germans reached the vital road and rail junction of Amiens, they would cut its armies off from the Channel ports of Rouen and Havre. On 26 March, at an emergency conference of generals and politicians, Marshal Ferdinand Foch was given overall command of Allied forces on the Western Front.

When the Germans struck on 21 March, the New Zealand Division was in Flanders recovering from the disaster of Passchendaele five months before and enduring a particularly grim winter in the Ypres salient. Alerted to the threat of a major German offensive on the Western Front, Russell had maintained a rigorous programme of training in the techniques of open warfare and the tactics of fire and manoeuvre. Section and platoon commanders were schooled in the use of ground, direction and control of fire, and quickness of decision in dealing with a range of battlefield situations. Once again, as he had done after the Somme and Messines, Russell weeded out men who were now too tired for war, and removed platoon and company commanders who were not up to the job.

On 25 March, the division was ordered to cut short its training and rush south to the old Somme battlefield where the British Army had already lost most of the territory won in the bloody fighting of 1916. There, with three Australian divisions, it would attempt to plug a 6-kilometre gap between two corps of the Third Army, through which German storm troops were now rapidly moving to threaten the key railway junction at Amiens. Russell noted in his diary: 'Word has come that we are to be ready to move south at once to the Somme to help hold up the German offensive, which has been let loose on a 50 mile front—the men very pleased I hear.'

But moving a division rapidly from one part of the front to another was a major exercise at the best of times. There were some 16,000 combat troops to be transported by train, truck or foot, along with their food, ammunition and supporting artillery batteries. There were the machine gunners with their weapons, field ambulance units with their medical equipment and supplies, the divisional transport and the men, wagons and horses that would keep a division mobile in the field.

Logistics aside, getting to the battlefront was an ordeal for men who had spent a hard winter in the trenches of Flanders and were probably well below their peak. Railway wagons and trucks took them most of the way, but the final leg of the journey involved a forced march of up to 70 kilometres in light fighting order, which meant that they were without packs, blankets or greatcoats. The fires of burning villages by night, the rumble of distant artillery, the crowds of French refugees and panic-stricken stragglers from British units streaming to the rear, left the men in no doubt about what lay ahead.

At 6 am on the morning of 26 March the 1st Battalion of the New Zealand Rifle Brigade passed through the village of Mailly-Maillet. They and the units that followed would attempt to fill the gap in the British line between the nearby villages of Beaumont-Hamel and Serre and drive the Germans back, or at least halt them in their tracks.

By committing his battalions piecemeal to battle without artillery support, Russell was taking an unavoidable risk. But by nightfall his men had cleared the enemy from the village of Colincamps and were holding a strong and continuous line from west of Beaumont-Hamel to north of the Serre road. By the morning of 27 March the New Zealanders had linked up with the Australian 4th Brigade at Hébuterne, closing the gap between two British corps and the road to Amiens.

The Germans counter-attacked all that day in an attempt to break through, abandoning their infiltration tactics for full-frontal assaults on the New Zealand positions. Well led by their NCOs and junior officers, the men fought back tenaciously and the line held. Russell's message to his commanders was blunt: the enemy had been held, the division was now protected by wire in front, on its flanks and to its rear. There would be no retreat.

Russell was well aware of what he was demanding. His out-numbered troops were fighting off repeated attacks—for 36 hours without the support of their artillery—and for three days they were short of food, shelter, blankets and warm clothes. The men coped by stripping deserted French houses, barns, cellars and gardens of whatever they could find, including wheat, vegetables, livestock and caches of wine. On the night of 28 March, it began to rain and the New Zealand trenches were soon knee-deep in mud and water. Captain George Tuck rated that week as one of the hardest in his battalion's history: 'How the men stood the terrible strain,' he wrote, 'I cannot tell.'[207]

Endure it they did, and on 30 March the division counter-attacked and captured the high ground of La Signy Farm, which gave it clear visibility over the Ancre valley and over the German posi-tions, along with nearly 300 prisoners and more than 100 captured machine guns. Although a small operation in tactical terms, this was the first successful offensive action taken by the British Army on the Western Front since the start of the Michael offensive nine days ear-lier. Russell's diary entry was brief: 'Melville and a battalion of Rifle Brigade carried out a very successful advance giving us good obser-vation of Serre—200 prisoners and 90-odd MGs.'

On 3 April, Russell wrote to Allen:

Before you get this you will know that we are in the middle of what is reputed to be the biggest battle on record. Our Division came in on [sic] the nick of time. There was a big gap, and by dint of hard marching we managed to fill it just in time . . . After spending the night in getting from one headquarters to another, making plans, getting orders etc, I remarked to the GSO1 that I was not sure that we were not in for a catastrophe. However, it turned out otherwise, and a miss is as good as a mile.[208]

If the tactical situation was fraught, the change of environment was much to the liking of Russell and his division. 'The men are all extraordinarily fit and thoroughly appreciate the change from the Ypres Salient, which was a disgusting spot,' Russell wrote. 'There it was nothing but mud, duckboards, carrying parties and general discomfort. Here we are on lovely open rolling country where wheeled transport can, by following the folds of the ground, get nearly up to the front line.'[209] Hailing the arrival of spring after a long hard winter, Russell quoted his favourite Roman poet, Horace: 'Nunc hyems abest redeunt iam gramina campis'—'Now the long winter is over and the grass returns to the fields.'

Russell relished the return to combat as a relief from the boredom and hardship of the Ypres salient. As the German attack faded, he wrote to his sisters: 'We are much to be congratulated on the fact that the Boche screwed up his courage to this point and came at us. I was afraid he would not and a dreary vista of interminable trench life faded into an uninviting distance.'

On 30 March, a successful counter-attack by British, Australian and Canadian troops marked the turn of the tide for the Allies, halting the German advance just 17 kilometres east of Amiens. On 5 April, 10 German divisions launched a fresh assault on the Third Army front in a last attempt to batter their way through to Amiens. At 5 that morning they began a heavy bombardment of New Zealand positions, perhaps the heaviest the division would face in the whole war. At 8.30 am, the German infantry attacked in an attempt to break through to Colincamps, now nearly 2 kilometres behind the British front line—only to be heavily repulsed by the fire of the division's machine gunners.

The German regiment that the New Zealanders fought against that day later acknowledged the 'colossal toughness' with which the New Zealanders had held the line south of Hébuterne. Captured German officers who had been in the attack described it as their most terrible experience of the war.[210] Corps commander Lieutenant-General Harper acknowledged the key role the New Zealanders had played in checking the German advance and closing the gap between the two British formations on the Somme.

By now, however, the Germans had outrun their artillery and lines of supply, and this, combined with the failure of their assaults on the Third Army front, brought the Michael offensive finally to a halt on 5 April, just 14 kilometres short of Amiens. With German losses at a quarter of a million men, Ludendorff was forced to concede that the enemy's resistance was now 'beyond our powers'.

The Germans, Godley told Allen, had not made anything like the progress they had hoped for: they had failed to capture either of the strategic points—Amiens or Hazebrouck—they had aimed for, or to separate the French and British armies, or to make any appreciable advance towards the Channel ports.[211] Churchill was equally dismissive. The Germans, he wrote, had failed to achieve a single strategic objective and had done little more than reoccupy their old battlefields on the Somme and the regions they had devastated a year before.[212]

Despite colossal losses, however, the Germans had made impressive gains in 15 days of battle. They had driven a huge bulge into the Allied line and recaptured ground on the Somme that had been won at such fearful cost by the Allies in 1916. They had taken around 1900 square kilometres of territory, over 1000 guns, and inflicted over 240,000 casualties on the British and French forces, including 90,000 prisoners.

Nearly 2400 of these casualties were soldiers of the New Zealand Division—once again a heavy price for a small national force to pay. The division, however, had fought its first defensive battle of the war for 11 days on end, in foul weather and without adequate food, shelter or clothing. It had taken over 400 German prisoners, along with 137 machine guns, and it had closed the gap in the line between Beaumont-Hamel and Hébuterne—albeit in the nick of time.

Ludendorff launched several other offensives in the following months, all of which followed the same pattern: 'shock attack, initial success, ultimate failure'. At a particularly dangerous moment in April, the British, in Haig's famous words, had their 'backs to the wall', but the line held and the German onslaught was finally halted.

Russell, however, was much impressed with what the Germans had achieved during the Kaiserschlacht: 'I admit we have nothing in the least to be proud of surveying the operations as a whole,' he wrote to his sisters in mid-April. 'We were superior in numbers and guns to the enemy in 1916 and 1917, and according to Lloyd George are at least even with him this year. And yet he has succeeded in as many weeks in doing far more than we did in as many months.'

Why had the Germans done so well? In Russell's view, it was because their soldiers were on the whole 'better educated, and more efficient and thorough, and better disciplined. If his men are told to do a thing—to stick it out in a trench, or whatnot—they do it. Not because they are braver men—I do not think they are as brave—but because they have learnt to obey. Democracy owes the Germans an enormous debt, if it has learnt the lesson of discipline and self-denial.'

Russell sensed that the war was now drawing to an end, with inevitable defeat for the Germans. 'There will be scares, unfounded rumours, perhaps disasters,' he wrote to his sisters, 'but at the end the wild beast will have exhausted itself, and we must then soberly set to work to put our somewhat damaged house in order.' He noted that the woods near him were full of wildflowers and enclosed some violets in the letter 'for luck'.

For the moment at least, Russell could afford to relax a little. Tom Seddon recalled riding with him to a conference of divisional commanders in the days after the German drive towards Amiens had been halted. 'I shall never forget that expedition. Our horses swung into a joyous canter and a General from whose brow the anxieties of previous weeks had been lifted recited snatches of poetry. It was "The Last Ride Together".'[213]

While conceding that his division had by now 'a great reputation' among the British armies in France, Russell was predictably still hard to please. 'Some troops, of course, fought well—most did—but some want training badly,' he wrote again to his sisters. 'Training and more training—we all want it. You can practise in war only what you have learnt in peace. It is a grave mistake to think that the battlefield is to be the schoolroom. It is too expensive.'

Russell was clearly worried by the division's sluggish response to the crisis of 21 March. Its failure to establish itself at Serre northwards to Hébuterne after first arriving on the Somme, he complained, had cost it a good many lives and casualties. He had subsequently been criticised by General Johnston for wanting to treat his infantry as if they were mounted rifles. 'I accept the criticism. I certainly do expect the New Zealand Infantry both in thought and action to be at least 50 percent quicker than the New Armies.'[214]

The Anzacs, however, had been critical of the performance of some of the British units serving alongside them during the Kaiserschlacht, and many derogatory comments had been made about their morale and fighting abilities. On 30 April, Birdwood directed his commanders to discourage negative comments about the fighting qualities of British troops compared to those from the dominions. 'We are the same blood,' he wrote to Russell in person, 'and the creation of friction by criticism is only playing the German's game.'[215]

The same issue seemed to trouble the New Zealand Government. In June, Allen wrote to Birdwood: 'There are some [NZ officers and men who have returned] who say that some of the "Tommies" can't or won't stand up to the fight. It is hinted that some are wanting in physique and have not that strength of purpose and will which makes for success ... There are ugly rumours about some of the British troops breaking and running.'[216] Much of this criticism, however, was unfair. While some British units broke as the Germans attacked in overwhelming force during the March and April offensives, others held out stubbornly or fought to the finish.

As the German offensive continued, the War Office stepped up its pressure on the New Zealand Government for more troops, asking that reinforcements be doubled for five months (from 800 to 1600 a month). The Government agreed, subject to the availability of shipping, and to the formation of a new tank battalion. Allen, however, was worried about the arrangements. He wrote to Godley: 'If that rate proceeds, we shall just about exhaust our manpower by May 1919, unless we reduce the age or find some other means of securing more men.'[217]

In mid-1918, the furlough issue emerged again after a decision by the New Zealand Government that no more men were to be given home leave. Angered by the decision, Russell, his brigadiers and other senior officers protested to Godley. Godley reported to Allen: 'They were most indignant in view of the fact that the sending of the limited number who have gone, and who it has been proposed to send, was to make up for the disappointment caused by the scheme for returning the original Main Body men in considerable numbers having failed.'[218]

Allen, however, was strongly opposed to the furlough in any form. In July he outlined its drawbacks to Russell, and particularly the problem of getting men back to the front after home leave:

At the present time we have had about 300 men returned and only 10 have so far re-embarked. Apparently when they get back here their nerves begin to go. Men plead sickness and a great many have been turned down on medical examination. Their friends begin to raise an outcry that they have done their bit and should not go back again. Other next-of-kin who have not been able to secure their relative's return are sending in applications day by day asking that their boys may be returned . . . The whole question bristles with difficulties . . . I am sure that it will result in considerable wastage to the Expeditionary Force at the front.[219]

The issue of venereal disease amongst the troops also resurfaced at this time, possibly because of the activities of controversial anti-VD campaigner Ettie Rout on the home front. Russell's approach to the problem, like Rout's, was typically pragmatic—all New Zealand soldiers going on leave in London and Paris should be compulsorily issued with prophylactics (condoms). He wrote to Allen:

I am so absolutely convinced of the urgent necessity of protect-ing, not only the men, but also the womenfolk of New Zealand, that I would not hesitate to support anything which gave a fair hope of mitigating the evil. Moral suasion has had 2000 years in which to do its work, and the result is clear evidence that we must support moral suasion with practical means.

The 'principal chaplains,' Russell assured Allen, had been consulted and had given him their full support.[220]

It was a bridge too far for Allen, who worried perhaps that news of a mass issue of condoms to the troops would provoke a public backlash in morally conservative New Zealand. He replied to Russell: 'I hope there is no need for this at the present time. I presume the chaplains and officers are being constantly reminded of the neces-sity of stiffening up the moral fibre of your soldiers, especially with regard to the question of immorality. I hope you have had a talk with the Prime Minister and Sir Joseph Ward on the subject.'[221] Whether Russell did so is not recorded.

Meanwhile, the war went on. The New Zealand Division remained active throughout the middle months of 1918, practising tactical manoeuvres by day and raiding German trenches by night. On 18 July, the division repulsed a 100-strong German raid, preceded by a heavy bombardment, on its own line. A mopping-up party that went out afterwards counted 32 enemy dead and captured 14 prisoners and three machine guns.

While the combined-arms training continued, there was no slackening in Russell's emphasis on the basics. A memo issued after a divisional conference in April noted that the discipline of the division required stiffening up, especially its standards of marching and saluting. It recommended that any battalion whose men were 'brought up' for non-saluting should be required to do a half-hour of saluting drill.

By now, however, Russell's health, and therefore his fitness to command, had become a serious issue. He was suffering from repeated bouts of bronchitis, and the rheumatism in his damaged wrist and broken ankle was troubling him. In early June, Haig alerted Godley that Russell had come to the head of the list of major-generals to be recommended for command of a full British Army corps, and that he might be required to take up a new command at any time.

By late June, the prospect had become a full offer, but Russell's response was ambivalent. He told Haig's private secretary that he was about to go to England for repairs to his wrist and ankle. In any case, he would insist on choosing his own brigade commanders before accepting the appointment. Godley felt that if Russell took up the offer of a corps, he should succeed him in command of the NZEF and Chaytor should, in turn, succeed Russell in command of the New Zealand Division. Russell seemed to be unenthusiastic about the prospect, which would in effect mean him taking responsibility for two separate forces. 'I do not welcome the idea,' he wrote in his diary on 27 June. '[I] think it a good thing a detached officer such as he [Godley] should command.'

Godley, however, stood his ground, recommending to the New Zealand Government that Russell should succeed him as NZEF commander. 'Should he not take my place, a rather anomalous situation would be created of my commanding the NZEF, Chaytor commanding the Division, Richardson commanding in England, and Russell in command of a British Corps with nothing whatever to do with the NZ Forces.'[222]

By mid-July, with Russell still on sick leave in England, the opportunity for a corps command had passed. General Lawrence, the Chief of Defence Staff, and Haig himself both expressed regret that the offer could not have been kept open, and hoped that another opportunity might arise in future. Russell's candid thoughts on the matter of a corps command are unknown, but he could well have accepted Haig's offer had he been confident that his health was up to the task.

Sick leave, however, was not without its compensations. Although on crutches, Russell was able to spend time with his sisters, Milly and Gwen, and his daughter Jan, at their home in Petersfield, Hampshire. In the evenings, Jan would read him Marcel Proust's letters and together they would practise their French.

By the end of July, Russell was back in harness, but his health had not noticeably improved and Godley was worried by the implications of this for the division. 'I am afraid Russell is rather seedy and cannot walk,' he wrote to Allen, 'and I am rather disturbed about it, as it is not right for the Division to go on for so long with him only half fit.' Godley thought the best solution would be for Russell to hand over the division to Chaytor and move to England where he would command the NZEF from a base in London.[223]

Russell had no disagreement with this. He was still very lame, and every winter his bronchitis was getting worse. A change of commander, he felt, would be a good thing for the New Zealand Division. He wrote to Godley: 'I have always been a strong believer in an occasional change of blood. It is true the Division is doing fairly well, but might do better still—but it will not do so until a new broom is installed.'[224]

Godley discussed the issue with Russell and Lawrence, and together they agreed that a change of command should be made. Russell would go to England to command the NZEF in Godley's place and Chaytor would take command of the division in France. Godley informed Allen accordingly:

> It may save Russell from a breakdown, and it will be of inestimable value to Chaytor and to NZ in the future that he should get a chance of a command in France ... Russell has commanded the NZ Division quite admirably for the three years that he has had it and I hope you will let him know that the NZ Government appreciates it.[225]

The switch of command was never made. The great British counter-offensive had begun a month before, and on 21 August the New Zealand Division took its place at the leading edge of Haig's '100 Days' advance that would end the war on the Western Front. In spite of his declining health, Russell remained in effective command of his division until the enemy was finally beaten in the field.

Chapter 18

The Advance to the Rhine

'On 21 August 1918 the NZ Division—in strength equivalent to a British corps of three divisions—advanced from their trenches on the Somme and never returned to them. For the next 11 weeks the New Zealanders were constantly moving forward. Well-trained, equally skilled in open warfare, trench warfare and the set-piece battle, the NZ Division was a superb fighting machine. For the remainder of the war . . . it was used as one of the spearhead divisions of the British 3rd Army.'[226]

At 4.20 am on 8 August 1918, supported by over 400 tanks, 2000 guns and 800 aircraft, the British Fourth Army began the advance that would finally end the war on the Western Front. A combination of armour, surprise and the fighting skills of the spearhead Australian and Canadian divisions produced dramatic results, and by the afternoon of that day the heaviest fighting in the Battle of Amiens was over.

Between 26,000 and 27,000 German soldiers became casualties of war that day, most of them surrendering to the advancing Dominion troops. Hundreds of artillery pieces, machine guns and

The NZ Division Advance:
21 August – 11 November 1918

mortars were captured. Although stiffening German resistance slowed the advance in the days that followed, a 13-kilometre hole had been punched in the enemy lines across a 19-kilometre front. For the first time since 1914, Allied forces were free to manoeuvre in open country.

The German high command reacted with shock and near despair. Ludendorff described 8 August as 'the black day of the German Army', a day on which it had suffered its greatest defeat since the beginning of the war. By the time the Battle of Amiens ended on 11 August total Germans losses were 73,000 killed and wounded, and nearly 30,000 taken prisoner. The Kaiser admitted to Ludendorff that the German armies could no longer win the war.[227]

Russell doubted that the Allies would succeed in giving the Germans the 'coup de grâce' in 1918 because of manpower constraints, and his feeling that it was too soon to push the raw American troops in battle. 'Without knowing what Foch and Haig have in their pockets,' he wrote to Seddon, his former aide-de-camp, 'I make a shrewd guess that there are not sufficient men available to do more than hold the Germans off with the help of a few counter-offensives, such as [has] been very successfully carried out.'[228]

Waiting with his division in reserve, Russell acknowledged the remarkable success of the Australian and Canadian attacks at the Battle of Amiens, though he was more than slightly envious of the reputation his fellow colonials were winning. 'No doubt,' he wrote to Seddon, 'our turn will come soon.'[229] He would not have to wait long. The New Zealand Division took its place in the front line of the great advance on 21 August as part of IV Corps of Byng's Third Army. It was by now a well-trained and battle-hardened division, its four brigades making it numerically the strongest on the Western Front. The Third Army itself was the strongest of the four British armies in France, containing 13 divisions, supported by 200 tanks, nearly 1500 guns and 10 squadrons of aircraft.

In dense fog and semi-darkness on 21 August, the Third Army launched a surprise attack north of Albert in what was the second major offensive of August 1918. The New Zealand Division's assault on the village of Puisieux at dawn caught the German defenders by surprise, netting over 200 prisoners and 30 machine guns. It was the first of many such captures the division would make in the coming months.

Russell's response was low key; he noted in his diary: 'General attack along our own and adjoining Corps fronts—fair success—our part a small one and [with] adjoining divisions converging we are practically squeezed out at the end of the day. Hart's bde carried our share and did it well—about 200 prisoners, our casualties well under 100 . . . Winston Churchill called after lunch.'

On 24 August, the New Zealanders advanced again, sweeping the enemy from Loupart Wood and the villages of Grevillers and Biefvillers to reach the outskirts of Bapaume. That afternoon Russell and his IV Brigade commander, Brigadier-General Hart, rode forward to inspect their frontline positions. Everywhere squadrons of tanks, armoured cars and artillery were on the move, while fighter and spotter aircraft flew low overhead. 'The whole scene,' wrote Hart, 'was very stirring and much less gruesome and awesome than the Somme, Messines, or Passchendaele.'[230]

The New Zealand division had now advanced 11 kilometres into German-held territory and was just 4 kilometres north of the scene of its bloody battles on the Somme in September and October 1916. Open warfare was now the norm: the roads were good, and the country was no longer pitted with shell craters. Horses and wagons could reach to within a kilometre or two of the battle line.

The next objective was Bapaume itself, in a struggle that would involve the division in one of the hardest-fought battles of its three years on the Western Front. The town occupied a commanding position and had already resisted heavy bombardment and several frontal attacks. Russell planned to avoid a direct assault on the town by enveloping it from the flanks and forcing the Germans to abandon it without a fight. Success did not come easily. It took further heavy bombardment and much hard fighting before the Germans finally pulled out of Bapaume to new defensive positions in the east. The final cost of victory was over 3000 New Zealand casualties, including 800 killed.

'The Boche is being well harried,' Russell wrote to his sister the day the Germans evacuated Bapaume. 'The gain of ground is distinctly valuable: it puts Amiens, Paris, the Channel ports out of the question for the Boche this summer—so that we are now in a position to wait for the development of American strength. This being so I hope we shall be working quietly with a minimum of expenditure of life and a maximum of ammunition. The latter can be replaced, the former not so.'

There was to be no respite in the coming days for the New Zealanders, or for any other frontline division of Haig's armies. On 30 August, they overcame stubborn German resistance to take the villages of Bancourt and Frémicourt. 'His [the enemy's] machine gunners are stout fellows, who fight until we are on top of them,' noted the NZEF's official correspondent. 'The German High Command is ruthlessly sacrificing them in order to save the artillery.'[231]

At Russell's direction, the New Zealanders advanced as they had done at Bapaume, bypassing villages and German strongpoints and leaving them to be mopped up by the units that followed. 'Villages are only obstacles,' he noted in his diary, 'not ends in themselves.' Russell kept in close touch with his troops by moving forward each day to advanced brigade headquarters. In this way, he gave his commanders both the freedom to plan their own battles and the support they needed to keep going.[232]

The New Zealand Division was now marching and fighting across open country almost untouched by war. Behind them now was 'the lacerated, too familiar landscape of churned-up shellholes, hideous walls of wire, miry battered ditches, stricken villages and blasted woods'.[233] Forests, valleys, ridges and spurs; rivers and canals; railway embankments and cuttings were surmounted one by one as the New Zealanders stayed at the cutting edge of the Third Army. Hart's diary noted: 'Our division still in the lead towards Berlin; there is usually an eastern bulge in the line when we go in.'[234]

On 31 August, the Australians captured Mont Saint-Quentin in one of the most brilliant actions of the war, and took the town of Péronne. On 2 September, Canadian and British forces broke through the Drocourt-Quéant Line southeast of Arras. In 12 days of stubborn fighting the Third and Fourth armies had driven 35 German divisions back across the old Somme battlefield, taking some 34,000 prisoners and 270 guns. The New Zealand Division took 1650 of these, and was now over 30 kilometres east of Hébuterne where it had first joined the offensive on 21 August.

On 9 September, Haig reported to Lord Milner at the War Office that in the preceding four weeks his forces had captured 77,000 German troops and 600 guns. Never in British military history had there been such a victory, he told Milner. Discipline in the German Army was clearly declining, and German troops were now unlikely to stand up to Allied attacks even in the strongest positions.[235]

The New Zealand Division had so far seen little evidence of that. They were now across the Canal du Nord, and on 12 September were ordered to capture Trescault Spur, just 5 kilometres from the great defensive wall of the Hindenburg Line. The Germans were determined to hold this ridge at all costs and had garrisoned it with some of their best troops, including a Jäger division.

In the dimly lit vault of a village cemetery, Russell and his staff directed the battle as attack was followed by counter-attack and the line swayed back and forward until midnight. Russell's diary mentioned nothing of the severity of the fighting, noting only that the division had met stiff resistance from a Jäger division 'of good repute'. While the New Zealanders had inflicted heavy losses on the Jägers and taken a large number of prisoners, the British 38th Division on the right, Russell complained, 'did nothing, which hampered matters'.

The problem was one that dogged Russell's men throughout the '100 Days' offensive—the failure of flanking British divisions to get forward in several major attacks, forcing the advancing New Zealanders into a vulnerable salient. A further limitation on the success of his division, Russell noted, was the general refusal of British divisions to attack, as the New Zealanders almost invariably did, in the dark. The official correspondent wrote on 15 October: 'Our men have made night fighting their specialty, which has resulted not only in the surprising of the enemy and the capture of villages, but has saved many casualties.'[236]

On 16 September, Russell wrote to Allen: 'The men really have done extraordinarily well during the last month, which has given scope for their innate qualities such as they have not had before.' His brigadiers and their subordinate commanders had shown plenty of drive and initiative, and the division was 'anything but a one-man show . . . There is no one but, if he were lost tomorrow, could be suitably replaced at a moment's notice. In this lies a great deal of our strength.'[237]

But with no guaranteed end to the war in sight, and still in indifferent health, Russell suggested again that the time had come for him to be replaced as commander of the New Zealand Division. He told Allen: 'I have now held the position for three years, during which time I have been remarkably well served by all the commanders and my Staff. The men have always played their part faithfully and honestly. I cannot say too much for their fighting qualities. Consequently it is not astonishing that the Division has earned a pretty good reputation, though I say it myself. At the same time I have noticed in almost every line of life that a change is sometimes good.'[238]

In mid-September, at a time when the division was taken out of the front line and put into reserve for two weeks. The men were entertained with platoon, company and inter-battalion football games, sprints and relay races. NCOs and other ranks were grilled on their experiences of the previous month's fighting, and a series of tactical exercises was arranged to put the lessons learnt into practice. Russell noted in his diary on 24 September: 'Inspected 2/Auckland and 1/Wellington . . . Men wonderfully fit and cheery—the turnout far ahead of what one would have got 2 years ago.'

On 29 September, the division was put back into the line with orders to capture La Vacquerie village, the Welsh and Bonavis ridges, and to secure bridgeheads across the St Quentin Canal and the Escault River. In a brilliantly executed night attack, Russell's brigades advanced nearly 6 kilometres across the mass of wire, trenches and strongpoints that was the Hindenburg Line, taking over 1400 prisoners, 44 artillery pieces and hundreds of machine guns. Welsh Ridge and La Vacquerie fell easily, and Bonavis Ridge after much hard fighting. Against stubborn German resistance, the division forced a crossing of the St Quentin Canal to capture the village of Crevecoeur, holding it against heavy shelling and repeated counter-attacks. Over 1000 prisoners were taken. Russell's diary noted drily: 'Attack (with British 62nd and 3rd Divisions) was tolerably successful on our part but sticky on left—consequently we gained but little ground and lost fairly heavily—it's useless to depend on British divisions—they may succeed or they may not.'

By 5 October, the whole of the heavily fortified Hindenburg system was in British hands. The 'wall of bronze in the west' that Germany's Imperial Foreign Minister, Admiral Paul von Hintze, had assured the German Reichstag would never be broken was now irretrievably shattered. 'The Hindenburg Line is gone forever,' intoned the NZEF's official correspondent. 'A great fire is burning in Cambrai ... The whole horizon is grey with smoke. Hindenburg's and Ludendorff's destroying angels are busy with their firebrands—aware of the disaster which has overtaken them.'[239]

The Germans were destroying everything that might be of use to their pursuers. Abandoned towns and villages were set on fire, and roads, bridges and railway tracks were destroyed. Dugouts, houses, roads and wells were infested with booby-traps. The New Zealanders forced German prisoners to go first into such places and either remove the booby-traps or be blown up instead of their captors.

In the Battle of Cambrai on 8 October, the New Zealanders broke through the northern part of the Masnières Line to capture the villages of Esnes and Lesdain, followed by Beauvois, Fontaine and Viesly. On 10 October, the division took the village of Briastre, liberating 172 civilians who had been trapped in their cellars by the fighting. It then forced a passage across the River Selle and fought its way up to the heights of Bellevue. Russell wrote to his family: 'The inhabitants of the villages we are now in receive us very cheerfully.

For them, as they say, La Guerre est finie—now that they are out of the House of Bondage.'

By 21 October, the New Zealand Division had advanced 65 kilometres from its start line on the Somme and taken over 6000 prisoners, 49 artillery pieces and nearly 1000 machine guns. A young officer wrote: 'One way and another we had hard fighting enough and it was mostly successful—always advancing and always mopping up lots of prisoners and guns . . . The attack of the Division was something like a series of waves breaking on the shore, one battalion after another pushing on.'[240]

On 23 October, the division made its longest advance of the counter-offensive—7 kilometres in a single day—to secure three bridgeheads across the Ecaillon River and capture the village of Beaudignies. Russell noted in his diary: 'NZ Divn attacks at 8.20: Everything went smoothly. Little resistance and few prisoners—the 3rd Divn did well on our left—the 37 Divn on the right were sticky, getting a bad start. By night we had reached the Ecaillon and secured 3 bridgeheads . . . an exceptionally good performance on the part of Btn Cmdrs Stitt and Hargest.' In the village of Solesmes, divisional officers bunked down in a beautiful old house which had once hosted the Kaiser on a visit to the Western Front.

The retreating German forces were now in a desperate state. Since 15 July, 250,000 German troops had been captured by the Allied armies, along with 4000 guns, and their supplies of fuel and ammunition were low. Everywhere lay the evidence of defeat— broken-down trucks and railway wagons, machine guns, trench mortars and abandoned stacks of military stores. Prince Rupprecht warned German Chancellor Prince Max: 'Whatever happens, we must obtain peace before the enemy breaks into Germany; if he does, woe on us!'[241]

The final blow on the Western Front was delivered by the British Third and Fourth armies in the 10-day Battle of the Sambre. The Fourth Army took over 4000 prisoners and 80 guns. The Third Army was even more successful, its biggest success being the capture of the ancient medieval town of Le Quesnoy by the New Zealanders on 4 November.

Founded in the eleventh century, the old walled town had been captured by French Kings Louis X1 in 1447 and Henry II in 1552, the Spaniards in 1568, and the Austrians in 1793. Its cannon had fired on the English army in the Crecy campaign of 1336; and the Duke of Marlborough had ended his last campaign there in 1711. Russell and his New Zealanders were its latest besiegers in one of the last actions of the war.

Initially, Le Quesnoy looked to be a tough nut to crack. It was protected by 16-metre-high ramparts and surrounded by a wide, deep moat. On and around these ramparts the Germans had sited field guns and dozens of machine guns. Taking the town by frontal assault would mean bombarding it in advance, causing heavy damage to historic buildings and much loss of life among its civilian population. As at Bapaume, Russell planned to avoid this by encircling Le Quesnoy while his other brigades pressed on through the Forest of Mormal towards the River Sambre.

The attack opened at 5.30 on the morning of 4 November. The town was steadily enveloped and German positions on the ramparts were deluged with smoke and drums of burning oil. Prisoners were sent into the town with a message demanding a German surrender, and a similar note was dropped by aircraft. Before any reply could be received, men of the 3rd (Rifle) Brigade scaled the ramparts by ladder, just as medieval soldiers might have done 600 years before. Under cover of Lewis gun and mortar fire, they took its 1000-strong garrison by surprise, and once New Zealand troops were in the town, the Germans readily surrendered. In the main square, the German commander handed over his revolver and 400 of his men to a young New Zealand captain.

The joy of the French population at their liberation was unbounded. The French tricolour flew at every window, and the townspeople flocking out of their shelters under the ramparts went 'joyfully hysterical'. Russell and one of his brigade commanders rode into the town, before going on to check the progress of their troops still fighting in the Forest of Mormal. A few days later, French President Henri Poincaré inspected a New Zealand guard of honour drawn up in the square and thanked them for what they had done for France.

That day, 4 November, was probably the division's most successful day of the war. It had taken Le Quesnoy, Rompaneau, Villerau, Potelle, Le Carnoy, Jolimetz and Herbignies. By 5 November it had reached the eastern outskirts of the Forest of Mormal for a total advance of 26 kilometres. Over 2400 prisoners, 84 field guns and nearly 300 machine guns had been captured.

Behind the lines, German resistance was now nearing its end. The German Navy had evacuated the ports of Zeebrugge and Ostend, and on 19 October Admiral Scheer had ordered all German submarines to return to their bases. On 30 October, sailors of the German High Seas Fleet had mutinied and refused to take their ships to sea for a final and decisive battle with the British Grand Fleet. The German army was by now in a critical state.

The end to hostilities was declared at 11 am on 11 November 1918. World War I historian and novelist John Buchan described what followed: 'There came a second of expectant silence, and then a curious rippling sound, which observers far behind the front likened to the noise of a light wind. It was the sound of men cheering from the Vosges to the sea.'[242] Hart's diary on the day lacked Buchan's literary flair, but probably reflected the feelings of most: 'So it is all over at last. Thank God for that. There was no jubilation. Each one asked himself and each other: "Now how soon can I get home?"'[243]

The terms of the armistice accepted by Germany were harsh but predictable: immediate evacuation of Belgium, France, Luxembourg and Alsace-Lorraine, and repatriation of all inhabitants of these areas who had been deported, imprisoned or held hostage. The German Army was required to surrender 5000 heavy guns and artillery pieces, 25,000 machine guns, 3000 trench mortars and 1700 aircraft. Sixteen battleships and battlecruisers, 8 light cruisers, 50 destroyers and all submarines were to be handed over to the Allies. All German troops in the east, including those in Russia, were to withdraw behind Germany's 1914 frontiers. Allied troops would occupy all of Western Germany up to the left bank of the Rhine, including three bridgeheads across the Rhine at Mainz, Koblenz and Cologne.

The Germans had been driven to defeat on the Western Front by the growing military superiority of the Allied armies and the enormous loss of men and weaponry. Bolshevik propaganda had also taken its toll, but a greater factor was the war weariness of the German troops and their awareness of the miseries being endured at home as a result of the British naval blockade. Despite their tenacious and skilful rearguard actions, the loss of morale and fighting spirit in the German armies was eventually irreversible.

The seeds of defeat, however, were probably sown much earlier. Travers argues that the decisive events of 1918 were not so much the last months of the war but the 115 days of the Kaiserschlacht, between 21 March and 15 July. This period, in which Russell's New Zealanders played an important part, cost the German army nearly a million men in casualties and prisoners, effectively destroying it as a combat force.[244]

For his part, Russell was pleased with what his division had achieved in the final months of the war. Between 21 August and 6 November 1918, it had taken 8765 prisoners, 145 guns, and 1263 machine guns, as well as large quantities of other war material. In the epic battles of Bapaume, Havrincourt-Epehy, Cambrai, the Second Battle of Le Cateau, the Selle and Sambre, the division had fought with skill and determination and shown an aptitude for open warfare that Russell always felt it possessed. Adapting rapidly to the switch from static trench warfare to a war of movement, the New Zealanders spearheaded the advance of Byng's Third Army for the 11 weeks from 21 August to the Armistice. Russell was now in command of a citizen army 'indistinguishable from a Regular formation, skilled and professional at every level. Despite strong defences and determined resistance, it was something the Germans could no longer match and defeat.'[245]

Allen regretted that Russell had lost the opportunity to command a British Army corps, although he was pleased that he was able to finish the war still in command of the New Zealand Division. He wrote to Russell: 'You have earned a great name here and, so far as I understand, at the front as well.'[246] Allen understood well. By now Russell had established a reputation as a first-ranked divisional general, and this had been acknowledged at the top levels of the British Army.

But Russell's soldiering was not over yet. The day after the Armistice there was some trouble in the ranks over the news that the division was to go to Germany on garrison duty instead of being immediately demobilised and sent home. Russell's diary of 13 November noted a disturbance in the form of a meeting called by 'an agitator of the name of King, who I understand, has achieved notoriety in NZ. Spoke to the men, and took no notice—think no danger but must watch out for Bolshevism.' The British high command had been preoccupied with the threat of Bolshevism since hearing of outbreaks in Germany in the last months of the war. Godley, in fact, had told Allen that the army of occupation might be used to put down Bolshevism in Germany.

Unrest in the ranks following the Armistice was not exclusively a New Zealand Division problem. Similar incidents were occurring with British, Australian and Canadian troops, and for much the same reasons—restless men fed up with war and military discipline, and wanting to get back to their families and the civilian life they once knew.

On 28 November, Russell's division began its 250-kilometre march to the German frontier through northern France and across Belgium. On the roads it encountered streams of German prisoners and civilians moving back, but in every town the New Zealanders entered—Bavai, Mauberge, Liège, Namur, Huy, Charleroi and Verviers—the welcome was the same. At Verviers, near the German border, the townspeople 'went mad as we marched in. Otago was in the lead on this march and girls hung garlands of flowers around my horse's neck as we went along and rushed the ranks to kiss any man they liked the look of . . . we stuck their flowers in our hatbands and the muzzles of our rifles.'[247]

After three days in Verviers, the division marched by night over the German frontier and entrained for the city of Cologne. On 20 December, the first battalion of New Zealand infantry crossed the Hohenzollern Bridge over the Rhine, followed closely by the artillery. 'There, under the great bronze statue of the ex-Kaiser himself, passed the long column of Diggers, guns and wagons, all pretty rough after their continuous trekking, but mighty serviceable looking in spite of, or rather because of, that fact.'[248]

With the hostilities now over, the challenge was how to keep the men 'amused, interested, and occupied' while on garrison duty in Germany. In August, Russell had written to Defence Minister Allen asking for information on the employment prospects in New Zealand for returned soldiers—where the shortage of labour was being felt, what lines of business were likely to be attractive, what the future of fruit growing and other industries was likely to be, in what areas public money was likely to be spent—'anything in fact which will give the men an idea of what they can look forward to on their return to NZ'.

By December 1918, 50 scholarships to British universities were in place and 50,000 pounds of government money had been earmarked for Russell's educational and vocational schemes. As Reg Gambrill put it: 'He [Russell] knew how men's minds could atrophy under the deadening influence of war but he did his utmost to arrest this easy, fatalistic drift.'[249]

The demobilisation of the division began at the end of December 1918, based on length of service. Inglis spoke for many, as the New Zealand troops packed their kit for their return to England and then by troopship for home: 'Notwithstanding the imperative call of home, it was sad pleasure to break with the old life and part from those with whom we had experienced what W.H. Nevinson has called "the highest of all human joys", perilous companionship in a cause they counted good.'[250]

Russell was unable to remain with his men to the end. On doctor's orders he handed command of the division over to Brigadier-General Napier Johnston, and on 1 February left again for the south of France to recuperate from a bout of bronchial pneumonia. His farewell message to his division acknowledged its exceptional fighting record. In its three years in the line, he wrote, the division had gained every objective given it. The only exception was Passchendaele, which had 'added yet fresh laurels for tenacity and resolution in the face of insuperable difficulties'. He urged the men, on their return to New Zealand, to lay aside class and sectional interests for the common good.[251]

All was not well, however, on the family front. By this time the Spanish flu epidemic was at its height; its final toll in New Zealand alone was 8000 people, and 20 million worldwide. A cablegram from Gertrude on 8 December told Russell that his immediate family was safe, but that two of her brothers, Edric and Cyril, had died of the flu. It was not the end of tragedy for the Russell family. Guy's younger brother Claude and his wife and only son died of tuberculosis just as the war in Europe ended, and his sister Evelyn of pneumonia. They were followed by Dick Riddiford, a former member of Russell's staff and the man he regarded as his closest friend in France. 'It is the loss of a brother,' Russell confided to his diary.

By now, Russell himself was also at risk. In early 1919, he collapsed in a train between Paris and Calais after spending two weeks caring for his sick sister Gwen, and his daughter Jan, who was recovering from the Spanish flu. Ill and exhausted by the strain of four years of unbroken command, Guy Russell was now badly in need of rest.

Chapter 19

I'll Soldier No More

'I have often felt that there may still be work left for me to do, tho' I don't seek it, feeling that if Le Bon Dieu wants anything of this humble servant he will make the call evident enough. I cannot imagine seeking place or power.'—Russell writes to his sister Milly four years after the war.

In April 1919, Russell returned to New Zealand in the troopship *Arawa*. Jan, who was with him, recalled the voyage home: 'In no time he was organising the care and occupation and recreation of his men and officers . . . Only once did exhaustion overtake him, this time when we were three days out from NZ. He had received a wireless [message] telling him of the civic receptions and speeches awaiting him in Wellington and Christchurch.' The issue now was whether he had the physical and mental strength to go through with all of them.[252]

The *Arawa* made landfall at Lyttelton in mid-May and almost immediately Russell faced the rigours of a civic reception in Christchurch. He stood first in an open vehicle as a squad of returned soldiers drew it through streets bedecked with flags and streamers and lined with cheering crowds. At the public reception that followed, Russell was formally welcomed by a powhiri performed by local Maori in traditional costume, followed by a somewhat florid speech of welcome from the Mayor of Christchurch.

Russell's reply paid due tribute to the fighting qualities of his division—'a reputation second to none amongst all the troops that fought'—and to those who did not return from the hills of Gallipoli and the fields of France. He quoted from the letter of a highly placed British officer who had been in a position to judge its performance: 'I think that you may always claim that the Imperial soldiers would sooner fight with the NZ Division or hand over to them, or take over, than any other troops in the field.' Many others, said Russell, had expressed similar opinions.

He told his audience that the New Zealanders were 'right out in front in Mormal Wood' at the end of the final offensive in November 1918, and had to be told by their commander (himself) to go no further. 'It was the Canterbury and Otago troops that had done it. They had left other troops on either side a bit behind, which is not always a safe thing to do, but it is a very good fault.'

Russell's speech at the mayor's luncheon was typically self-effacing. He paid generous tribute to his corps commander Lieuetenant-General Godley, 'to whom the success of the New Zealanders was largely due'. Under its first commander, he said, the division had achieved a standard of discipline and devotion to duty as high as any unit in the British Army.

At a parliamentary luncheon in Wellington, Russell was named New Zealand's 'Ariki Toa' (Fighting Chief). In reply, he directed the attention of his hosts to the needs of the many thousands of returning soldiers, who after the rigours of war service now required 'personal service and human sympathy' as much as they needed financial support. 'The men do not want charity as it is generally understood,' Russell told his distinguished audience. 'What they want is love, real personal help, the helping hand.'

The civic reception at a packed Hastings Municipal Theatre—his last—was preceded by a vigorous haka by Maori soldiers who had fought under Russell's command. Russell acknowledged the fighting skills of the Maori contingent on Gallipoli, and the non-combatant but 'arduous, important and dangerous work' they carried out as a Pioneer battalion on the Western Front.

If his New Zealand Division could claim to be the happiest in France, he told his audience, it was because he had impressed on every one of his young officers and sergeants that 'one soldier's duty was to look after another,' and this spirit had gone through the division. The address ended on a religious note: God had helped the Allies to win the war against Germany and the teachings of the New Testament must now be their guide. The welcomes now over, the former commander of the New Zealand Division could retire to the family seat at Tunanui to recuperate as best he could. It would be a full two years, much of it spent in bed, before he recovered his old energy and zest for life.

Russell's mind, however, was far from inactive at this time, and he kept a close watch on the international situation. As early as 1920, he foresaw the rise of Germany and Japan in the years after World War I, and the need for New Zealand to be prepared. Germany, he argued, was intent on regaining a premier position in Europe and the world, and was determined to have its share of raw materials and an outlet for its population. The British Empire could either cave in to such demands or go again to war.

New Zealand governments, however, had other priorities, and had imposed heavy cuts on defence spending in the years following the end of World War I. In 1922, the Territorial Force was reorganised and its 30,000 establishment ceiling reduced. The result was a revival of the pre-war National Defence League (NDL), with Major-General Sir Andrew Russell as its president. The league's manifesto, released in April 1920, described itself as a non-political organisation dedicated to 'a white New Zealand; to secure the immunity of the country from invasion; to educate the people of the country upon such measures of defence as may be considered necessary'.

A sound system of defence, the manifesto stated, would ensure that New Zealand was protected from invasion and able to discharge its responsibilities to the defence of the Empire. Starving the defence forces of money, however, would commit ill-trained and equipped men to combat in future wars. In support, the manifesto quoted an American secretary of state: 'To thrust untrained citizens into the field is nothing short of death by Government order.'[253]

Specifically, the league wanted the strength of the Territorial Force maintained at 20,000 in three brigade groups, with three months' compulsory military training for all young men reaching the age of 18, followed by four more years of service in TF units. The defence of Australia and New Zealand should also be regarded as 'one and indivisible', with the general staffs of the two countries meeting regularly to discuss plans for joint and mutual defence. Underlined in the manifesto was the role that universal military training should play in training the youth of the country in good citizenship and how to work together for the common good. Good citizens, the manifesto concluded, were the stuff of which good soldiers were made.

The league's 'White New Zealand' policy reflected the deep-seated insecurities about Asian immigration felt by many New Zealanders in the first decades of the twentieth century. In the 1920s, it reflected its authors' view of New Zealand and Australia as two 'outposts of Western civilisation' isolated in the South Pacific and, therefore, vulnerable to over-populated Asian nations seeking resources and living space. A major decline in living standards and cultural extinction would surely follow, they argued, if the gates were opened to large-scale immigration by foreign nationals.

Meanwhile, the 'slump' that began in 1921 had hit the Russells at Tunanui hard, as it had others in rural New Zealand. Prices for meat and wool were falling, credit was becoming tight, and neighbouring farmers in Hawke's Bay, including some soldier-settlers, were facing bankruptcy. Russell reduced his farm operating costs by cutting back on farm development work, reducing domestic staff to a cook and a maid, and cutting the wages of all his employees by 25 percent.

It was done at a meeting of station staff at which Russell explained the precarious financial position he was in and his need to cut costs. He made them an offer: accept redundancy or work on at Tunanui on reduced wages. They unanimously chose the latter, reasoning no doubt that a job, even for less, was better in hard times than no job at all. By such measures, and with the help of 'a little nest egg of war bonds' bought during the war, the Russell family survived the slump.

Guy Russell had worked hard over the years to ensure that his sisters in England had a secure source of income from interest on the mortgages they held over Tunanui and investments he made in New Zealand on their behalf. Now times were tough and those interest payments were just another cost. After telling Milly that he was sending her 1000 pounds, he warned: 'You will have to sell War Loan. I simply cannot strain my own resources beyond a certain limit because I have to meet my interest payments to you and others, and as you know I am helping several men—a very ticklish job at the moment . . . thank heavens I didn't go for making money [for] myself and so now have some to spare for helping others.'

The one positive outcome of the 1921 depression, in Russell's eyes, was the damage it had done to the country's speculators and profiteers. In April 1921, he wrote to Milly: 'You laughed at me for my scorn of money and contempt of the "get rich quick"—well! I can only say I am truly thankful that I was born a slow coach in these matters, for nearly if not all of the people who have been profiteering these past few years are coming to ground and find that their profits were paper ones . . . So being able—so far—to pay my way and able to stand a long siege, naturally I feel happy—tho' poor.'

Meanwhile, Russell was again involved in matters to do with the closer settlement of rural land. Big Hawke's Bay landowners, including his near-neighbours Lowry and Shrimpton, were selling off parts of their holdings to be cut up into farms for returning soldiers. Russell was doing the same: by 1920, three small farms had been sliced off the original Tunanui station and leased, with right of purchase, to returned soldiers who had worked on the run before the war. 'NZ is quickly becoming a nation of small farmers,' Guy wrote to his family. 'It must be right. Tunanui will shortly be only 4500 acres—and so it goes on.'

Initially, the resettlement venture was not a success because wool and livestock prices fell dramatically as the slump hit home, and the new settlers were unable to exercise their right of purchase. Russell, however, was sympathetic to the plight of his lessees and ensured that they suffered no loss of capital, unlike many of the soldiers settled on similar units by the Crown.

In 1921, the elder of Russell's two sons, Andrew, applied to enter Sandhurst as an officer cadet but failed on medical grounds—a great disappointment to his father. Guy decided that Andrew should now focus his energies on a degree at Oxford University and imported a tutor, A.B. Sackett, from England to prepare him for the entrance examination.

Under Sackett's tutelage, and although not a natural scholar, Andrew passed the entrance exam and entered Oxford in June 1923. That year also, his younger brother John entered Sandhurst, re-establishing a Russell family link with the British Army that went back four generations. His father saw it as a matter of principle, writing to his family in England: 'Our family owes one of each generation to the Service to which, after all, we owe our rise in the social scale.'

Chapter 20

The Years of Service

'The men who had marched off to the cheers of an admiring and supportive public returned to an unsympathetic and uncaring society, and a government which showed little interest in the plight of men who had been seriously wounded. While the public gave its ready support to the erection of expensive monuments to the dead, those who had returned quickly became the forgotten victims of the war.'[254]

By 1921, Russell had recovered enough of his old strength to consider the needs of men who had fought under his command and were now struggling to fit back into society. In 1922, he was elected president of the NZRSA, accepting the post more from a sense of duty than any desire for post-war prominence. For 12 critical years of its history, Guy Russell would give the NZRSA a high public profile and strong leadership, ensuring that its policies were heard—if not always acted on—by the governments of the day.

While commanding his division in France, Russell had given considerable thought to the problems that disabled soldiers would face on their return to New Zealand. In 1917, he wrote to Sir James Wilson:

The question above all others that has got to be tackled in sober earnest by you in New Zealand is how to make those of us who have the misfortune to lose an arm or leg or our eyesight into useful and self-supporting members of society . . . Of course, the same spirit applies to the widows and dependents of men who are killed. We cannot put our hands too deeply into our pockets to provide for them so long as the money is wisely and economically spent.[255]

Early in 1920, Russell had admonished veteran World War I commander Lieutenant-Colonel Reg Gambrill, after meeting him by chance in a Gisborne street: 'Don't forget that you were privileged to command men overseas. Now that we are back it becomes your duty and privilege to look after them in civil life.'[256]

The organisation Russell was now to lead had been set up in 1916 to lobby the Government and private employers to give preference to returned servicemen and to negotiate land settlement, pensions and housing issues on their behalf. It had declared itself entirely non-sectarian and not affiliated to any political party. For its first five years, the association was ably led by Russell's predecessor, Dr Ernest Boxer, at a time when disputes over its organisation and non-partisan approach to political action had threatened to dismember it.

Since 1919 the association had been heavily involved in the repatriation of soldiers who had fought overseas in World War I. Russell, as the new president, applied himself to the issues with vigour, leading delegations to the prime minister and Cabinet urging better pensions for widows, disabled ex-soldiers and their dependants. He chaired regular meetings of the Dominion Executive and Dominion conferences, attended local branch reunions, unveiled war memorials, made speeches at Anzac Day services, and addressed officers' clubs on defence issues.

Russell was also the NZRSA delegate to regular meetings of the British Empire Service League (BESL), which had been set up to combine ex-servicemen's organisations throughout the Empire into one imperial organisation. On the RSA's agenda at these meetings were immigration, Empire trade and defence, but its main concern was Britain's obligation to the welfare of the 13,000 British ex-servicemen and their families who had migrated to New Zealand under the post-war free passage scheme.

These were the desirable immigrants, for the association's immigration policy—like that of Russell's National Defence League—was unequivocally racist, and for much the same reasons. Immigration was to be encouraged by deliberate government policy, but only for 'white' people of exclusively British stock. In part, the policy was driven by a fear that a pool of cheap migrant labour would compete with returned soldiers struggling to regain their place in society. Russell supported the policy from the start, telling the 1921 annual conference: 'We did not want it ever to be possible for a mixture of races to take place in this country.'[257]

Immigration policy was also closely linked to defence and national security. Urging the Government to do more to encourage immigration from Britain, the association's 1924/25 annual report warned: 'This Dominion must look to a fully occupied country as its chief defence—other countries could do with fresh fields for their millions—and if money is not sufficiently invested in order to populate New Zealand with our own stock, the time may come when the decision will not be left in our own hands.'

The immediate issue facing Russell's presidency in 1921, however, was not immigration but the slump of 1921/22 and its impact on the jobs and pensions of widows, returned soldiers and their families. Spiralling inflation during the war and post-war years had severely reduced the purchasing power of war pensions and allowances, and the RSA had been agitating to have them increased and automatically adjusted to the cost of living.

On 23 September 1922, a public meeting addressed by Russell endorsed a resolution urging the Government to increase pensions by 75 percent for soldiers' widows with children, widowed mothers whose sons were their sole support, and a pension of over 50 percent for ex-soldiers with a disability. At a quarterly meeting of the association the next day, Russell and his councillors confirmed their support for a scheme to employ 1200 ex-soldiers on hydroelectric development, and agreed to take it before the prime minister and Cabinet.

The result of this persistent lobbying was the establishment of a War Pensions Commission in 1922 to take submissions on the pensions issue. This was followed by the War Pensions Act in 1923, which resulted in pension increases for a large number of returned soldiers and their families. In the words of NZRSA historian Stephen Clarke, the Act 'was a major victory for all returned soldiers and war dependents, and a tribute to the persistence of the RSA.'[258]

In the employment area, some useful gains were also made. In 1921—Russell's first year as president—the association pressured government agencies to give employment preference to returned soldiers, and for relief work programmes to be set up. When the preference proposal was turned down, the RSA established its own employment committee and set up a relief fund to assist urgent cases of hardship. Proceeds from the inaugural Poppy Day Appeal in 1922 were divided among local associations, and these paid the wages of unemployed ex-soldiers on relief work during the winter of 1922.

Russell's address to the Dominion Council in July 1922 focused on another victim of the Depression—the returned soldiers who had settled on the land after the war. Prices for primary produce, and particularly for butterfat, had fallen and many of these men were now unable to pay even their grocery bills. Russell recommended a revaluation of their land, an adjustment in rents, and an exploration of ways to enable dairy farmers to improve their stock and, therefore, their production. The result of the latter proposal was the development of the RSA's pure-bred-stock scheme, by which ex-soldier farmers could draw on a pool of stud bulls to improve their dairy herds. Russell initiated this by writing to a number of his farmer friends seeking donations of pedigree stud bulls, and in 1924 he donated a Friesian bull of his own to the pool. By the end of that year the association had 40–50 stud bulls in its inventory.

A serious problem in the early years of Russell's presidency was a fall in membership that threatened the very survival of the RSA. During the slump, numbers had fallen from a peak of 57,000 in 1920 to less than 8000 by 1925. The reasons for this were not exclusively economic—men returning from the war were looking to the future, not the past, and many were turning their backs on wartime experiences and associations. By the late 1920s, however, membership was on the rise again. Ten years had passed since the end of the war and ex-servicemen were looking to escape, however briefly, from the pressures of civilian life and experience again the wartime comradeship they once knew. By this time, also, increasing numbers of veterans were coming forward with various wartime-related physical and psychological problems and needing access to medical treatment. Others were looking for help with pensions and employment.

As the Great Depression of the 1930s bit deeper, the RSA worked closely with the Government to improve the position of its members on pensions and in employment. In 1929, it secured the appointment of a Rehabilitation Commission; in the early 1930s, the establishment of the Disabled Servicemen's Re-establishment League, and in 1935, the War Veterans' Allowances Act. In conjunction with local authorities, the association also took an active part in the management of unemployment-relief schemes around the country.

By September 1931, 1000 pounds in relief was being distributed every year through the RSA's network of district branches, either in the form of subsidised work schemes or as direct grants of food, clothing and fuel. In the words of Stephen Clarke, 'The RSA had once again become a major social provider and powerful pressure group as it took up the cause of the incapacitated, the unemployed and the impoverished returned soldier.'[259]

Clarke attributes the RSA's success in the 1920s and 1930s to 'the politics of patriotism', which in the climate of the times was difficult to oppose or ignore. Other factors at work were the association's status as the predominant organisation representing returned servicemen, and the calibre and status of its leaders—notably Russell and vice-president Bill Perry.[260] The fact that the association was not allied to any political party also enhanced its influence, as did the fact that a growing number of Members of Parliament were returned servicemen who were in sympathy with the aims of the association. Among them were future prime minister Joseph Gordon Coates, and Tom Seddon, son of Liberal Prime Minister Richard Seddon and a former member of Russell's wartime staff.

The RSA's efforts in the defence area, however, met with little success, despite frequent resolutions urging the Government to maintain a well-manned and -equipped defence force. The RSA supported the fledgling League of Nations, but believed that until the league took a tougher line on international issues the best guarantee of world peace was the military power of the British Empire, and specifically the security provided by a well-equipped Royal Navy. This was not militarism as it would commonly be described at the time, writes Clarke, but the desire to see peace maintained through collective security.[261]

In 1930, the RSA protested vigorously at cuts in the defence vote, which reduced the numerical strength of the Territorial Force and put an end to compulsory military training (CMT). The following year it went further, urging that a commission be set up to inquire into the defence of New Zealand. In spite of the rise of fascism in Europe in the 1930s and growing tensions in the Asia–Pacific region, the Government, for the most part, remained silent. New Zealand was not the only nation to neglect its armed forces in the post-war years. The American army, for example, dwindled in numbers and faced ever-decreasing financial votes, as did the armed forces of most of New Zealand's former allies.

The RSA persisted with its lobbying, however. From time to time it was supported by the National Defence League, with which it had a logical relationship given that Russell now headed both organisations. In 1935, however, the RSA rejected a bid by the right-wing New Zealand Legion, with which Russell was also involved, to unite both organisations into a National Unity Movement. The RSA 'wisely' continued to follow a moderate and bipartisan political path.[262]

By 1933, Russell's ninth year as president, the strain was beginning to tell: 'RSA conference—re-elected—a pity,' his diary noted in June. In 1935, at the age of 67, Russell had had enough and tendered his resignation to the Dominion Council. A grateful and no doubt regretful council passed a unanimous resolution acknowledging his 'guiding influence in placing the NZRSA on its higher plane of membership and consolidating its place in the social structure of the community'.

In his 12 years as president, Russell provided the RSA with strong and stable leadership, and handed over to his successor a growing and vibrant organisation. Clarke observes that his presidency 'combined an officer's sense of duty with genuine concern for his former soldiers, who in turn greatly admired their old chief'.[263] Russell's successor, Bill Perry, wrote that Russell brought to the affairs of the RSA 'the same drive and ability as he gave to everything to which he put his hands'.[264]

But it was not all over yet. In 1938, Russell led the NZRSA contingent to the celebrations marking the 150th anniversary of European settlement in Australia. After an official farewell to the contingent at Parliament in Wellington, thousands of Wellingtonians thronged the wharves to give the 2000 World War I veterans a rousing send-off.

On arrival in Sydney, the men were greeted by a flotilla of ships and small boats, cheering crowds, and an air force flyover, before marching to the cenotaph for a wreath-laying ceremony. The march to the Sydney Domain after the Anzac Day dawn service involved 50,000 'Diggers' marching twelve abreast, with the NZRSA contingent led by Russell in the place of honour at the front of the column. Over half a million Sydneysiders came to watch.

The farewell to the New Zealanders was almost as impressive—10,000 people gathered on the wharves at Darling Harbour. Bands played wartime tunes, ferries hooted, fireworks exploded and thousands of streamers fluttered in the breeze. The links the Anzacs had forged in the crucible of war 20 years earlier had clearly endured—and would endure again, if under some duress, in the greater conflict to come.

Chapter 21

The Maverick Politician

'I am starting electioneering on a bad wicket. The Reform people—out and outers—do not know what to do. They entirely dislike my claiming independence of a binding obligation. A few have listened to my arguments—that I offer my time, my ability, and my judgement—that if they refuse the last named they must do without the other two.'—Although he is the Reform Party's candidate in the 1922 general election, Russell refuses to give unequivocal support to the party's policies.

In 1922, Guy Russell sought nomination as the Reform Party's candidate in the 1922 general election. In doing this, he was following an honourable family tradition: his uncle, Sir William Russell, had represented Hawke's Bay as an MP for 21 years, had held several ministerial portfolios in the Atkinson ministries, and was Leader of the Opposition for six years.

In August 1918, Russell had been offered the opportunity to stand as a Reform Party candidate in the place of the retiring Hawke's Bay MP. He turned it down. 'It is very good of Vigor-Brown to keep this seat warm for me,' he wrote to MP Tom Seddon. 'Tell him I am deeply grateful, but that I do not aspire to the seats of the mighty.'[265] Russell had declined the offer on grounds of poor health and because, after five years out of the country, he felt he was out of touch with domestic issues. His move into politics now was made with mixed feelings, and again mostly from a sense of duty.

Many of Russell's beliefs, however, did not fit easily with those of his adopted party. There were differences of opinion with the party hierarchy over his support for closer land settlement and for the establishment of business cooperatives along the lines of existing farmer organisations. In 1919, Russell had written to his sisters: 'If I go into politics (as I suppose I shall or must), I foresee trouble for me all round, because I have little patience with the rich or with the working man, but a good deal of sympathy with the poor.'

Because of his independent stance on particular issues, Russell doubted that his party would endorse him as their candidate in the upcoming election. If not, he was determined to stand as an independent, as he made clear to Allen: 'Whoever votes for me votes for the man and not the party—the party may change more than the man.'[266] The party hierarchy, however, swallowed its reservations and picked Guy Russell to contest the Hawke's Bay seat in the 1922 general election against the Liberal-Labour candidate, Gilbert McKay. Russell judged his chances of winning the seat to be slim, perceiving a lack of common ground between himself and much of his voting base. Voters, he thought, would have little sympathy with his values of self-discipline and service to society, and the 'ordinary working man' would also distrust someone of his social position and class: '"How can he have anything in common with me, he's not in my class"—says the unthinking toiler ... I've got to overcome it somehow or I'm no good—at any rate in politics.'

Busy with RSA affairs, Russell approached the coming election campaign with no great enthusiasm. 'I could spend my whole time in writing memorials and travelling on soldiers' business connected with the RSA, let alone this wretched political business,' he wrote to his sisters. 'However, I made up my mind at the Front that, if spared, it was up to me to more or less devote myself to other people, so it's all in a day's work.'

The beginnings of the campaign were not promising: Russell was still at odds with his party over policy issues and determined to be his own man. His election speech was delivered in the Hastings Municipal Theatre on 4 December 1922. It covered a range of topics and ended on a religious note with a call for the destiny of New Zealand to be shaped in accordance with divine law.

Reform Party officials would have been dismayed by Russell's opening words. From the start, he refused to make an outright commitment to the policies of the party he hoped to represent. He had been placed in an 'arbitrary' position during the war, he told his audience, and was heartily sick of it. He reserved the right to his opinion, and to criticise any measure, 'either for or against, constructive or destructive'. He would not give unthinking adherence to any party, but in the interests of stability would vote with Reform on matters of confidence.

Russell described himself to his audience as a 'convinced socialist'—an ideology light years from that of his adopted party. However, he explained that this did not mean he supported communism—which had been tried and found wanting; instead, he was referring to the Latin meaning of the word: 'neighbour'. It meant helping other people and combining in a common effort for progress, rather than the law of the jungle and survival of the fittest.

The speech outlined policies that were Russell's focus for the next 20 years: closer land settlement; increased immigration, particularly by people of British stock; and the need for strong, well-trained armed forces. Closer settlement, Russell argued, would encourage more men with capital and farming experience onto the land. Every new family settled would increase the demand for labour and for services from the towns, and thus the growth of secondary industry. This in turn would boost employment, discourage the dumping of goods from countries where labour was cheap, and assist the defence of New Zealand by making it more self-sufficient. A dedicated land bank, he argued, should be set up to give suitable men access to capital to purchase land and stock.

Linked with a 'progressive' land policy would be controlled immigration of 'kith and kin' from the British Isles. Increased immigration would not only meet the growing demand for labour but would boost the country's population. This in turn would help to make the country more secure against potentially aggressive nations attracted by New Zealand's unpopulated open spaces.

As a further insurance against such possibilities, defence spending should be kept up, and compulsory military training expanded to ensure the country and the Empire were supplied with 'first-rate fighting men'. More aircraft should be bought to strengthen the air force and deter attacks on New Zealand by potential raiders. The British Navy, he reminded his audience, was currently the only thing that stood between New Zealand and any threat of invasion.

Other key themes included better support for returned soldiers, profit sharing between employers and their workers, and a national unemployment insurance scheme. In the first case, Russell wanted pension increases for men who were over 50 percent disabled as a result of their war service. To help returned soldiers who were having difficulty paying off loans on their farms because of the Depression, the Government should revalue their land and 'wipe off the arrears'.

Profit sharing was Russell's most radical proposal, given the farming and small business electorate he hoped to represent. If it was widely adopted, Russell declared, profit sharing would result in 'goodwill and mutual esteem from top to bottom', and would greatly increase production. It would also increase the wealth of the country instead of diminishing it, as industrial strife was currently doing. He told his audience that profit sharing had already been tried by the Russells on the family property at Mount View, near Whanganui, and would be repeated at Tunanui 'once times got better'.

On 6 December, the *Hawke's Bay Herald Tribune*—solidly for Massey and his Reform Party—came out strongly for Russell. It warned voters against giving the reins of government over to a Liberal-Labour coalition that had 'no more chance of pulling together than a coster's donkey and an untamed mustang from the plains of Lenin's land'. But it was not enough to swing the result. Russell was narrowly beaten on election night by Gilbert McKay, 3903 votes to 3552. Reform was re-elected with just under 40 percent of the popular vote.

Russell accepted his defeat with good grace and apparent relief. It was, he told his sisters, 'an escape from an uncongenial life, uncongenial companions, and a possible lowering of one's standards'. Duty done, he could now return to farming with a clear conscience. Russell was in good company—few returned soldiers were nominated by any of the parties in the post-war years, and most of them were defeated.

There would be no more forays into the political arena for Russell, in spite of efforts to get him to stand in the 1935 general election. 'When will they realise I am not a politician as politics go today,' he wrote to his sisters that year. 'One has all the influence one wants without writing MP after one's name.' In the meantime, his mind and energies would be directed elsewhere.

In the early 1920s, Russell put his weight behind a government-supported scheme that would encourage young men educated in British public schools, with farming aspirations and some capital, to emigrate to New Zealand. Candidates who were approved would be found work as cadets on 'suitable and congenial farms'. When they were ready to start farming on their own account, they would be advised how best to invest their capital.

Russell became president of the scheme's managing body—the New Zealand Association of Public Schools of Great Britain—and actively promoted the scheme for over 10 years.

The cadets who spent time on Tunanui were introduced to most facets of the station's work: mustering sheep, harvesting crops, felling trees, milking the house cows, and packing fencing materials by horse to distant parts of the farm. Russell wanted his young workers 'on the ball' early each day, and he would turn up in his old Ford truck to check that they were properly breakfasted and ready for a day's labour. Cadet Edward King wrote of his experience:

> Life at Tunanui for a cadet was a mixture of being a rouseabout, learning the elementary rudiments of farming, and of being a young man learning some of the social graces expected of one in that area. From Monday to Friday I took my meals with the station hands in the cookhouse . . . On the weekends I was expected to don a dinner jacket and present myself to the Big House for dinner on Saturday night, brunch on Sunday and for high tea and bridge. Sir Andrew and his lady were always entertaining house guests from overseas, so I met some very interesting people.[267]

Guy Russell would quiz his guests on their general knowledge and attempt to draw them into debates on the leading issues of the day. According to his daughter-in-law Ros, he would sit at the head of the table like 'a benign guru' and gently bait the young men until they did not know what side they were on. However, it was all done kindly: 'He was interested in what they thought and what they had read and did not make anyone feel that their ideas were banal or commonplace.'

The cadet scheme seems to have been an overall success. A survey by the association of 500 cadets in 1936 found a failure rate of only 5 percent; and another 5 percent with business qualifications who had found a more suitable occupation in the towns.

At Tunanui, however, the results of the scheme were mixed. In November 1923, Russell noted the 'the lack of drive' of two of his cadets and vowed to knock them into shape. Both would be required to put in an hour's work before breakfast, he told his sisters—one milking the cows and the other helping him with the horses. 'It has been made perfectly plain to them that if they do not like my ways, there are other stations who may welcome them . . . or the reverse.'

In some cases, 'the reverse' held true, at least after the cadets in question had come and gone. In 1931, Russell noted that two or three 'Old Etonians' who had worked on Tunanui had offended their next hosts with their 'hypercritical, even supercilious, attitude to things in general'. By 1935, his enthusiasm for the scheme was flagging: 'These cadets are an eleventh plague,' he complained, 'but I suppose they must be kept going for the future of farming.'

The puzzle is why the scheme did not focus on young New Zealanders with farming aspirations, character and capital, instead of graduates from British public schools. Russell's correspondence is silent on the matter.

Chapter 22

Lobbyist and Political Activist

'I'm so busy now paddling my own frail and leaky canoe that I've no time or energy for national causes. Indeed I bid fair to become a back number and remain one. I'm sorry in a way because I am so interested in public questions but I recognise my limitations.'— Guy Russell writes to his sister Milly in 1927 as he struggles to stay solvent.

By the late 1920s, Guy Russell's life had settled into a discernible pattern—RSA lobbyist, defence activist and struggling farmer. At the 1924 council meeting of the National Defence League, he revisited his familiar themes: continued support for universal military training; the proper equipment of New Zealand's defence forces; and closer defence links with Australia.[268]

The command of the Pacific Ocean and the security of its trade routes, Russell warned, were no longer in the safekeeping of the British Navy. Australia and New Zealand were 'two dangerously isolated outposts of Western civilisation' and vulnerable to threats from other nations in the region. New Zealand therefore had three options: an 'understanding' with the United States, whose navy could provide the

shield that the British fleet had provided until now; an alliance with
an Asiatic power, possibly China; or self-reliance, based on cooperation between the two countries most affected—Australia and New
Zealand.

The first of these options—an 'understanding' with the United
States—was not practical, he concluded, because of the limited range
of the American fleet without a base at Guam. The second—an alliance with China—was ruled out in the short term because of the
'political chaos' in that country and its distrust of foreigners. The
third recommendation—self-reliance supported by defence links
with Australia—made better strategic sense. In cooperation with the
British Admiralty, the two countries could pool their naval resources
and establish a naval base in Australasian waters. Aircraft and submarines, combined with artillery batteries at selected ports, would
be New Zealand's best defence against raids, which were more likely
than armed occupation of the country by an enemy force.

Universal military training should be maintained, Russell argued,
not only for defence but for social reasons. It would teach discipline
and self-control, 'encourage national corporate feeling, good citizenship, and inculcate in youth the ideals of devotion, self-forgetfulness
and ungrudging service not measured by pecuniary reward'. These
recommendations—like similar ones from the RSA—for the most
part fell on deaf ears.

In 1924, Russell's Uncle William died, bringing to an end the
opening chapter of the Russell family's New Zealand story. It was
William and Guy's father 'Ham' who had broken in the first scrub-
covered acres that became the Tunanui and Flaxmere stations, living
rough and borrowing heavily. It was they who then battled through
the courts for nearly 15 years to have their freehold purchase properly legalised. When Ham deserted New Zealand for the comforts of
Europe in 1879, it was William who managed the Russell estates while
in the first years of a distinguished 30-year career in colonial politics.

That year, Guy and Gertrude Russell sailed to England to visit family, including their sons—John, now at the Royal Military College, Sandhurst, and Andy, now studying at Oxford. On the itinerary of a planned 'Grand Tour' was business connected with the British Empire Service League; a visit to the former family seat at Lausanne in Switzerland—where he introduced his sons to mountaineering, as his father had earlier done for him—and a tour of old battlefields at Gallipoli and on the Western Front. They would be away from New Zealand for over a year.

In May 1925, Guy and Gertrude, along with 450 other ex-soldiers and dignitaries, visited Gallipoli for the unveiling of the New Zealand memorial on Chunuk Bair. Together with his former commander, General Godley, Guy tramped across the old battlegrounds where over 10,000 Anzacs had died just 10 years before. The original tracks and trenches, however, were by now much weathered and overgrown. Russell's diary noted: 'I climbed to my old HQ on Walker's Ridge. Barely recognisable, though I guessed its position. Here and there a clip [ammunition], a bit of mess tin etc, still showed in the scrub. I expect plenty remains hidden.'

Although he was not a British citizen, Russell was invited to take an active part in the 1924 British general election on the side of the Conservatives. He was not averse to the idea; as he told his sisters, he considered the Conservative leader Stanley Baldwin to be a man 'prepared to stand or fall by what he considers good for the country . . . So different from old Massey.'

The result was some campaigning on behalf of Conservative candidates, including the prominent MP Leo Amery, who was then Secretary of State for the Colonies and Dominion Affairs. Russell spoke before audiences in Birmingham and Uxbridge and to 1000 people at a political meeting at Bow. His speech—to Labour and Communist party supporters in the main—was drowned out by a mass singing of 'The Red Flag'. 'A queer lot,' Russell noted in his diary, 'but not ugly.' The Conservatives won a landslide victory that election, taking nearly 70 percent of the seats at Westminster.

Frequent illness dogged the Russells on their trip through Europe. Family letters covering their tour of Belgium, France and Turkey are a litany of sicknesses suffered en route, with one or the other of the family bedridden in hotels with heavy colds, flu, bronchitis and other ailments. Gertrude, prone to depression and a range of minor illnesses, seemed the worst affected.

In July 1925, their daughter Jan married Royal Navy officer Vero Kemball at Holy Trinity Church in London. The congregation included two former governors-general of New Zealand—Jellicoe and Liverpool—Lady Birdwood, the wife of Russell's commander at Gallipoli, former defence minister Sir James Allen, and former NZMR Brigade commander Brigadier-General Edward Chaytor.

Returning home that year meant a return to the demands of station management in hard times. In September 1926, Guy wrote to his sisters: 'Last year's balance sheet appalling. Loss on Tunanui 3000 pounds, so with my own savings am 4000 pounds poorer than I was this time last year.' The year 1927 he rated his 'worst ever' because of reduced carrying capacity, very low lambing, a poor wool clip, and losses in cattle.

Gertrude, with her own sources of income and much better off financially than her husband, was still able to indulge her love of gambling—on horse racing and also on the stock exchange. The year before, Russell noted with some unease that she had '£700–£800 out at present in wild gambles'. He himself did not mind spending 200 pounds on artificial fertiliser, where the results could be seen, but he did not enjoy risking money on what he could not control.

On the morning of 3 February 1931, a magnitude 7.8 earthquake—New Zealand's most destructive—struck Hawke's Bay. Napier and Hastings were hard hit; more than 250 people were killed and many thousands more were injured. Tunanui got off comparatively lightly: chimneys on the station, including those of the homestead itself, came crashing down and some damage was done to workers' cottages. Riders along the ridge above the homestead saw great clouds of dust, shaken loose by the tremors, rising out of the deep gorges on the station.

Tunanui was now feeling the impact of a drought that had started the year before. Russell's accounts for 1930/31 recorded another 'devastating loss', and those for the following year were not much better. Conditions had become so bad by November 1932 that Guy suggested to his sisters that they might have to take over Tunanui, presumably because he was finding it difficult to service their mortgages over the run: 'Indeed I am beginning to look at it as yours already, and to resign myself to taking orders.' By now, he was only just holding his own, cashing up a 3000-pound life insurance policy and making further cuts to staff wages. Guy told his sisters that he could reduce costs still further, but did not want to sack any of his staff as that would only add to nationwide unemployment. 'Although I've made a 40% cut in wages, it now costs me 5 sheep per week per man, while 3 years ago it only cost me 3 sheep. We can't go on for long on this scale. Something must and will crack.'

With the Government proposing to double taxation on large properties like Tunanui, Guy told his family in England that his options were to sell some more of the station and so get out of the class of 'big' landowner, or to simply 'grin and bear it': 'The place can just about stand it as it is getting into a good payable state, but wool and meat are both falling.'

By this time, Russell's sons, Andrew and John, were moving in a similar direction to their father's from 40 years earlier. Andrew, now a successful Gisborne farmer after buying a 4000-acre (1619-hectare) property in a mortgagee sale in 1928, had joined a mounted rifles unit and now held a commission. John had completed officer training at Sandhurst and had been posted to the 1st Battalion of the Border Regiment, his father's old unit, and was serving with the British Army in Mesopotamia (modern-day Iraq).

John's lust for active soldiering in the Middle East rather than the life of a garrison soldier in England mirrored that of his father in the

1890s. He differed from his father, however, in his impatience with military history and theory—perhaps a reflection of the difference in their intellectual interests and capabilities. An active life in the open, doing things, had far more appeal for John. Russell was confident that this 'rascal' and 'irresponsible youth' would make a good soldier, but was worried that John's unwillingness to study the theoretical side of his profession might limit his prospects of promotion.

At the end of the 1920s, Russell was still actively involved with the RSA, attending council meetings, leading delegations, visiting branch associations and generally advancing the interests of its members. Among the initiatives he proposed was a scheme to settle returned soldiers and British migrants on volcanic pumice country between Rotorua and Taupo. He envisaged that the scheme would be financed jointly by the New Zealand and British governments, on condition that 60 percent of the required labour would be admitted from 'overseas'.[269] Russell discussed the proposal personally with Prime Minister Gordon Coates in August 1928, but what happened to it subsequently is unclear.

By now, however, Guy Russell was growing tired of the relentless round of public activities; he complained to his sisters that he was attending too many public functions and making too many speeches. 'They are a nuisance. I am not an orator and would fain avoid limelight and publicity.' As always, the life of the mind was not neglected in the hectic round of farm management and public activities: 'I've a host of good books in hand, and read them several at a time. Sir Edward Grey we're reading, when the family will listen after dinner. I'm determined that tho' Andy has to lead a strenuous outdoor life, his mind shall not starve for want of good reading and food for thought.'[270]

Chapter 23

The 'Four Colonels' Affair

'Our position here is not encouraging. No hope of the Navy being in force in these waters for a year or so, so we are thrown back on our resources, and very slender they are. Looking at the problem from a soldier's point of view, I can only say it is desperate if Japan is after an unpopulated and fertile country. Difficult to make people understand the danger. And what can you do with a Government that doesn't understand the problem, and perhaps doesn't want to?'—Russell writes to his sisters as war breaks out in Europe in September 1939.

The 1930s saw no let-up for Russell, now well into his 60s; but the burden, as always, was mostly self-imposed. The first year of the decade brought new challenges to his leadership of the RSA and the National Defence League, in the form of an announcement by the Government that it intended to cut the naval, military and air force vote by 50 percent.

The NDL responded in June 1930 with a statement under Russell's name protesting that the overhaul of the armed forces in the early 1920s had already cut these forces to the irreducible minimum.[271]

The 30,000-strong Territorial Force that existed before the war, the statement said, had been steadily reduced and was now under 17,000, and the length of service cut from seven to three years. What was more, 75–80 percent of those in training were under 20 (the war service minimum age), which meant that no more than 4000 men could be mobilised in the event of war.

The statement noted that the Permanent Force—'the keystone to the whole structure'—had been cut from 1134 in 1920 to just 489; schools of instruction and drill centres had been closed, and training camps had been cancelled for three years. Expenditure on New Zealand's land and air forces in 1929 had amounted to 1.48 pence per head of population—'not even the cost of a twopenny tram fare!' Any further cuts in defence spending would put the country over the danger line. The position New Zealand now found itself in, the statement read, had been made more acute by the demise of Britain's naval supremacy, on which the country's defence had traditionally depended. It posed the question: 'Is New Zealand prepared to place the onus for her defence upon the shoulders of an already staggering Mother Country?'

The policy statement was released at the same time as a delegation to Prime Minister Forbes and Defence Minister Cobbe, led by Russell himself. Russell's diary of 28 June noted that the proposal to cut defence spending by 50 percent had been successfully blocked for the time being, and that this would give the league breathing space until the next election. A year later, Russell led another NDL delegation to Wellington to protest at a government plan to repeal the universal military training provisions of the Defence Act. The attempt failed. By special general army order that year, the Territorial Force was put on a voluntary footing and a reduced peacetime establishment. In the years that followed no territorial regiment was ever up to full strength.

Russell continued to speak out on defence matters across the country—to some effect, he thought. In April 1933, after a tour of the South Island, he reported 'a growing desire for more common sense in public affairs, and disgust with the purely party attitude displayed'. By the end of the year, he felt that the country's pacifists had at last been routed, and the government was making an attempt to put New Zealand's defences in order. 'If we are to get it in the neck,' he wrote to his sisters, 'let us at least do so fighting and not like rats at the bottom of a funk hole.'

In 1935, Russell's old corps commander, Lieutenant-General Alexander Godley, made an official visit to New Zealand. In spite of the many harsh things said about Godley during the war, he was apparently well received wherever he went, much to Russell's relief. Included in the tour was a dinner at the Hawke's Bay Club, hosted by former officers of Godley's old command, the New Zealand Division, and a stay at Tunanui. After it, Russell noted: 'He is a very charming person, full of talk, jokes, reminiscences, and anecdotes.' This was not the Godley the New Zealanders knew at Gallipoli and on the Western Front, when he had often seemed arrogant, uncaring and cold.

By 1935 the situation in Europe was deteriorating, and John—now five years out of the British Army—and his brother Andy were serving in volunteer mounted rifles regiments and attending annual camps. In May, Russell, in full military uniform, presented the Hawke's Bay unit with its new standard (guidon) before a crowd of 7000 on a strip of land on the Napier foreshore brought up out of the sea by the 1931 earthquake.

That year also, Michael Joseph Savage came to power at the helm of a new Labour Government. Russell was impressed with Savage's commitment to Christian ideals, but unimpressed with what he saw as his 'wishy-washy humanitarianism'. He was particularly critical of the Labour Party's defence policy, which he considered was more concerned with the protection of New Zealand's shores than with the defence of the Empire as a whole. 'A fatal error if this is so,' he wrote to his family, 'since the greater includes the less.' Although New Zealand 'might prove a hornet's nest to an invader, he would certainly stand off and smoke us out by raiding our shipping and trade till we came to terms i.e. free entry for his nationals and favourable trade terms.' The primary focus of the government's policy, Russell felt, should be the defence of the Empire 'since only within it, and free from external dictation, can we work out our own salvation'.

Two years later, Russell chaired a meeting of army officers, all of whom had held senior commands in World War I and had served in the Territorial Force in the years after the war. The meeting resulted in a memorandum expressing the group's concerns about the strength and training of the Territorial Force and 'the vital necessity of ensuring New Zealand's preparedness for the emergencies which now threaten the Empire'. The document recommended that the Territorial Force be established at 16,000—well below its strength in 1914, but the bare minimum for the Dominion's requirements.[272]

In 1938, Russell became embroiled in what came to be known as the 'Four Colonels' episode. Four Territorial Force colonels—Spragg, Macky, Wilder and Gambrill—had been growing increasingly concerned at what they saw as government indifference to the state of the Territorial Force in the face of a deteriorating international situation. All four officers had seen active service in World War I under Russell's command.

The colonels were convinced—as was Russell—that if a global war eventuated, New Zealand could not rely on the Royal Navy and the British Army for its defence, and would have to provide its own. If the British Empire was defeated, New Zealand would inevitably be annexed by the victorious enemy power when the peace treaty terms were settled. On the other hand, 'distance and a determination to preserve independence, backed by a well-trained and efficient home defence army could provide for our salvation if we were prepared'.[273]

The immediate problem, in the eyes of the colonels, was that salvation could not be achieved with the meagre resources then available. In May, they published a 'manifesto' which claimed that the organisation and the current numbers of the Territorial Force were not sufficient for the defence of New Zealand. The document alleged low morale in TF units as a result of 'successive reductions in strength and lack of public support'. It expressed the colonels' fear that the current 'skeleton force' would disintegrate unless definite support was provided by the government and people of New Zealand.

In taking this bold step, however, the four colonels had bypassed the army chain of command and broken King's Regulations. The reaction was swift: all four were immediately placed on the retired list, which meant that they were effectively sacked from the Territorial Force. Russell thought the four colonels had made a tactical mistake in not resigning before making their stand publicly, but he was prepared to help to reinstate them. In May the following year, he approached the Chief of General Staff, Major-General Sir John Duigan. From Duigan, he secured an agreement by which the four would write seeking re-employment in the Defence Force, but admitting that what they had done was outside King's Regulations. As Russell understood it, the whole episode would then be forgotten and the officers would be employed in the same positions they would have occupied had they not broken the rules.

The colonels duly complied but, despite Duigan's assurances, their approaches were rejected by the army secretary. Expecting a different result entirely, Russell felt betrayed: 'If Duigan has wittingly gone back on his word, he stands convicted. It may be he was too weak to stand up to other influences,' he wrote to one of the four, Lieutenant-Colonel Reg Gambrill. In the event, he urged Gambrill not to resign his commission: 'If you do so, I shall feel inclined to do so myself as a protest against the treatment meted out to you and the other three.'[274]

Duigan may well have gone back on his word—and done so with malice. He was one of two staff officers whom Russell had sent home from France in 1917, and he had allegedly sworn to get even with that 'bloody sheep-farmer general' when the war was over. Gambrill himself speculated that someone within the defence establishment 'was paying off an old score against the General'.[275]

Two years later, the demands of war intervened in the colonels' favour. Spragg had died in the meantime, but with experienced officers in short supply Macky and Wilder were reinstated and appointed battalion commanders in the second echelon of the NZEF. But in spite of Russell's efforts, Gambrill, possibly because of his ringleader role in the affair, was not reinstated. He was eventually posted to the Home Guard as area commander of the Cape Runaway to Mohaka district.

In the last years of the decade, Russell relentlessly toured the country, putting the NDL's case to meetings in towns and cities throughout the North and South islands. In March and April 1938, he addressed meetings in 14 South Island towns, including Christchurch, and 10 towns in Taranaki. His target audiences included branches of the Farmers' Union, Women's Institutes and other community organisations. Everywhere his message was the same: the Government needed to act urgently to assure the country had a level of military preparedness that would make it impervious to attack, whatever happened overseas. If war broke out 'in our backyard', the British Navy would be unable to help for at least a year and New Zealand would be thrown back on its own, very slender resources.

Russell told his audiences that New Zealand should have in readiness a small but highly efficient and mechanised expeditionary force underpinned by compulsory military training. As the League of Nations had by now shown itself to be 'a broken reed', the country's defence should also be based on the British Commonwealth of Nations. Without that protection, New Zealand would be easy prey and its people would have to do the bidding of whatever country controlled it. It was not a question of invasion but isolation—New Zealand would be cut off from the rest of the world, and other nations could dictate their terms.

Widespread apathy, Russell recognised, was his biggest enemy. The challenge was to convince 'the man in the street' of the problems the country faced without being viewed as 'a militarist, a warmonger, and an alarmist'. The Labour Government, which should be taking the lead in these matters, he complained, was failing to do so because it was 'honeycombed with pacifism and League of Nations union propaganda'.

The links between increased population and defence were again a consistent theme. In March 1937, Russell warned members of the Palmerston North Rotary Club that an unoccupied country like New Zealand was a danger and a liability. New Zealanders had to show the world that they had a right to their country by using the land; no one nation had any more right than any one individual to monopolise thousands of acres of unused land.[276] The answer was more people, but from where? A natural increase in the birth rate was unlikely, as the birth rate in New Zealand had dropped from 41 per 1000 in 1880 to 16 per 1000 in 1935. Immigration was the only practical option—although the country at that time did not have the public or private resources to finance large migration schemes. Russell suggested that the government look to Scandinavian countries as well as Britain as a source of immigrants, as British workers with ambition and energy—the type needed in New Zealand—were finding ample work in their home country.

For nearly two decades now, Russell and the NDL had been warning governments about the parlous state of New Zealand's defence forces. He was annoyed that in spite of this—and his position as president of the league—successive governments had never consulted him on matters to do with the defence of New Zealand. He wrote to his sisters: 'I have never been called into consultation by the powers that be; being unpopular in having tried to warn the Government of what was in front of us, tho' I have never said latterly I told you so.'

In June 1939, however, Russell met with Prime Minister Savage to discuss defence issues, after which his diary noted: 'I hope I put some ideas into his hands.' Russell was concerned at the lack of senior officers with the experience to command in the field, and a shortage of trained junior officers. Although the Labour Government appeared sincere in its wish to make the country more secure, he wrote to his family, 'they still think a brave but untrained man is a soldier instead of what he is—merely a potential soldier'. Army training, or the lack of it, was only part of the problem. In his recent study of the inter-war years, historian Gerald Hensley observed that government decision-making in the defence area was by this time (the late 1930s) in a state of paralysis. 'Lack of money was only partly the reason; there was a lingering reluctance to make decisions.'[277]

In the early 1930s, Russell's activism took a quasi-religious turn. He became a member of the British Israelites, a Bible-based movement that was particularly influential among Britain's royalty, military, clergy, and the colonial middle classes. Among its supporters were Queen Victoria, King Edward VII, King George VI, Admiral of the Fleet Lord Fisher, Field Marshal Earl Roberts, Rudyard Kipling, and even New Zealand's Prime Minister Bill Massey. Massey is reported to have written: 'British Israel truth is God's truth. It is, therefore, bound to win. It is winning now all along the line.'[278]

The movement was founded on the premise that the Anglo-Saxon/Celtic peoples of Britain and her dominions were descended from the 'lost ten tribes' of Israel. It held that the Royal House of Britain was descended from King David, and that the British nation had a key role to play in 'God's great plan' for world order. Russell attended the second annual congress of the British–Israel Federation of New Zealand in 1931, where he declined the offer of the presidency but agreed to be its patron.

Some members of the New Zealand branch of the movement, however, took biblical interpretations of history to extremes. Its general secretary, D.D. Ince, predicted 'a cataclysmic world conflict in which the combined hordes of Russia/Germany will descend upon Israel' no later than 1936. A great earthquake would 'rend the Mount of Olives in twain', causing the Empire's enemies to turn their weapons on each other, slaughtering millions. In the light of this 'terrible day of the Lord,' wrote Ince, the federation was justified in its efforts to warn the masses about what was to come, and the need for New Zealand to be better prepared militarily.[279]

Russell's attitude to this kind of thinking is unknown, but the basic doctrines of the British Israelites made sense to him in the unstable international environment of the 1930s. He wrote to his family: 'It's provoking but in line with B.I. (British Israelite) interpretations of scriptures—we are in for a deuce of a time— the fascist states have so much to recommend them—opposed to communism, with which we are white-anted; opposed to usurious capitalism, which is riding us—and itself—to downfall; showing capacity for self-sacrifice, which we haven't even—as a nation— dreamt of.'

Russell's support for the primacy of the Bible in national affairs, however, went beyond the British Israelites. In August 1931, he was part of a delegation to the prime minister seeking the introduction of Bible teaching in New Zealand schools. Once again, his family in England bore the brunt of his disappointment: 'The usual courteous reception and non-committal reply. PM says issue to be decided by each MP according to his convictions and conscience. He might more truthfully have said "according to his election pledges".'

The delegation's case was not helped by a split between those who gave the proposal full backing and the aggressively anti-Catholic Protestant Political Association (PPA), which felt that it did not go far enough. In any case, said the PPA, the proposal was 'the offspring of an agreement with the "Scarlet Woman"', i.e. the Catholic Church, and therefore 'parleying with the devil himself'. 'Heaven help us from our friends,' was Russell's comment when it was all over.

At this time, Russell was also giving active support to the New Zealand Legion, a Bible-based, right-wing political reform movement. Founded by Dr Campbell Begg, a hospital surgeon and decorated World War I veteran, the legion 'articulated the frustration of conservative, small-town New Zealand at the Depression and the ineffectiveness of the traditional parties'.[280] It believed that the existing political system, in which the votes of elected MPs were controlled by the party whips, was wrong: all MPs should elect and appoint the prime minister and Cabinet—not just those of their own party. If necessary, the same MPs should revoke those appointments by a majority vote in Parliament. Along with a major reform of the party system of government, the league wanted Bible teaching put in its proper place 'as the guide towards the solution of material problems'.

Russell's interest in the movement was sparked by a meeting with Major Sherston, a former British Army officer, during his visit to England in 1924. Sherston later emigrated to New Zealand and took up farming in Hawke's Bay, and they became good friends. In January 1933, Russell's diary noted: 'Sherston's views on present political bankruptcy coincide with my own. Almost the view that we need a fresh start, doing away with party government, not quite socialism nor yet fascism, rather a combination.' On the basis of their beliefs and distinguished war records, Russell was prepared to support both Begg and Sherston to the hilt.

Russell saw the legion as essentially an ethical rather than a political movement, and one that would cut right across party divisions. Its stress on the need for Bible-based policy at national level appealed to him, and in May 1933, he accepted an invitation to become its regional chairman. In September, he spoke to a large meeting of the legion in Christchurch, and subsequently addressed many other meetings around the country.

In spite of the efforts by Russell and others to maintain public interest in the legion's policies, it ultimately failed to gain traction. From a peak membership of 20,000 in late 1933, it was practically extinct by the end of 1934. In 1935 its founder, Dr Campbell Begg, left New Zealand for South Africa, and by 1937 Guy was referring to it as 'that abortive movement'.

There were many other demands on Russell's energies during this decade. He was by now a Hawke's Bay county councillor, and there were defence and business matters still to be seen to, along with the never-ending struggle to keep Tunanui and the other farming properties financially solvent. By now, John Russell had resigned his commission in the British Army and returned to New Zealand to help his father on Tunanui. In 1933, just as his father had done 40 years before, Guy handed over the day-to-day management of Tunanui to John, while keeping a tight grip on the station's finances. That year he wrote to Milly: 'I'm turning myself into a forester, spare shepherd and handyman with an overseeing eye.'

Four years later, Guy leased 1500 acres (607 hectares) of Tunanui to John with the right of purchase within five years, creating a new sheep and cattle station he named Gola. Despite his earlier doubts, he was confident that John would settle down and succeed as a farmer. 'He's a good worker,' Guy wrote, 'his weak point being book work and too generous an attitude. However, having to provide the pounds, shillings and pence will steady too generous a habit.'

Russell's farm management methods had by now begun to attract attention. A 1935 edition of the national magazine, *The Weekly News*, published a full-page feature on Tunanui in which Guy Russell was acknowledged for his close study of modern farming methods. His efforts to establish a Friesian cattle stud at Tunanui were judged 'a considerable achievement' because the land had a carrying capacity of only one and a quarter sheep per acre and the cattle were given neither supplementary fodder nor concentrates. Other progressive features noted were the planting of lucerne for winter and drought cattle feed, and the introduction of rotational grazing.

At this time, Russell was also taking an interest in the testing of different grasses and clovers at a plant research station in Palmerston North. Seed should never be selected blindly, he wrote to his family. 'It's just as important to select your seeds as your rams or bulls . . . As you know, I'm a fanatic on improvements. Too much so perhaps.'

On the business front, however, there were problems aplenty, including those thrown up by Russell's directorships. He was by now a director of Barraud and Abraham (B&A), an ailing Palmerston North general merchandise, shipping and insurance company. Realising that the company had to be put on a sounder financial footing if it was to survive the Depression years, he persuaded his fellow directors to agree to a major reorganisation of the company, including a change of manager. Russell approached the company's mortgagors, the Bank of New Zealand, with proposals to restructure its debt. The bank declined, instead demanding that another 30,000 pounds be raised by a fresh issue of shares secured against whatever equity remained in the company. It also wanted all directors, except Russell and J.B. Williams, sacked.

Russell would later blame the bank for the firm's ongoing problems, which would not have occurred had it accepted his proposed rescue package. 'Don't trust banks overmuch,' he wrote to his sisters. 'They understand money and its manipulation better than they understand men and things.' Russell's efforts to rescue the company eventually bore fruit: its chairman and board acknowledged that his firm action as a director and his careful stewardship of the company's assets had effectively saved it from bankruptcy.

Russell's approach to finance matters was, by his own admission, iconoclastic. In the 1930s he developed an interest in the doctrines of Douglas Social Credit, although not officially a member of the movement. He was, as he put it, 'a fellow worker in the same vineyard trying to discover what is wrong and how to remedy it'. He felt that the system proposed by Douglas was too complicated, but agreed with the movement's argument that sufficient purchasing power was not being made available to buy the goods produced by the farmers of New Zealand.

Frustrated by continuing low prices for meat and wool, Russell joined an organisation called the Stable Currency League and stumped the North Island speaking to audiences on the need for monetary reform. The anomaly of the current situation, he argued, was that a huge increase in agricultural production since World War I had been accompanied by a drastic fall in farm produce prices and a loss of farmer confidence. Farmers could only be sure of good prices for their meat and wool if the currency, then secured against the gold standard, was devalued. This would be mildly inflationary but would increase the money supply, which in turn would result in a rise in farm produce prices. 'Today a bale of wool brings about six pounds; devalue the currency and it would bring 12 pounds,' Russell told his listeners.

In the early 1930s, Guy and Gertrude Russell became involved in an attempt to rescue their eldest daughter Kath and son-in-law Bill Deans, then farming Sandown station near Darfield in Canterbury. Bill had lost a leg in the Palestine campaign 15 years earlier and was not coping with the physical or financial demands of station management. At current low product prices, the Deans were unable to reduce their bank overdraft or pay the interest on their loans and were facing bankruptcy.

With typical energy, Russell set to work 'to get the place in order', cutting the station's expenses, persuading the bank to reduce its interest rate on the loans, and appointing a working manager. Guy's assessment of Bill's Dean's abilities was blunt: 'Fact is, he's no businessman, nor farmer,' he wrote to his sisters. 'Brought up as a gentleman farmer. Many others like him in Canterbury. No good nowadays. A farmer has to be something of a scientist, more of a businessman, and wholly a hard worker.' Bill Deans resembled the Russells' other son-in-law, Mowbray St John—another failed farmer—in his 'utter want of business ability, but without his conceit'.

In large part due to Guy and Gertrude's efforts—she providing the bailout money and he the management skills—the Deans kept Sandown. The whole exercise, however, strengthened Guy's opposition to the current financial system: 'The whole system of interest on financial credit appears to me ludicrously wrong. A system under which the world has arrived at the absurd point of owing itself more money than it can ever hope to repay.'

Despite his strenuous efforts to economise, Russell's own financial position during the depression years of the1930s appeared to be as dire as that of the Deans, whom he and Gertrude had successfully rescued. To his family in England he wrote: 'I'm living on my director's fees, to which B&A contribute £50 plus expenses, and in the proud position of having £7.10.00 in hand with about £20 due; so I can see the New Year in with a light heart.'

Despite the Depression, social life was not neglected at Tunanui. Socials in the Sherenden hall were attended by neighbouring farmers, station hands and their wives. The younger Russells—Jan, John, Andy and Margot—would sing or perform on stage; songs and other musical items were interspersed with dances. Guy Russell set up a fortnightly debating club which drew a steady number of local farmers and their workers to discuss selected topics of the day. Among them were the benefits of immigration and the threat of Bolshevism, two of his consistent interests.

Attendance at Sunday church services in the hall—always sparse—was a different matter. The fault, Guy surmised, lay with both the message and the messenger. In the backblocks at least, the Anglican Church seemed to have little appeal to 'the wage-earning class', and the parsons entombed there appeared to be of the wrong sort. The one taking the services in 1933 seemed unable 'to get alongside the working man'; the incumbent in 1939—'old Anderson'– was kindly, well-meaning but dull. What the congregation needed was a fire-breather of the John Wesley stamp. Despite the dull sermons, Russell always attended local services—'saluting his maker', he called it. He was also an active member of Sherenden's meagre flock, and over a post-service cup of tea would regularly challenge the pastor on why he said a particular thing during the sermon of the day.

On both the public and the private fronts, the 1930s had been a demanding decade for Guy Russell. At 72, however, he could take pleasure in the fact that he was still 'in harness and trying to earn an honest living' at an age when many of his Victorian forebears were either fully retired or long dead.

Chapter 24

The Threat from the North

'To be brutally frank, we have not the troops trained or equipped to stave off even a small attack.'—Gordon Coates, World War I veteran, former prime minister and member of the War Cabinet, warns current prime minister Peter Fraser eight months before the Japanese attack on Pearl Harbor in December 1941.[281]

The 1940s should have seen Guy Russell comfortably retired from public life and active farming, but again it was not to happen. In large part this was because of the outbreak of war in Europe in 1939 and in the Pacific two years later.

In early 1940, General Bernard Freyberg, recently appointed to command 2NZEF, invited Russell to Wellington to discuss the coming deployment of New Zealand troops to the Middle East. Russell thoroughly approved of Freyberg's appointment to the top operational command in the New Zealand Army: 'a good fighting man in whom the men will have complete confidence,' he wrote to his family. 'He is only 49 and I imagine well-preserved. I do not believe in old generals; saw too much of them in the last war. All right as far as experience goes, but there's no doubt that with advancing years the dash goes out of a man and caution gets too good a hearing.'

In June 1940, Russell was called again to Wellington to give Prime Minister Fraser his thoughts on the military situation in Europe, and asked to become a member of the War Council. If he accepted, he would join NZRSA president Bill Perry, MPs L.G. Lowry and E.T. Tirikatene-Sullivan and they would work in tandem with a War Cabinet made up of senior members of the Labour and Opposition National parties and chaired by Fraser himself.

Unlike the War Cabinet, however, the War Council had no executive powers. It could make recommendations to the War Cabinet and attend its meetings to discuss various phases of the war effort, or to approve decisions before they were finally adopted. The Secretary to the War Cabinet and later the first Secretary of External Affairs, Alister McIntosh, later described the council as little more than 'window dressing'. On the basis of his experiences as a member of it, Russell himself would have wholeheartedly agreed.

Reluctantly, Russell accepted Fraser's offer to play what he expected would be an active part in his government's wartime planning. Ironically, just a month before he had lambasted it for what he saw as its continuing inaction on the defence front: 'You get wonderful accounts of what we are doing and of what we intend to do,' he wrote again to his family. 'But it's mostly talk and there is a growing feeling of the necessity of a more whole-hearted effort. It's rather difficult for a Government composed mostly of men who took no part in the last war personally, except perhaps as conscientious objectors, to put their whole heart into it. It means getting into reverse gear.'

Russell found Fraser himself 'an enigmatic personality; not altogether pleasing. I much prefer the blunt, downright approach to problems of Dick Seddon, the best leader that NZ, or should I say Lancashire, has given us.'[282]

Russell attended his first meeting of the War Council on 19 August 1940. Agenda items for the 22 months Russell would serve on the council ranged widely from the employment of women in the armed forces to wartime publicity and propaganda, coast-watching and the defence of Fiji. In the first seven months of 1942, the council considered reports on improving the security of cargo vessels and troopships bound for Britain and the Middle East, and on the mobilisation of the RNZAF in response to the outbreak of war with Japan. It assessed the steps being taken to minimise damage to aircraft and stores in case of an enemy attack on New Zealand airfields, and the reinforcement of the RNZAF's reconnaissance squadron in Fiji with Hudson bombers.

The council was advised that 4000 men of Territorial and National Military Reserve units had been mobilised to guard key New Zealand ports and other vital installations. It was told of the acute shortage of rifles and communications equipment for the Home Guard, and delays in the arrival of armoured vehicles for the mounted rifles units. It was informed of the action being taken to release labour from the army for essential primary and secondary industry. It considered a report on compulsory military service for Maori, who at the time were not required to register for war service. A recommendation from Russell on the appointment of military area commanders was accepted.[283]

Having no executive powers, however, the council could only endorse these reports, and in some cases recommend further action. It was not a situation that Russell was at all comfortable with. In October 1941, as the threat of war in the Pacific grew stronger, British Army General Sir Guy Williams was called in to report on the country's defence preparations. Williams briefed the War Council on his findings and Russell agreed with 80 percent of his views. Otherwise, he told his sisters, the meeting 'was [as] futile—useless—as the last'.

Russell, however, was to have a larger role in shaping his country's preparations for the coming war with the Axis powers. In September 1940, after discussions with War Cabinet, he accepted appointment to the key post of Inspector-General of Military Forces. His overall responsibility was to inspect and report on the state of the country's home defences, notably its coastal defences and the equipment and training of its forces. Russell described himself to his family as the 'humble inspector of the home front in the most distant and least important of the Dominions'. His recommendations, however, would reflect the Russell of old—detailed, incisive and unsparing where deficiencies in organisation, equipment or training were identified.

The problems facing the men responsible for the defence of the New Zealand homeland in late 1940 were daunting. The effective forces available for home defence were now a 31,000-strong Territorial Force and a 9000-strong National Military Reserve (NMR), both largely untrained and poorly equipped. They had no tanks or anti-tank weapons, fighter aircraft or anti-aircraft defences, and were short of artillery, machine guns and mortars. The country's existing naval and air forces were incapable of detecting and then defeating an invasion by sea. As historian F.L.W. Wood put it: 'The means of stopping an enemy force from reaching the country were as slender as those for dealing with it once it arrived.'[284]

By now the protection provided by the British naval base at Singapore was also very much in doubt. In June 1940, with Britain now at war with Germany, the New Zealand Government was told that if France fell, Britain would not have sufficient naval forces to confront both the German and Italian navies in European waters and the Japanese fleet in the Far East. For Fraser and his Cabinet, it was a seismic shock, sweeping away at a stroke the whole basis of New Zealand's defence preparations and early strategy decisions.[285] In July 1940, Fraser told a secret session of Parliament that there was no longer any significant Allied deterrent to Japanese aggression in Southeast Asia and the Pacific. He rated the odds of Japanese intervention in the region at one in three; and the odds of a Japanese raid on New Zealand at one in five.[286]

The country's preparedness for a possible attack by Japanese forces was now rapidly assessed. A number of factors had to be taken into account, including the forces the enemy was likely to deploy, where they might land, what their objectives were likely to be, and what forces the defenders could muster against them. Threat assessments supplied to Russell assumed that the most likely aim of any attack on New Zealand would be to secure a sustainable base for Japanese operations in the South Pacific rather than a full-blown invasion of the country. This base would be large enough, however, to allow the Japanese to defend it effectively and to supply their troops from local resources.[287]

Provided that the enemy could protect their sea communications, New Zealand could expect to face an initial invasion force of 30–40,000 troops, supported by warships and aircraft carriers. Against an enemy fully equipped with modern weaponry, the defenders' lack of firepower would put it at a severe disadvantage. It was assumed, however, that the defenders would have some things in their favour—a superior knowledge of the country's communications and resources, 'the natural resourcefulness and initiative usually found in the majority of New Zealanders', and the fact that they would be fighting to defend their homeland. The defending force would have to be prepared for the common Japanese tactic of landing their troops where they were least expected, often on distant, difficult and, therefore, poorly defended parts of an enemy coast.[288]

Coastal defence was a key part of Russell's brief as inspector-general of military forces, and in spite of his age he approached the task with typical energy and focus. For 10 months, he toured the country by air, car and on foot, inspecting harbour entrances and points on the coastline likely to be vulnerable to landings by invading forces. He assessed plans for their defence, reported on troops in training and their equipment, and on commanding officers and their staffs. He attended military manoeuvres and inspected transport facilities and road communications.

The coastal defence plans Russell reviewed would have given his employers little comfort. A tactical exercise based on a section of the west coast of the lower North Island between Waitarere and Tangimoana assumed a beach landing by 20,000 Japanese troops supported by naval guns. Opposing it, until reinforcements arrived, would be lightly armed units of the Home Guard and the NMR. A plan for the defence of the Nelson area assumed an attack by 500 enemy troops, supported by a warship and aircraft, for the purpose of securing an airfield from which an attack could be launched on Wellington. Another plan assumed an attack on a section of the Hawke's Bay coastline, which would be opposed in part by blowing up several key bridges and building a floating boom to stop enemy craft going up the Ngaruroro River.[289]

Russell's itinerary for October 1940 included a visit to Trentham camp in the Hutt Valley to inspect the training of prospective officers; and another to Titahi Bay, north of Wellington, 'to have a look at this country in case of invasion in Porirua Harbour vicinity'. It was followed by a flight up the coast to Paekakariki and back via Judgeford 'to spy out tactical problems', and several visits to Northland, whose coastline was considered particularly vulnerable to attack from the sea.

In November 1940, Russell was in the South Island, inspecting the King Edward barracks, Burnham Military Camp, the Taieri Elementary Flying Depot and the coastal defences of Port Chalmers. The Southland Regiment quartered at Forbury was appraised with a horse-breeder's eye: 'Of the battalions I have inspected, this was one of the best I have yet seen. The men were not tall, but their faces were well set; clear-eyed, deep-chested, and well muscled up. After inspecting the Regiment, the men marched past and in my opinion they were good.'[290]

In March the following year, Russell inspected the approaches to Wellington harbour, attended a conference on the defence of North Auckland, and watched army units on manoeuvres. In an echo of 1914, just before sailing for Egypt and Gallipoli, Russell was highly critical of what he saw: 'Too much and too confusing umpiring—bad section and platoon leading—no drive in attack. Field training very deficient.'[291]

Russell's first report to the minister of defence and chief of general staff recommended that the air force be urgently equipped with long-range reconnaissance aircraft, both for the defence of the country and for the protection of ships leaving and approaching it. The reports that followed concentrated largely on deficiencies· in the training and equipment of the Territorial Force. His report for June 1941, for example, concluded that although the calibre of TF personnel was excellent, the force was not yet sufficiently trained or equipped for active operations. Many deficiencies, he observed, were due to 'lack of attention to the little things, which may lead to disaster, and is a sign of slack discipline'.[292]

Russell's reports targeted the lack of experienced officers, especially for staff work—the result of what he had earlier seen as the Government's failure to keep Defence Force manpower at adequate levels. To meet the need of New Zealand's forces for younger men as leaders, Russell recommended that all officers be placed on the reserve list when they reached the age of 50.

Reports on the manning, training and equipment of the Home Guard occupied a significant amount of Russell's time. By 1941, the Home Guard was a volunteer force 100,000 strong; its purpose to provide guards for vital installations, reinforce the TF if necessary, and provide an auxiliary force for home defence. Where no other forces were available, it would provide the first opposition to any enemy landing on the coast of New Zealand. Russell, however, recommended that the Home Guard not be used as active troops but as guards for key installations like powerstations, gasworks, bridges and petrol dumps, and for auxiliary functions such as traffic control, coast-watching, communications and transport. At this point, the effectiveness of the force was limited by a shortage of arms, equipment and uniforms, as well as effective direction and supervision.

Better planning and coordination of local defence efforts was a regular refrain. Ten days after the Japanese attack on Pearl Harbor, Russell wrote to the Chief of General Staff, Major-General Sir Edward Puttick, to complain about the organisational 'chaos' he found in Hawke's Bay: 'Everyone keen as mustard, pursuing his own line of action, taking orders from no one.'[293] More serious, in Russell's view, were deficiencies in the military planning needed to meet a raid or a major attack on New Zealand. No one, for example, seemed to know where the reserves of ammunition and explosives were sited, and plans for the rationing of the Home Guard and Military Reserve in case of an emergency were vague. The appointment of local military commanders, he told Puttick, would improve the coordination of anti-invasion preparations around the country.[294]

However, Russell was having difficulty getting his recommendations accepted and actioned—possibly because of the strained relationship between himself and the Minister of Defence, Fred Jones. Russell found Jones 'slow on the uptake' and told Prime Minister Fraser quite bluntly that he was 'no good' as minister of defence. He wanted Jones sacked and replaced by Labour Minister Bob Semple or Gordon Coates, a World War I veteran, ex-prime minister, and now a member of the Wartime Cabinet.

In January 1941, Russell recommended that Colonel Row—'a good fighting soldier with tactical nous'—be sent to Egypt to familiarise himself with modern troop-training methods. When the recommendation was turned down, Russell fired in his resignation. The defence chiefs blocking the proposal ultimately backed down, and Russell was able to report to his sisters that for the moment he remained at his post. By the end of June, though, he was ready to go. He felt that too many of his recommendations had borne little fruit and that his usefulness to the country was now at an end. 'The whole machine is very sticky,' he wrote to Fraser. 'I certainly cannot, as an Inspector-General, who after all has no executive power, succeed in getting the machine moving as it should . . . I could contribute more to the war effort by attending my farm and hoeing weeds.'[295] With the appointment of General Williams as military adviser to the New Zealand Government, Russell resigned as inspector-general of military forces, recommending that the inspection role be passed over to army headquarters and district commanders.

But the decision to resign went beyond mere frustration. Russell was exhausted by his efforts and, at the age of 73, felt that the job should be given over to a younger man. 'For in the last 10 months,' he wrote to his family, 'I have been continually on the move, have seldom slept in the same bed three nights running, have motored thousands of miles, and have tried to stow away in my mind numberless details (and my mind is rapidly becoming a sieve). So nature says hold hard awhile.' The relief of his resignation was palpable: 'I'm out of the [military] saddle—not bucked off, however, but a graceful descent on my own volition. I'm like a dog off the chain or a boy home from school.'

Off the chain Guy Russell was, but there was still work to be done on the War Council. A key council meeting in December 1941, immediately after the surprise Japanese attack on the American Pacific Fleet at Pearl Harbor, confirmed his view of the Government's chronic slowness to react to the threat or onset of hostilities. 'PM gave a jittery talk on the situation,' he noted in his diary. 'Many steps being taken now in a hurry which should have been set afoot months ago.'

Fraser had reason to be jittery, for these were probably the darkest days of the war for New Zealand. Simultaneously with the attack on Pearl Harbor on 6 December, Japanese forces had landed in Malaya and the Philippines. Two British battleships, *Repulse* and *Prince of Wales*, were sunk by Japanese aircraft on 10 December. Churchill confirmed what was now quite obvious: as a result of the losses inflicted on the American and British forces, the Japanese had full naval control of the Pacific and could attack with force at any point in the region.

In January 1942, the Japanese invaded Burma, New Guinea, the Solomon Islands and captured Manila, Kuala Lumpur and Rabaul. With Japanese forces moving rapidly south, the American authorities warned the New Zealand Government that an attack on Fiji—seen as vital to the defence of New Zealand—could be expected at any time after 10 January.[296]

The Fraser Government now ordered a general mobilisation. The strength of the Territorial Force was rapidly increased and by March it stood at 67,000 men—the equivalent of three divisions, if only half the official estimate of what was required for the defence of New Zealand. The National Service regulations were amended to provide for the conscription of civilian manpower. The army began training selected men from the Home Guard for commando and guerrilla units, setting up operational bases and accumulating stores.

In mid-February, 'impregnable' Singapore fell after a short siege and 130,000 British, Indian and Australian troops became prisoners of war. Three days later, the Japanese attacked the Australian mainland, bombing the city of Darwin and killing nearly 250 civilians. A similar raid on New Zealand—if not a full invasion—now seemed likely and there was a good chance that the country would face it alone. Singapore had fallen, Britain was preoccupied in Europe, and in the wake of Pearl Harbor there was 'serious talk' in American political and military circles about abandoning Australia and New Zealand to the Japanese.[297]

On 8 March, Fraser broadcast to the nation, outlining the measures the Government was taking to defend the country. He warned New Zealanders that they faced the most critical situation since the war in the Pacific began. Any Japanese attack, however, would be vigorously resisted. 'Let there be no doubt,' he declared, 'if there is a raid, we will repulse it. If there is an invasion, we will hurl it back.'

Unlike Fraser, neither the British chiefs of staff nor their New Zealand counterparts believed that there was any real threat of invasion. At the most, the Japanese might aim to capture the northern screen of islands from New Guinea through New Caledonia to Fiji and perhaps Samoa. This would cut Australia and New Zealand off from the United States and from reinforcement or essential imports, and might compel the two nations to seek a separate peace with Japan. Russell and his National Defence League, however, now felt that their warnings had been vindicated, if too slowly acted on.

In June 1942, Russell resigned from the War Council in what he called 'a mute protest against its futility', and in spite of Fraser's efforts to dissuade him he would not change his mind. 'We do not really pull any weight,' he wrote to his family, 'the decisions are made before the question comes before us, we merely endorse.' Fraser's letter of acknowledgement was soothing. Russell and his colleagues, he wrote, had 'brought a breadth of vision and wealth of experience to the Council table which had crystallised many a difficult situation'.[298]

Russell, however, had been making more personal contributions to the war effort. He had helped to organise a group of local bodies and associations into a committee that would oversee the interests of men called up at short notice to serve in the forces. He had given active support to a government scheme to bring some 5000 child evacuees out to New Zealand, and had made a financial contribution to the war effort through 'patriotic funds'.

In the meantime, the old general sensed that the tide of war was turning in favour of the Allies and that there was now little chance of the Japanese getting a foothold in New Zealand. His tolerance of pacifists and conscientious objectors, however, had not improved. There were too many of them in the country, he complained to his sisters, and the Government's reliance on them for political support was making it seem 'weak and inconsistent'. To ensure that such people did not 'profiteer for conscience sake', Russell suggested that they be made to do work of national importance at army rates of pay.

The COs were not the only targets of Russell's acerbic pen. He mocked the enthusiasm of New Zealand's trades councils and labour unions for 'the sacred cause of liberty so ably served by the terrorists of Moscow.' Russian communism, he argued, had no value in terms of creating a better world. It was wrong in principle and practice, and a bar to progress. He would fight against it 'to the last'.

Russell was cheered, however, by the performance of the New Zealand troops against German and Italian forces in the Middle East: The soldiers of 2NZEF, he thought, could well outperform those of the division that had fought under his command 25 years before. 'More power to them,' he wrote to his family. 'The New Zealander has only to get out of his country and escape from the enervating climate of social security to come into his own. His virtues are undeniable but they must have a chance.'

Russell had been encouraged too by the good reports of his son John, including one from General Freyberg himself. John Russell had won the Distinguished Service Order for his performance in Greece and Crete and was now in command of the 22nd Infantry Battalion with the rank of lieutenant-colonel. In June 1941, John was in hospital in Cairo with slight shrapnel wounds to his back and arm; a year later he was dead, killed instantly when he stepped on a mine during frontline fighting in Libya against Rommel's Afrika Korps.

Russell and his younger son had shared similar character traits—natural qualities of leadership, inexhaustible energy, and a concern for efficiency and the welfare of the men under their command. He took the loss very hard: 'I feel as if part of myself has gone and life never to be the same again,' he wrote to his sisters. 'I feel empty. But one mustn't hug any grief, it's selfish. But oh for the touch of a vanished hand and the sound of a voice that is still!'

In his letter of condolence, John's brigade commander, Brigadier-General Howard Kippenberger, described an action the day before John's death in which John had personally rallied a retreating platoon of his men to repulse an attack by two battalions of German infantry spearheaded by 15 tanks. 'We have lost many fine officers in this battle,' Kippenberger wrote, 'but none will be so hard to spare as your son.'[299] Attached to the letter was a photo of John's grave in Libya, but Guy Russell did not have the heart to show it to his wife.

By this time he had received other letters from men who had served with John, all of them extolling his courage and leadership. It was comforting to know that John had won the love and respect of his men—to Russell's mind the highest tribute that could be paid to a commander in the field. His son, he wrote, had 'lived a good life, left a good record, and met a soldier's end'. Guy handled his grief by writing regularly to his dead son for 17 years afterwards in long, very personal letters that could never be sent. In one of them, he wrote: 'I wish you were here, and every morning look at the track and imagine you riding down it on the old grey horse.'

Guy could take some comfort from the news that his remaining son would not be going away to fight. Although he was now a major in the Territorial Force, Andy had been rejected as unfit for service because of persistent kidney trouble. Gola, however, still had to be managed, and John's widow, Ros, and her three young children supported, physically and emotionally. In spite of his age, Russell took to it all with his usual courage and determination. Every day he would gallop up to the homestead (he never walked or cantered his horse) and do basic chores around the homestead—cutting firewood, carting coal and weeding the garden. Although he was not good at fixing things, he would wrestle with the water pump, which invariably seemed to break down during the hottest weather.

Supporting his grieving daughter-in-law emotionally was more difficult—'keeping her spirits up and interests alive', as he put it. Ros appeared to lose heart with her husband's death and buried herself in constant work. She never spoke of him either to her father-in-law or to her children. Because of their age, the young ones barely remembered their father, and Russell was able to distract them with stories of his bear-hunting exploits in Kashmir or climbing mountains in Switzerland, along with much-embellished favourite fairy stories. Russell's efforts to communicate with his grandchildren, however, did not always meet with success. His grandson, John Russell, recalled that his sister Rachel was 'a quiet little girl' and the general often had difficulty getting her to talk. 'Eventually he would smile and say, "Well Rachel, it's much better to say nothing and let the world think you are fool than to open your mouth and tell the world that you are!"'

As with his own children, Russell's grandchildren were taught to face and overcome their fears. As a six-year-old, young John was made to climb a steep rock face on Tunanui, with his grandfather following closely behind to make sure he did. He derived great amusement from loading the running-boards of his ancient Ford with grandchildren and driving erratically around a paddock trying to shake them off—an exciting but probably low-risk activity, given the age of both the vehicle and its driver. 'Granny Russell would go so crook at him when she heard about it,' John laughed.

In 1946, Ros married prominent left-wing journalist, farmer and politician Ormond Wilson. Wilson had become the youngest MP in the 1935 Labour Government and was the owner of Mount Lees station in the Manawatu. Russell initially dismissed Wilson as 'one of those pink-flavoured intellectuals who, having come into a good income, has never done a hard day's work in his life, but considers that he is fully qualified to run the world'. He would later concede that Ormond was essentially 'a decent fellow', and that the match was a chance for happiness again for Ros after four years of widowhood. It would also provide a steady male influence for her three children that he now felt too old to provide.

But with his ingrained distrust of Labour Party politicians, Russell was determined that his John would grow up free from left-wing ideas and attitudes. His own grandfather, 'the Colonel', had done much to mould his character and ambitions; now he would attempt to do the same for his only grandson. In later years, John Russell would acknowledge the huge influence 'the General' had had on his early life as mentor and role model.

John Russell seemed set to follow his father and grandfather into the army, but eventually chose to take up farming at Tunanui. The decision was a disappointment to Guy Russell, as it broke a father-to-son tradition of military service going back nearly 200 years. In the end he was philosophical, recognising that 'youth must follow its own star'. His grandson, however, would not abandon his earlier ambitions entirely; he served for several years as a territorial officer in the 4th Armoured Regiment after completing his compulsory military training in 1956.

In spite of his age and flagging energies, Guy Russell kept abreast of new techniques in farm management as well as he could. Aerial topdressing was applied to Tunanui pasture when the technology was still relatively new. Chisel ploughing was introduced in an attempt to limit the damage to the soil done by conventional ploughing. His interest in cultivation now stretched to growing lettuces in the horse dung produced by the 'mucking out' of the stables on Tunanui.

Russell also kept a close eye on the progress of the war, which was now turning slowly in favour of the Allies. He still heartily disapproved of Fraser, however—for his pacifist activities during World War I, and for the wartime censorship and loss of civil liberties imposed under his name. Under the emergency regulations introduced in 1941, the Government had cracked down hard on communists and pacifists speaking in public and publishing or disseminating their material. Some were jailed, and the communist *People's Voice*, the radical journal *Tomorrow* and the Christian Pacifist Society's *Bulletin* were banned. A government censor was appointed with the power to open any private mail that might contain 'seditious' material.

Though the curbs on civil liberties were temporary, Russell, like others of his countrymen, feared that in fighting a war for the defence of liberty, New Zealand was in danger of losing its own. 'This Government,' he wrote to his family, 'can't stand up to the slightest criticism, and the powers invested in the censor are being, like the wireless, used for party political ends, in a manner which reminds one of Goebbels. And even Labour supporters are beginning to realise that it is not necessary to be a German or a follower of Stalin to live under a dictatorship.'

By war's end, Russell's opposition to wartime controls was undiminished: 'Everyone heartily sick of the authoritarian methods employed by the Government, implemented through an overgrown bureaucracy.' As for the prime minister himself, a family letter noted sourly: 'Our Mr Fraser has just landed after a world tour, during which he has walked the ruins of Cassino and told the British public what a "magnificent job" NZ is doing. And that's the man who in the last war was a conscientious objector and declined to take off his hat when the national anthem was played.'

The criticism was hardly fair. Fraser had never been a conscientious objector, although as an active pacifist he had opposed conscription in 1916 and had spent a year in jail because of it. His abandonment of pacifism and reincarnation in 1940 as the hardline leader of his country's war effort was no act of hypocrisy or road-to-Damascus conversion. Through the 1930s, Fraser had become steadily aware that pacifism and support for the League of Nations were no answer to the aggressive fascism of Hitler and Mussolini. Only military force, he concluded, could effectively stop such people and guarantee a lasting peace. To that end, Fraser was prepared to curtail civil liberties for the duration of the war in the interests of supporting the Allied war effort.

With the war finally won in Europe and the Pacific, Russell began once again to take an interest in closer land settlement. His argument was essentially the same as 20 years before—large landowners across the country should be encouraged to offer land for sale and subdivision and give the Government 'first refusal'. In this way, partially developed country in private hands and unused Crown land could be made considerably more productive. Most important, closer settlement would encourage the population growth New Zealand needed to help secure it against potential aggressors.

Russell was pragmatic: he knew that selling off land would come at a cost, not only to himself but to other landowners who had broken in large tracts of the New Zealand back country over many years. He wrote to his sisters: 'Some of us will not like parting with land on which we, or our fathers, have spent a lifetime of work and interest, but we must look on it as the price we pay for our children's future.'

The Government, however, was already moving in this direction with a pledge that returned soldiers would get a better deal than they had received after World War I. A Minister of Rehabilitation was appointed in 1943; legislation was introduced to control land values, and a land sales commission was given the power to acquire land for servicemen's farms.

In 1946, Russell sold Gola to the government for soldier resettlement, reducing his holdings to 1500 acres (607 hectares)—just big enough to occupy one shepherd and himself fully, but not too fully. 'Thought I was able to run Gola while Ros and the children were there,' he wrote to his grandson John. 'Now I shall be glad to see it sold. I'm aging, I know it, and don't want to be bothered any more with a big place. Indeed, one has reached a stage where one no longer looks forward to fresh fields to conquer, but rather to the past.'

The Russell domains had seen plenty of change over the years, and particularly to the old Twyford station that Guy had once managed but now lay on the outskirts of Hastings. 'John motored me round the old Flaxmere-Twyford block which he had never seen,' Guy noted in his diary. 'Explained to him how the 1897 flood went. I could hardly recognise the paddocks I knew 40 years ago. Now homesteads, orchards, plantations everywhere.'

Chapter 25

'Too Many Ghosts on Memory's Stage'

'The husbandman [farmer] is the most fortunate of all men because for him there is no retiring age. He continues in the same old groove, till declining faculties, mental and physical, gradually shake off his mundane cares till he reaches the blessed stage of "contemplation", and in due course of nature draws up his knees like old Abraham and surrenders.'—Guy Russell, now 83, looks to the end times.

The 1940s had seen a steady decline in the physical capabilities of the old general, although his mental faculties were still acute. He no longer did any hard physical work, content to ride around Gola and Tunanui keeping an eye on things, but leaving the day-to-day supervision to his managers. Except for meetings of the Hawke's Bay Farmers' Co-operative and the shareholders of Mount View station, he had shed the appointments to the various boards and trusteeships that had once kept him so actively engaged.

His thoughts now often turned to the past. In his letters to his son John, he confessed to going over in mind the many things they had done together. He was doing the same with his father and mother, and all those with whom his life had been intimately connected—'so perhaps, as I hope, when we meet again, we shall not feel strangers'.

In 1947, Guy arranged for a brass memorial to John to be placed in the Hastings church where he and Gertrude were married over 50 years before. It would go alongside memorials to John's first cousins, Bob, Phil and Nick Williams; Bob was killed in the South African War of 1899–1902, and Phil and Nick while serving with the Royal Flying Corps in World War I.

Much had changed for the Russells in the years after World War II. The homestead was no longer bustling with family, servants and important visitors. Guy and Gertrude were now on their own and living a very simple life. The only servant was a cowman-gardener, and from time to time sheep could be seen wandering on the once well-used tennis court.

There were ongoing problems of farm management, however. The summer of 1945–46 brought a double disaster: the worst drought Guy Russell could remember, and his old nemesis, a plague of rabbits. The result was no water for stock as dams and springs on both properties dried up, no grass growth, and therefore no winter feed. Stock had to be sold off or they would starve. The drought was followed by a chilly August, again the coldest Russell could remember: 'Practically no growth, and cattle hanging on thanks to a few pounds [of feed] a day apiece,' he wrote to John. 'Just enough to last to Sept 13th. After that they'll have to live on sunshine unless the grass starts to grow.'

In 1947, at the age of 79, Russell admitted at last that the time had come to hang up his work boots and bridle: 'There's no disguising the fact that the old machine is very, very second hand, and though a coat of paint may hide the fact, it's no longer fit for hard work.' Despite arthritis in his knee, however, he was still active about the farm, provided he drove or was driven.

In 1949, for the first time since arriving home in 1919, Russell attended the dawn service on Anzac Day as a spectator rather than a speaker. Attendance at the RSA conference that year was passed up because he was 'not up to the travelling', and his doctor, Sandy White, had told him to take a great deal of rest. The old warrior was definitely slowing down, but his prodigious energy and drive were not yet spent. That year, he drove himself to Havelock North to visit the dying Sir John Duigan, who had finished his military career as chief of general staff. If Duigan had done him the harm he once vowed to do, Guy Russell was obviously now prepared to forgive.

He also had energy enough for some social activities. A diary entry in March 1950 noted: 'Sorting up glad rags for Thursday's dance at Waipukurau. Motheaten but Gertrude has made them at least respectable . . . Met old 1914 acquaintances, among others, Peyton, who used to drive me in France.' In October, he attended a reunion of the Main Body of the NZEF at Hastings: 'Great success. About 300 there, including [Brigadier-General] Hart and Tim Wilder.'

The ranks of World War I veterans, however, were thinning steadily and Russell was beginning to feel bereft. 'Only a platoon left of company, only a company left of the battalion I knew at full strength,' he wrote to A.B. Sackett, Andrew's tutor from the 1920s. 'Well, it is all in the natural course, but I do miss my old "cobbers" as they, like autumn leaves, fall at the approach of their winter.'

Guy Russell's sister Gwen died in 1945; and Milly in 1953. When their home, Heath House, was sold the following year, the family connection with England was all but broken, and the sibling relationship that had sustained Guy for over 80 years was at an end. He spent an emotional day in June 1954 sorting through the various documents, letters and artefacts that he had now inherited. 'Rather a melancholy business,' he noted in his diary. 'Too many ghosts appear on memory's stage.'

Nevertheless, he maintained his interest in defence issues and international affairs generally. His letters to John in the late 1940s revealed an anxiety about what he saw as a drift towards another world war, and the need to 'stir the country up to its defence responsibilities', particularly in the Pacific. He noted communist efforts to end Dutch rule in Indonesia, and reiterated beliefs nurtured from his days as a defence lobbyist in the 1920s and '30s: 'The Asiatic is becoming not only race conscious; his many millions constitute a danger to our empty lands, here and in Australia.' For the activities of Jewish nationalists in post-war Palestine he had nothing but contempt: 'Using all they can—murder included—to antagonise British and Arab.'

In the early 1950s, Russell took a close interest in the progress of the Korean War and the post-war alignment of nations with Russian-dominated communist or Western blocs. He felt that the West would ultimately prevail in the so-called Cold War, but Westerners would have to overcome their preoccupation with materialism and cease to 'make a fetish of comfort, pleasure and a cotton wool-padded life'—a reference, no doubt, to what he saw as the negative aspects of New Zealand's well-established welfare state.

In October 1954, Guy felt he was not strong enough to attend the 40th anniversary celebration of the departure of the Main Body of the NZEF from New Zealand for Egypt and Gallipoli. 'In spite of appeals to come,' he wrote to John, 'this dog won't run; rather I should say, can't run.' For their diamond wedding anniversary on 5 August 1956, Guy and Gertrude got up just in time for a family party and the obligatory cutting of the cake. The party was attended by 30 close friends and family, including three of their original bridesmaids; and it lasted until 5.30 pm when the old couple retired early to bed. Apparently exhausted by the experience, Gertrude stayed there for several weeks. By now, Russell was hoping to outlive Gertrude because he could not bear the thought of her being left alone in the big house at Tunanui. His letters to his dead son were also growing more infrequent. The time was now close, he wrote to Sackett, when he would be leaving his 'personal glades and mansions'.

With the 'young folk' and servants nearly all gone, Guy felt that the grand Tunanui homestead was now too big for two old people to manage on their own. He thought the Salvation Army might be interested in buying it, plus 50 surrounding acres, as a farm school, and began discussions with army officials to that end. The homestead was saved for succeeding generations, however, when his grandson John decided to live there himself (later with his wife Phillida and family), and it remains in the Russell family to this day.

In 1957, Tunanui put one more demand on the old man's reserves of energy and commitment. His farm manager had contracted the cattle-borne disease leptospirosis and was off sick for over six months. At the age of nearly 90, Guy was compelled to take up the reins again, this time with help from former Tunanui manager Alick Shaw. Riding a horse was now out of the question; instead he roamed the paddocks in a Land-Rover with the manager or a farm hand to open gates and do any 'dirty work'.

Social activities had by now become increasingly burdensome. A diary entry in February 1958 records Russell's difficulty in coping with a visit by Chief Justice Barrowclough and several members of his own family—'too many to talk to, at any rate for a bad day'. That year also, he retired as a director of Hawke's Bay Farmers' Co-operative after 52 years of service, and his extensive tree-planting on Tunanui finally came to an end. Physically, it was now beyond him.

In October, Russell's last remaining sister, Gertie, died in England, leaving him now the only surviving member of Ham Russell's family. A last visit to an old family haunt on the farm in April 1959 reminded him of the part Ham and his brother William had played in breaking in Tunanui nearly a century before. His diary noted: 'Got Fox to take me as far down to the point at which you can look down to the mouth of the Konini and see the cutting on the far side used by the old coach road to Mowhango first used by my father 100 years ago.'

The issue of who would take over Tunanui on Russell's death, however, had been settled. His surviving son Andy had been farming successfully near Gisborne for 30 years and had no desire to take on the management of Tunanui. The heir to the station, Russell decided, would be his grandson, John Russell, now about 20 and no longer headed for a career in the Regular Army. The great 9350-acre run of the early 1900s, however, had been reduced by land sales over the years to just 1430 acres (578 hectares).

By 1959, Guy was working 'in the lowest gear' as he watched his physical energy fading and felt his mental processes slowing down. In 1960, the last year of his life, much of his day was spent in bed. Failing eyesight made it difficult for him to read, and increasing deafness left him out of many conversations between family and friends. His interest in the running of Tunanui was strong right to the end, though. Four or five times a week he would meet with Kerridge, his current farm manager—but not always to his satisfaction, as he found it difficult to teach the latter how to 'foresee and plan'.

Questions of religious education still engaged him, however. In August that year he wrote to Governor-General Lord Cobham on matters to do with the Council for Christian Education, a lobby group of Protestant churches that wanted to see religious education included in the primary school curriculum. In Russell's opinion, it would be easier if children were introduced to 'the reality of the spiritual world' at their mother's knee—if the Plunket Society could teach young mothers how to keep their children in good physical health, could not something similar be provided to meet their spiritual needs. At the moment, he told Cobham, the council had no sound foundation on which to build.

Later that year, Cobham visited Tunanui in person; and so did his wartime contemporaries Willy Wood and Hugh Crosse—now among the few survivors of the original officer corps of the New Zealand Division. In October, Russell wrote a last letter to his family, to be opened after his death. In it, he acknowledged his good fortune in being born into a family of strong religious faith 'to whom family ties were sacred'. He credited his happiness and success over a long life to over 60 years of marriage to Gertrude, who had shown him 'unfailing love and wise tolerance of short-lived and surface stupidity'. The letter ended with a strong affirmation of his Christian faith: 'Oh Lord, my strength and my redeemer, as my old father used to say.'

Guy Russell died on 29 November 1960. The funeral service was held at St Matthew's Anglican Church in Hastings two days later. Canon K.F. Button gave the sermon; and the Bishop of Waiapu, the Rt Reverend N.A. Lesser, gave the eulogy. Six hundred official mourners attended the service and hundreds more congregated in the streets outside the church, some of them old soldiers who had served under Russell at Gallipoli and in France. The official party included Governor-General Cobham, representatives of the Government and the RSA, members of local bodies and other prominent Hawke's Bay citizens.

The casket was draped with the Union Jack on which lay the Sword of Honour that Russell had won at Sandhurst in 1887, together with his army cap with its General Staff badge and red band. With them were the insignia of the many honours and orders conferred on him during his service in World War I. The pallbearers that day were the Chief of General Staff, Major-General Leonard Thornton, Major-General Sir William Gentry, Major-General A.S. Wilder, Brigadier-General M.C. Fairbrother, Rear Admiral Peter Phipps and Air Vice-Marshal M.F. Calder.

The coffin was strapped to a gun carriage and, preceded by a military guard of honour, moved in slow and silent procession through the streets of Hastings to the crematorium. Four 25-pounder guns of the Royal New Zealand Artillery fired, at 10-second intervals, the 13-round salute to which the general was entitled. The escort presented arms, the bugler sounded 'The Last Post', and the coffin slipped away.

Bishop Lesser's eulogy that day ended with the poignant words: 'Death is but a coming of age of the soul, and Andrew Russell is, to use the words of the early church, "born into eternity".' A committed Christian and firm believer in the after-life, Russell would have expected no less.

The ashes of three Russells—the general, his wife Gertrude, and their eldest son Andrew—lie under two limestone boulders on a high spur overlooking Tunanui and its grand homestead in the valley below. The view is back over Hawke's Bay rolling hill country, ravines and pine forests to the blue line of the Kaweka Range. The pioneering farmer, intellectual soldier and devoted family man who once called England home is at home at last on that hill.

Conclusion

A Consummate Commander

'An inspiring commander of New Zealand troops, combining the practical common sense of a colonial farmer, a familiarity with Western Europe unusual among his divisional colleagues, and some background in the British army. Undemonstrative and self-effacing, straight-talking, responsible, determined, Russell epitomised the New Zealand citizen-soldier of the First World War.'[300]

A sample of writers on the science of military leadership indicates that outstanding commanders must have five essential qualities: courage, intelligence, good health, fighting spirit, and the ability to command the affection and loyalty of their soldiers.[301]

According to the doyen of military theorists, General Carl von Clausewitz, courage is of two kinds: physical and moral. Physical courage is defined as indifference to danger; moral courage is the willingness to accept responsibility and to make hard and often unpalatable decisions. Intelligence, says von Clausewitz, is the possession of a penetrating mind that can cut through 'the fog of war'. Fighting spirit is defined as 'the will to win', and includes a willingness to take risks and to be decisive in command rather than waiting for things to happen. It is also the ability to inspire troops in defeat, giving them the will to endure in seemingly hopeless circumstances. By these definitions, outstanding military leaders are those who 'combine extreme professionalism in the realising of military goals with warm humanity which earns them the lasting affection and loyalty of their men'.[302]

There is no doubt that Russell had huge reserves of physical courage—or perhaps simply a well-demonstrated lack of fear. As a young officer serving with a British garrison regiment in northern India in the late 1880s, he was remembered by his fellow officers as a skilful and fearless horseman, polo player and race rider who excelled in 'hard-ball games and wild sports'.[303] At Gallipoli and in France, Russell was equally fearless, taking big risks to keep himself in touch with frontline conditions. A former platoon commander recalled his commander

> striding along the front-line trench—ignoring shellfire—with gas respirator at the 'alert' and carrying his well-known stick. A pleasant 'good morning,' perhaps a question about snipers, trench mortar fire, or other enemy activity, then the general's short, sturdy figure would briskly disappear around the next traverse. Such an inspection—often very dangerous—would be an 8 or 10-mile walk in difficult conditions amongst his men. No wonder he had the complete confidence and respect of every Digger.[304]

Russell was 'a very popular man with all us fellows and a first-rate soldier', wrote a trooper who survived Gallipoli. 'No fear, always made his rounds no matter what was doing ... He is as hard as nails. At one time we were in a direct line of fire from a Turkish battery and the shells were dropping unpleasantly close, but the general didn't hurry while he explained what he wanted.'[305]

Russell claimed to being personally untroubled by combat situations. 'I never remember in France or on Gallipoli being in the least disturbed or anxious. It was just part of the show,' he wrote to his family a quarter of a century on. Was this due to iron self-control or simply a lack of any sense of fear? Russell's grandson, John Russell, believes the latter; he describes his grandfather as a man who simply did not know the meaning of fear—nor could he easily understand those who did.

That fearlessness never deserted him. In the late 1930s, Guy Russell, then about 70, was charged by a bull while inspecting cattle yards on a property at Ngatapa, near Gisborne. Russell did not flinch or run, but grabbed a loose fence batten and hit the animal hard across the nose. The now very angry bull backed off and charged again. Russell stood firm and again whacked him across the nose, this time breaking the batten down to a stump. The farmer whose property it was called in the dogs and the bull finally called it quits.

Russell's moral courage was unquestionable. It was demonstrated in his willingness to challenge the decision of a superior officer at Gallipoli that would have wasted the lives of 100 of his men, and to take full responsibility for the disastrous attack of his division at Passchendaele, even if the situation had been caused by the misjudgement of others. A refusal to attack, as Russell effectively did at Gallipoli, could have had serious consequences. Officers of the British Army who knew that an attack would inevitably fail and complained beforehand risked being disgraced or sacked. As a result, most commanding officers of the time felt compelled to attack regardless of the likely outcome.[306]

Intelligence in the military sense includes the ability to plan effectively and think tactically, even in the extreme conditions of battle. It includes the ability to learn from experiences and mistakes—a commander's own and those of his colleagues, allies and enemies. Intelligence in a military commander is the ability to recognise that soldiers who are well-trained, disciplined and properly cared for fight better and for longer than those who are not. It is manifested in the flexibility of mind needed to adapt to new ideas and technologies, and the energy and will to apply them.

Pugsley makes much of Russell's planning and tactical skills, arguing that Russell was one of the few commanders in the British Army with any ability in this area. His tactics at Messines, writes Pugsley, showed he was one of the more innovative divisional commanders in the British, French and German armies; and anticipated the tactics employed by the Germans in their March offensive in 1918.[307] Meticulous planning and attention to detail, he notes, became Russell's hallmark for every operation in the field.

Russell's tactical abilities were evident in the foothills attack at Gallipoli on 7 August 1915, and at Messines two years later. Stewart, the division's historian, wrote, for example, of his 'lightning insight into tactical situations' and his ability to remain calm and resolute in periods of crisis or confusion.[308]

As historians of World War I are inclined to observe, however, the opportunities for tactical brilliance on the Western Front were very limited: 'The rifle, the artillery piece, the machine gun, barbed wire, and the spade locked up the front. Until a mechanical means of mobility could be found—as it was later in the primitive tank—the tactics of advance and penetration were exercises in futility.'[309]

After the Somme battles of 1916, the British high command made strenuous efforts to improve the tactical efficiency of its armies, and these continued until the end of the war. For a variety of reasons, however, many commanders failed to effectively integrate these tactics into the training regimes of their divisions. By contrast, Russell ensured that the latest tactical lessons handed down from Haig's headquarters became an essential element of the training of the New Zealand Division and were carefully rehearsed before each battle. Like Monash in command of the Australians, Russell was not so much a tactical innovator as a highly successful imitator.

The results of Russell's training regimes were most clearly shown in 1918 as the division moved from static trench warfare to a war of rapid movement. New artillery doctrines were developed and the infantry trained in tactics that mirrored those of the storm troops in the great German offensive earlier that year. Towns and villages were outflanked and encircled rather than being attacked frontally. Night attacks were the norm, taking the enemy by surprise and reducing casualties.

Effective tactics and planning were one thing; support for the men who would have to fight was quite another. Experience of combat on the Somme had given Russell a firm appreciation of the link between sound administration, proper attention to the health and wellbeing of his men, and their fighting spirit. From late 1916 on, Russell gave this area his special attention. He closely monitored the condition of his units with regular visits to the frontline, demanded improvements, then ensured that his commanders carried them out. If subordinate commanders were not up to the job, Russell sent them back to New Zealand.

Russell's approach to disciplinary problems was equally uncompromising. He recognised that poor discipline was largely due to a failure in command at officer and NCO level. He addressed the problem by insisting on the training of his commanders at all levels, with particular emphasis on his junior officers and NCOs. The result was a major improvement in discipline and a steady decline in the number of courts-martial.

Overall, the New Zealand Division could claim to be a comparatively well-disciplined unit. There were just over 2000 courts-martial for the 100,444 New Zealanders who served overseas in the NZEF, compared to 23,000 courts-martial for the 331,814 Australians who served with the AIF, and 18,000 courts-martial for the 458,218 Canadians who served with the Canadian Expeditionary Force (CEF). The percentage of New Zealand courts-martial to troops in theatre was less than one third of the Australian rate and half that of the Canadians.[310]

Flexibility of mind and willingness to accept new ideas were other factors in Russell's success as a battlefield commander. Such qualities were in not in good supply among the senior British commanders of World War I. Where flexibility and imagination were required to address what seemed intractable military problems, many of them offered only more of the same—frontal attacks on strongly held positions, grinding battles of attrition and huge casualties. A long military career, Pedersen observes, tended to engender a narrowness of mind, and one that did not adapt easily to new ideas.[311]

Russell's experience was very different. He had offset the five years he spent in the British Army in the late 1880s with a broad range of intellectual interests—military history and tactics, economics, international affairs and the study of languages. These, combined with the practical, business and administrative skills gained as a pioneering farmer, gave him a mental flexibility and general knowledge that were not typical of the officer class in the British Army of the time.

The combination of intellectual skills with effective administration, training and discipline produced impressive results. Pugsley concludes that in tactical skill, level of training and performance, the first New Zealand Division on the Western Front far outclassed the second New Zealand Division that fought in North Africa and Italy in World War II. 'After their Somme experience of 1916, the New Zealanders were always one step ahead of everyone else.'[312]

During his three years in command of the New Zealand Division in France, Russell had to endure persistent rheumatism as a result of falls from horses, lumbago, and repeated bouts of influenza and bronchial pneumonia. By August 1918, Godley was worried that the division might now not have a fully fit commander.

A key question is whether Russell's state of health affected his performance during these final critical months. Military historian Glyn Harper believes it did, concluding that Russell was by this time on the verge of physical collapse. As a result, he was out of touch with his frontline troops by the Battle of Bapaume, and was conforming in most ways to the stereotype of a 'Chateau general'. It would have been better for both Russell and his division, Harper suggests, if he had been replaced before the Allied advance that finally ended the war on the Western Front.[313]

There is little evidence of the 'Chateau general' in Russell's performance at this time, and no evidence at all that his health affected his command of the New Zealand Division in the last 11 weeks of the war. Russell was well forward with his brigades up to and including the capture of Le Quesnoy, guiding and supporting his commanders as they pushed on towards the German frontier.

There is no doubt, however, that Russell was tired and ready for a change of command. If he turned his back on Haig's offer of a corps out of loyalty to his New Zealanders, he also recognised that his health was simply not up to it. Had Russell accepted Haig's offer, however, he would have been the only territorial soldier to rise to the command of a British corps in World War I.

By common agreement of his superiors, Russell was an aggressive and determined commander. It was shown in his attacks at Hill 60 on Gallipoli, on the Somme and at Messines. It was demonstrated most notably in the final months of the war as the New Zealand Division spearheaded the advance of Byng's Third Army, pushing the Germans back in action after action.

Stewart noted Russell's ruthless determination to attack and keep on attacking the enemy, while remaining calm and clear-headed under the stresses of combat.[314] Voltaire described it as that 'calm courage in the midst of tumult, that serenity of soul in danger, which is the greatest gift of nature for command.'[315]

As for his ability to inspire troops in defeat, Russell was involved in only two operations that could credibly be described as such. These were the evacuation of Gallipoli in December 1915 when he commanded the 20,000-strong rearguard; and on the Somme in March 1918 when his division plugged the gap in the British line during the great German offensive that almost won them the war. In both operations, he provided efficient and highly effective leadership. In both cases the element of inspiration is harder to identify, but the results speak for themselves.

Pugsley states that Russell was respected but not loved by the

A big risk-taker—Brigadier-General Russell inspects his trenches on Gallipoli, May 1915.

In the Gallipoli trenches—a sniper with a periscope rifle and an observer with a periscope.

Major-General Sir Andrew Russell, Western Front, 1916.

An elite division under a hard taskmaster. Russell inspects his troops before they go into action on the Western Front.

NZ soldiers display their trophies—German Pickelhaube helmets—after the Third Battle of the Somme, October 1916.

NZ troops en route to the front line on the Western Front, 1917.

Into harm's way—NZ troops march through the French town of Bailleul en route to the front.

New Zealand infantry in training for the attack on Messines, May 1917.

Russell (left) and the British Commander-in-Chief, General Sir Douglas Haig, inspect NZ troops in France.

Safe for the moment—NZ troops at rest in a trench on the Western Front.

Equipment on, bayonets fixed and ready to go—NZ infantry prepares to go over the top.

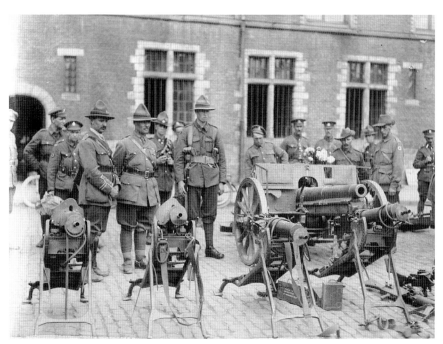

Spoils of war—captured German machine guns are inspected after an NZ Division attack.

NZ artillery in action on the Western Front.

A machine gun company cleans up after the NZ division's attack on Bapaume,
August 1918.

men of his division; Harper claims that the New Zealand soldiers he commanded respected him for his competence but did not warm to him as one of their own. Failing to win the affection of his men cost Russell his 'well-deserved' reputation as an outstanding military commander.[316]

The evidence in both cases suggests otherwise. As early as February 1915, Major A.A. Martin attested to Russell's popularity with officers and men of the NZEF as they trained in Egypt for the Gallipoli landings. Later in 1915, a published letter from a member of the Maori contingent at Gallipoli had this to say: 'In Guy Russell we have one of the finest brigadiers and bravest men to be found anywhere. Everybody respects him because he knows his job, and is game, tactful and considerate, and all those under him would do anything for him.'[317] Early in 1916, a letter from a trooper of Russell's mounted brigade expressed similar feelings:

> He [Russell] is absolutely a white man, and we of the old brigade, well, we love him. He is as game as the best of them, and when the trenches were being shelled by the Turks, he was always there in the thick of it. No dugout king about him. Besides that, he looked after we men of the mounted brigade like a father. He also has a brigade of the Australian light horse under his command, and they think the world of him.[318]

In January 1918, the last year of the war, an infantryman under his command wrote:

> ... the respect—almost veneration—in which our own Divisional Commander, General Russell, is held by everyone under him. There is not a trace of aloofness about him, and he walks around the battleground here and takes just as many risks as anyone. One day I saw him with some of his brigadiers sitting on the duckwalk, yarning away and knocking bits of dirt round with

his stick. This was at a spot where, as the saying goes, 'a fellow wouldn't want to say good day to his best girl'.[319]

Colonel Hugh Stewart, who served under Russell as a battalion commander in France, summed up Russell thus:

> His first thought was always for the comfort and well-being of the troops under his command. He always insisted on every possible provision being made for them in billets, on the march, and after an action; he was always very human and sympathetic, and a sound judge of character. To a man, the division had unbounded confidence in and unlimited regard for their commander.[320]

Lieutenant-Colonel Reg Gambrill, who served under Russell both at Gallipoli and on the Western Front, wrote: 'Those under whom he served and who were privileged to serve under him almost without exception honoured, respected, and loved him.'[321]

In these accolades lies the enigma of Russell's command. On the one hand, there is the tough and uncompromising disciplinarian; the commander with little tolerance for slackness or incompetence, ruthless in his drive for efficiency and sparing with praise. On the other, there is his ability to command the widespread respect, and even affection, of the men who served under him. Underlying this was Russell's inspirational frontline leadership and genuine care for their wellbeing, in or out of combat.

Judgements of military skill, however, must be made in the context of their time, and in 1914 Russell and his fellow commanders faced a revolution in military affairs comparable to that brought about by the microchip in the Gulf War of the early 1990s, in Afghanistan 10 years later, and in the recent US military intervention in Iraq. World War I was the first truly technological war, fought for the first time with tanks, submarines, aircraft, powerful artillery, and automatic weapons with high rates of fire.

Doctrines of warfare shaped in the nineteenth century and based on infantry and cavalry were being rendered obsolete by defensive strategies based on quick-firing artillery, machine guns, trenches and barbed wire. As Eric J. Leed put it: 'The superiority of defensive fire-power over attacking troops was the one, obvious, unquestionable fact of life and war—both for the staffs and the troops in the front line.'[322]

In the light of such dramatic changes in the technology and tactics of warfare, Russell and his fellow commanders could and did make mistakes. Those who learned quickest from their mistakes, like Russell and Monash, became the outstanding commanders of World War I.

The similarities between Monash and Russell as military commanders are intriguing. Monash—lawyer, civil engineer, archaeologist, botanist and part-time soldier—is described by A.J.P. Taylor as 'the only general of creative originality produced by the First World War'.[323] At one point in the war he had been mooted as a replacement for Haig as commander-in-chief of the British armies on the Western Front.

The two men, however, got on well. If Monash resented Russell's knighthood at Gallipoli in 1915, he was also able to describe him as 'a splendid fellow and a close friend of mine . . . urbanity itself, without weakness.' The two commanders shared a range of attributes. Both were citizen-soldiers of high intelligence, strong character, conspicuous organisational skills and strength of purpose. Both had studied the military profession with a thoroughness few regular soldiers could match, and meticulous planning was at the heart of every operation each of them undertook.

Both men gave priority to the conservation of manpower and to the proper care and welfare of their troops. Monash's concern for the welfare of his men, however, was pragmatic rather than sentimental. The fighting soldier, he wrote, should be given food, rest, and be made as comfortable as possible—not for humane reasons but because he needed to be kept going as 'a fighting machine'. Russell would have agreed with all of this, but his concern for his men had a solid humanitarian base.

Both Russell and Monash gave close attention to the techniques practised by other commanders within the British armies, as well as those of French and German formations. Both showed an ability to assess and learn from their mistakes. As a result, tactical training in both forces was a combination of battlefield experience and the recommendations that came down from Haig's headquarters.

Russell, however, was the frontline soldier that Monash was not. After the August offensive at Gallipoli in 1915, Monash was never seen again in the front line and effectively lost touch with his fighting troops. His physical courage was also called into question. Major-General Tim Harington, Plumer's high-performing chief of staff, noted acidly: 'He would tell you which duckboard needed repairing, but never in his life went near a front-line trench.'[324]

By contrast, Russell had to see things for himself, and at considerable personal risk. When his division was in the trenches he would tour the front line several times a week, inspecting his units and the conditions under which they were fighting. Russell also differed from Monash in his approach to planning for major attacks. The former would involve his subordinate commanders at all stages of the planning process. Monash simply told his brigadiers how to deploy their battalions, instead of allowing them to prepare brigade plans within the framework of a divisional scheme.[325]

Russell was no stranger to the day-to-day brutalities of war. Gallipoli had given him a foretaste of the realities of frontline combat well before he reached the Western Front; and, if his letters to family are any guide, hardened him to them. 'I don't find the responsibility [of command] worries me,' he wrote to his father, 'and really one feels that in this war at least you can't make omelettes without breaking eggs, or beat the enemy without risking and losing lives.'

The essential humanity remained, however, despite the decisions that Russell knew would cost the lives of his men. After Hill 60, he regretted the loss of so many of his mounted troopers, while at the same time showing sympathy for a brave and dogged Turkish enemy:

> What a miserable force war is! Killing people whom you don't even see, and certainly don't have any feeling against, is poor form. If it were Germans, it would, I hope, feel very different. But those poor fellows, ignorant peasants from Anatolia, whose hearts, like mine, are turned to their little homes and crops . . . It's all too sickening.

With such instincts went a strong reluctance to squander the lives of his men on essentially futile attacks. The most notable example was his refusal to authorise the attack at the Nek on Gallipoli in May 1915 that would have seen 100 men slaughtered for no tactical gain. The same instinct was at play during the last German offensive on the Western Front in 1918. Russell wrote to his family:

> I am studiously avoiding any firework shows such as corps and army commanders love; sideshows which consist in flourishing a big stick in the face of the Boche, and losing some of your best men in order to show that you are not afraid of him. If I am allowed, I mean to keep them for the big show which cannot be far off, and when we shall want all our men, and all our best men.

One of those men was Jim Burnside, who was to take up land near the Russells at Crownthorpe after the war. When a German machine-gun post had defeated all attempts to silence it, Burnside was ordered to make a last attempt. Before going over the top he met Russell on one of his frequent inspections of the front line. 'Where are you going, Burnside?' the general asked him. 'I'm going to knock out that machine gun, sir,' said Burnside. 'No you're not,' said Russell, 'you'll get yourself killed.'

A standout feature of Russell's style of command was loyalty to his senior commanders, whatever his private beliefs about their competence. When Godley came under attack in Parliament in 1917, Russell jumped to his defence, telling Allen that in his capacity as commander of the NZEF, Godley had done everything possible to see that the organisation ran smoothly and that 'everyone got fairness and justice'. When Hamilton was sacked as MEF commander at Gallipoli late in 1915, Russell was reluctant to accept criticism of his superior's performance before the full facts were known. He felt that Hamilton had been unlucky, and that his bad luck had been compounded by Winston Churchill's incompetence and the poor generalship of Stopford at Suvla Bay during the Allied offensive on 7 August.

But then a paradox: this man of loyalty, compassion, and concern for the welfare of his soldiers was also willing to sign warrants for the execution of 28 of his men, five of whom were subsequently shot by firing squad. By 21st-century standards, Russell would be judged 'a hard bastard', but he commanded at a time when the psychological effects of prolonged trench fighting were little understood. His priority was the fighting effectiveness of his division, not the mental condition of men who would not—or could not—face the stresses of frontline combat.

Russell and his division spent nearly three years on the Western Front. They achieved much, but at a high cost—nearly 12,500 were killed and many more would return home bearing the physical and emotional scars of battle. The acknowledgements of their battlefield skills, however, were generous. The French Army Orders of November 1918 noted that Russell had

led to countless victories a splendid Division whose exploits have not been equalled and whose reputation was such that on the arrival of the Division on the Somme Battlefield during the critical stages of March 1918, the departure of the inhabitants was stopped immediately. The Division covered itself with fresh glory during the battles of Ancre a la Sambre, at Puisieux au Mont, Bapaume, Crevecoeur, and Le Quesnoy.[326]

In a foreword to the division's official history, Haig wrote that no division in France had built up for itself a finer reputation, whether for gallantry in battle or for the excellence of its behaviour out of the line. Towards the end of hostilities, Haig's private secretary told Russell that the New Zealand Division was rated first equal with the élite British Guards Division as a fighting formation on the Western Front. An unnamed general on Haig's staff is said to have told Major Lindsay Inglis that in his opinion, and that of many others 'who ought to know', the New Zealand Division was the best in Europe.[327]

The accolades for Russell himself came from men well qualified to give them. Lieutenant-Colonel Geoffrey Pridham, a British regular officer and member of Russell's staff, described him as 'the beau ideal' of a general to serve. 'I have had many, and if I was going out fighting again I should only feel perfect confidence and trust if I were going under you or Smith-Dorien.'[328]

YMCA director Jim (later Sir James) Hay, wrote:

[Russell] combined in a unique way military leadership of a high order with an acute awareness that the 20,000 men under his command were human personalities, their well-being regarded by him as a great trust and his constant concern. He also knew, better than anyone, the closeness of the relation between contented and well cared for troops and their efficiency as a fighting unit.[329]

Captain Tom Seddon left the post of Russell's aide-de-camp in April 1918 with a deep respect for the character and abilities of his general:

Every detail of every operation undertaken he gave his closest personal attention. A senior officer failing to carry out the minutest instructions was interviewed and reproved, but never, never in the presence of other officers. He understood officers; he understood men. He had the highest sense of duty. His heart and soul were in his work. His endeavours were wholly for the Division, for the men he admired, the Division from which he could not sever his connection to undertake a higher command.[330]

Russell minimised the role he had played in his division's success, but Pugsley is in no doubt about what he achieved in two and a half years of command on the Western Front:

At Messines in 1917, at Passchendaele in victory on 4 October and defeat on 12 October, and in the battles of 1918, the NZ Division proved itself a superb, professional fighting machine, despite its amateur status. This largely reflects the calibre of its commander, Andrew Russell, who achieved his goal of producing one of the best divisions in France.[331]

In later years, Guy Russell would tell his grandson John that the New Zealanders were the 'finest men' any general could command and he felt it an honour to have done so.

In character, Russell can credibly be compared with the American commander on the Western Front, General John Pershing—a man of stubborn determination, physically tough, morally of indestructible fibre, and impervious to popularity.'[332] He could also be matched with his nineteenth-century exemplar, General Sir John Moore, for inspirational leadership, humanity and moral courage.

Allowing for obvious differences in rank and fame, Russell perhaps comes closest to the Duke of Wellington—a commander who put the efficiency and welfare of his army above all personal considerations, and one who was both a great humanitarian and strict disciplinarian. Wellington took full blame for his failures and refused to sacrifice lives unnecessarily. He kept an open mind to new ideas, took great pains in his planning, moved among his troops and always had 'to see things for himself'.[333]

The attributes that Russell shared with these men made him the consummate fighting commander he was, both at Gallipoli and on the Western Front. As a result of his generalship and the fighting skills of the 20,000 'diggers' he led, the New Zealand Division established a reputation from the Third Battle of the Somme on as one of the most effective fighting divisions in the British Army.

A Man for His Time

> To me, and to hosts of others who knew him, [General Russell] bore the marks of greatness. Like all big men his outstanding characteristic, stemming from a deep religious faith, was humility.'—Sir James Hay, director of the YMCA during New Zealand Division's deployment on the Western Front.

Guy Russell was a man formed by his time—the late nineteenth and the first decades of the twentieth century, and place—for the most part New Zealand of the same period. This was a country quite foreign to modern experience. The overwhelming majority of New Zealanders considered themselves British, and their patriotism was 'instinctive and almost absolute'.[334] This was a time of moral conservatism, enforced in the main by the dominant Protestant middle class, of which Russell was a conspicuous member. It was a time when 'the press was always right, the family unit rigid, men would die for a belief, a broken engagement could cause social disgrace, mothers were saints, and liquor was demon'.[335] Yet it was also a time of major social advances that, for a while, made New Zealand the 'social laboratory of the world'.

It was also a time of economic depression when nearly half the male workforce worked on the land, and over 70 percent of the country's export income came from meat, wool and dairy products. It was a time of overwhelming reliance on Britain for trade, defence, investment and immigration. In this time major land reforms put thousands of small farmers onto land carved from Crown land and the estates of big landowners like the Russells.

Inevitably, Guy Russell was a product of all of these influences, and they all played a part in shaping his values and attitudes.

Russell was a natural conservative, steeped in the values of the military, the Anglican church, and the colonial land-owning class of his ancestors. He had little tolerance for those who might threaten the moral and material foundations on which his world was built—militant unionists, communists, pacifists, conscientious objectors of any sort, and most left-wing politicians—although he admired Liberal Prime Minister Dick Seddon and maverick Labour politician John A. Lee.

Guy Russell extolled the virtues of obedience, self-discipline and self-denial, and expressed profound distaste for a society dominated by materialism and the pursuit of pleasure and comfort. The training of his troops in Egypt and France, for example, was not simply a matter of inculcating military skills but the self-discipline needed to ensure good citizenship. In February 1916, he wrote to his father: 'I am a fanatic on the subject of our becoming pretty good, because I feel it is up to us to bring back to NZ the right ideas, and so introduce an element of discipline and right feeling into the Dominion, and pass it on to the next generation.'

But the man who was so much a conservative in many respects could also admit to being a 'convinced socialist'. This had nothing to do with doctrinaire socialism or communism—which he despised—but with working for the common good; giving practical help and support to one's neighbour; rejecting entirely the survival-of-the-fittest approach to human existence. The evidence of that 'socialism' was the years of service Guy Russell gave to returned soldiers after the war; the practical help he gave to struggling farmers during the Depression years; his support for the break-up of large estates (including his own) to put returned soldiers on the land; and the introduction of profit-sharing on his properties at Tunanui and Mount View.

Guy Russell despised the speculation and profiteering, valued thrift and hard work, and demanded the maximum effort from all his staff on Tunanui. 'They say I work my men too hard,' he wrote to his sisters in 1932. 'All I can say is that it seems to suit them.' Not excluded were members of his family. When his sons Andy and John went up into the attic to sleep off the effects of a night of hard drinking, Guy climbed after them early the next morning with two stiff whiskies. 'There, drink that,' he ordered, 'and get back to work!'

Although a large run-holder with a good business brain, Guy Russell seemed indifferent to the accumulation of wealth. As he wrote to his sisters, 'I confess I'm more concerned with "doing things" than with making money and business, but have no wish to throw stones at those who are ... good at making money, when I reflect on how much harm can be done by the feckless.'

Doing things, combined with a strong sense of duty to family and country, drove the critical decisions of Guy Russell's long life. Duty to country influenced his decision to volunteer for overseas service, and take on the burdens of senior command in 1914, despite having a growing family and heavy farm-management responsibilities. Duty explained his decision to enter politics in the post-war years, even though he would have preferred to have stayed away. Duty influenced his involvement, as director or board member, in a vast array of public, private and community organisations both before World War I and after it. An ingrained sense of duty explained why in 1939, at the age of 72, he accepted Prime Minister Fraser's offer of a seat on the War Council and the demanding position of Inspector-General of Military Forces.

Beneath the undemonstrative exterior, Russell was a man of strong humanitarian instincts. They showed in his genuine regret for deaths of friends and brothers-in-arms, and in the small acts of kindness for fellow officers for whom he had a special regard. In 1919, Russell made provision for Bess, the horse ridden by Colonel Powles in Palestine, to be shipped back to New Zealand. After Lieutenant-Colonel George King died at Passchendaele, Russell arranged for King's horse to be shipped back to New Zealand at war's end.

In the 1920s, Guy and Gertrude Russell became surrogate parents to King's two children, Edward and Nancy; they paid for the two to attend private schools (Christ's College and Marsden), and regularly invited them to spend the holidays at Tunanui. Edward began his working life as a farm cadet at Tunanui in the 1930s, and later went on to become a group captain in the RNZAF.

Russell also made a special effort to help men who had served under him overseas to get their first start on the land. In the 1920s, he leased several blocks from the original Tunanui property to these men, and kept a watchful eye on their progress. He provided sheep for at least one small farmer at Crownthorpe during the Depression, and gave a stud bull to another who was setting up a dairy farm at Otaki.

Russell was no stranger to hard times, and these made him compassionate towards those who had suffered similar losses and hardships. He knew only too well what it was like to struggle to make farming viable in the depression years of the 1890s, 1920s and '30s, saddled with debt and the many burdens of frontier farming—floods, droughts, pest infestations, and the ever-fluctuating prices for meat and wool. With several premature deaths in his family, including those of his mother, brother, and younger son John, he was also no stranger to personal tragedy.

In spite of his military achievements, a knighthood, and position as a member of the landed gentry, Guy Russell was a humble man. When he was promoted to major-general and divisional commander in November 1915, he wrote to his family from a dugout on Gallipoli: 'I really feel hardly equipped for the job. However, you can't well refuse, and if I can't do it justice—well! they must just turn me out. In the meantime I must do my best.' After his sister Milly was awarded the MBE for war services in 1919, Guy wrote: 'Like the DCM or MM, it represents really a far higher personal achievement than all my gaudy ribbons which are earned for one by others.'

Over the years, many distinguished men were guests of the Russells at Tunanui. Among these were Lord Kitchener of Khartoum, the Prince of Wales and his royal retinue; Governors-General Jellicoe, Bledisloe, Liverpool and Cobham, and Guy Russell's old commander, General Sir Ian Hamilton. After World War II, visitors included Eighth Army commander General Sir Oliver Leese, Major-General Howard Kippenberger, and Chief Justice Sir Harold Barrowclough. Russell received them all hospitably, but nowhere in his diaries or letters is there any hint of pride in the status conferred by such visitations.

Quite the contrary, in fact. In August 1923, the Russells hosted a visit to Tunanui by Lord Jellicoe, his wife and family, and their retainers. Most prominent citizens in his position would have been flattered; Russell regarded the whole affair—which included arranging a hunt for Lady Jellicoe and golf for His Lordship—as 'rather a fag and expense'. 'A sigh of relief will be heard,' he wrote to his sisters, 'when his and her Excellencies, two ADCs, the two Miss Jellicoes, and the valet and maid drive away through the mud at the woolshed gate.'

Russell's political beliefs were an intriguing, and sometimes confusing, mix of rural conservatism and practical socialism. He was a candidate for the conservative Reform Party in 1922, but as a 'convinced socialist' supported and promoted the idea of land reform. Tying up much of the nation's productive land in the hands of wealthy runholders, Russell felt, was not only an inefficient use of resources but socially unjust. He wrote to Dan Riddiford in 1931: 'We have got to realise that the country comes first, and if you or I are holding land which could return a good living and support more people if cut up, why not?'[336]

As a farmer and businessman, Russell was frequently hostile towards the trade unions, particularly those in the primary industries.

In December 1926, he wrote to his family: 'These wretched freezing employees are giving no end of trouble. Strikes and rumours of strikes, going slow etc. Much of it the consequence of the "Preference to Unionist" policy, which gives the leaders a tyrannical hold over the rank and file. Trouble ahead I think.' While accepting that some employers exploited their workers, Russell felt that the unions had exceeded their role. Pay and working conditions should be fair and the responsibility of the employer, he argued; they should not be imposed by union pressure or government legislation.

Russell's attitude to the welfare state created by the Savage Government was ambivalent. On the one hand, he conceded its value in providing a safety net for the many who had fallen on hard times in the depressions of the 1920s and '30s. On the other hand, he felt it encouraged too much reliance on the state at the expense of individual initiative and hard work. During the early 1940s, he wrote of the 'enervating climate of social security' that he felt existed in New Zealand. A few years later, he was regretting the 'sad results' of welfare for Maori society generally and for 'a good many of the Pakehas'.

With this went a strong suspicion of state power, which in later years Russell saw as a potential threat to individual freedom. On post-war reconstruction in the mid-1940s, he wrote to his sisters: 'The main issue is whether we are to be state-controlled and governed by bureaucracy or given a reasonable amount of latitude to work out our own salvation. But I'm a rebel by nature. Didn't old Cruickshank find me so at Harrow?' For the same reasons Russell opposed the rise of fascism in post-war Europe and the threat of communism in the Asia–Pacific region in the 1950s. These too he saw as threats to individual freedom.

The state, he argued, should interfere as little as possible with private enterprise. It should nationalise only when private enterprise could not efficiently cope with large projects such as afforestation and electric power generation, or when private enterprise was in a position to apply 'a stranglehold on the community'. The state, however, should be responsible for the support of the old, the sick and the genuinely disabled.

Russell's long flirtation with the Social Credit Party and currency reform ideas reflected his anger at a monetary system that seemed unable to deliver farmers a profitable return from the sale of their produce. He was attracted to the New Zealand Legion in the 1930s because of its emphasis on Bible teaching as a solution of material problems, and his frustrations with a party system of government that seemed unable to solve the problems of a long-running depression.

Guy Russell was a man of wide intellectual interests, among them military history and tactics, international affairs and economics, English and French literature. He played the cello indifferently, enjoyed classical music and opera, and spoke French and German fluently. His knowledge of Shakespeare's plays and poetry was prodigious, and his letters to his family were peppered with Latin quotations from Virgil, Horace and others. In France, when the pressures on him were at their height, he would often read far into the night on these and other subjects that interested him.

Hitler and the rise of fascism in Germany, the expansion of communism in Europe, the activities of the League of Nations, and the growing threat of Japan in the Asia–Pacific region were all of great interest to him in the 1930s. After the war, Russell was a member of the Royal Institute of International Affairs (Chatham House), and carried on a regular correspondence on international issues with a number of friends and acquaintances overseas.

Religious belief ran deep in Guy Russell's psyche and sustained him from youth into old age. Happiness, he believed, must have a spiritual base, and death was not the end. Christian ideals should underpin the social, economic and political life of the nation, and then all the rest—economics, politics, international affairs—would fall into their proper place. Christian education, and particularly Bible study, should be part of the school curriculum as part of a child's equipment for life.

Guy Russell was an Anglican by birth and upbringing, but in later life he was attracted by Presbyterianism, whose 'more straightforward' approach to spiritual matters contrasted with the 'somewhat flabby' Anglican presentation of the Bible: 'Too indefinite, too lukewarm. No hard hitting,' he wrote to his sisters in 1941. 'Not that insistence on hell-fires and eternal damnation comes into my philosophy either.'

Underlying his commitment to organised religion lay an unwavering belief in the afterlife. In July 1916, he wrote to his dying father: 'Well! we've got to grow old whether we like it or not, just as a soldier has to take his chances, however formidable they appear. But I am happy to think that neither of us looks on the inevitable other than with cheerfulness which defies dread or dismay.' Death, Russell wrote to his son John in 1951, was 'only the sleep that is necessary to a new birth and renewed energy'.

Meanwhile, a belief in the Almighty could bring peace to troubled souls. His daughter Jan recalled an incident involving her father that made a lasting impression on her: 'We were debating "happiness" in the social hall. Most of us had treated the subject rather light-heartedly. My father came last, and it was obvious that he was going to be serious. I fully expected him to say that his greatest happiness was his family, but quietly he said: "The peace of God which passeth all understanding."'[337]

Guy Russell was not afraid of dying, and had no fears about a future life. His daughter-in-law Ros was with him at the end: 'The day before he died he asked me if I thought that St Peter would overlook his many offences. I said I was quite sure that all the trumpets would be sounding on the other side. Then we said goodbye just as though he were going off somewhere for the weekend. It has been a very great privilege to have known such a man.'[338]

There is little doubt that Guy Russell's relationship with his wife Gertrude was responsible for much of the happiness he found throughout his long life. Both partners in the relationship were strong personalities, of the same social class, and committed to family and church. Gertrude had a shrewd business sense and was well-off in her own right. While Guy managed the station, serviced the bank loans and extracted what profits he could, she provided many of the 'niceties of life' at Tunanui.

Gertrude, however, shared none of her husband's intellectual, political or community interests. Her focus was the farm, her family, and the running of the Russell household. Spiritualism and faith-healing were other interests of hers, along with an obsession with her health that bordered on hypochondria. Their grandson John remembered the copper wire spread around the house as a cure for rheumatism; the coloured wools that were supposed to have a ben-eficial effect on individual organs of the body—heart, liver, kidneys or brain. He recalled his grandfather being fed a tonic containing strychnine, which in small doses is a stimulant for the heart. Because he had not taken his normal dose for three days, Guy decided to tri-ple it. 'Bloody near killed him!' John recalled.

The infrequent visits to Tunanui by Guy's England-based sisters, Milly and Gwen, were often a trial for Gertrude. The three siblings would chatter away in French, each capping the other's quotations from French literature, leaving her entirely out of the conversation. Ros speculated that such differences may have led Gertrude subcon-sciously to take refuge in ill health. If his wife's constant bouts of depression and minor illnesses placed any noticeable stress on their relationship, Guy Russell does not mention it in his letters. He speaks of Gertrude with tolerance and constant concern—if at times with some exasperation. 'I don't think the General had any regrets,' their daughter Kath recalled, 'he neither longed for the moon nor cried over spilt milk; he was entirely philosophical. His brain was never idle and he was always taking up a new cult like the British Israelites or Social Credit.'[339]

He was, however, a great tease, and on occasion this would exas-perate his wife so much that she would threaten to go and live with one of her many relations in the Wairarapa. Their granddaughter Mary Cave remembered sitting at the dining room table at Tunanui talking with her two Russell grandparents about cremation. 'Grandfather looked at Gran and said, "Gertie, when you die, I'm going to keep you in a little box in my waistcoat pocket, next to my heart!" She wasn't very amused.'

Russell saw marriage as being essentially indissoluble, even if it was hard on one or other of the parties. As he wrote to his family: 'It seems the only way to keep the family together and the family counts for more than the individual. For better or worse. There's no getting behind that and at the same time keeping one's self-respect.'

His wartime liaison with the Swiss countess, Madame Lili de Condolle, temporarily damaged that relationship, although there is no evidence that the liaison was other than platonic. Guy enjoyed the company and friendship of other sophisticated and intelligent women during his time overseas. While training his troops at Zeitoun in 1915, he visited Anna Boutros Ghali, a well-educated woman of some status in Cairo society. During his service in France, he called regularly on Baronne de la Grange ('Lady Anzac'), a wealthy aristocrat of French/Belgian origins and hostess to a number of other British Army generals.

For Guy Russell, however, wartime service meant years of absence from his wife and family. He did not see four of his five children for four whole years, and he felt the deprivation keenly: 'There is nothing that I feel more in this war than the fact that I am losing so many interesting years of my children's lives,' he wrote in 1917.[340]

While Russell's letters reveal his close care for his family, through many of them runs a strong thread of nostalgia for 'home', and home was not New Zealand. In spite of his colonial birth and his years of struggle with the land, there was always a part of Guy Russell that was forever England.

Most exceptional characters have their quirks and failings, and Guy Russell was no exception. Daughter-in-law Ros observed that he was 'decisive and confident in everything he did, could make up his mind instantly, and, as he saw everything in black and white, this, perhaps, made him insensitive to the feelings of others. Lack of courage he could not understand.'[341] That lack of understanding could make him impatient with family members who showed fear.

Guy Russell could be impatient also with family members whose mental processes were not as quick as his own, and with most kinds of technology. 'Secretly, we enjoyed the occasions when he tried to telephone and could get no answer from the exchange,' recalled Jan. 'He was thoroughly frustrated, as he was with any piece of machinery that wouldn't obey him!' According to Kath, her father had no feeling for machinery and certainly no ability to fix it if it malfunctioned. 'Presumably, he could change a tyre, but that was about all.'[342]

Always decisive, Guy Russell could be impetuous and prone to hasty decisions. His grandson John recalled the farms he bought that failed to make an adequate profit and were later sold. He recalled the case of Dave Bottom, a woodcutter on Tunanui in the 1920s. 'Dave came to work one morning after a night on the booze and obviously the worse for wear. On the way he ran into the general who asked: "And what's the matter with you Bottom?" (he called everyone by their surnames). "I've had a bit too much to drink sir, and I'm not feeling the best," croaked Bottom. "You're sacked!" said the general, and Dave slunk off to pack his swag.

'En route, he met Lady Russell who, seeing his woebegone expression, asked him what the trouble was. "The old man's sacked me because I came to work drunk," said the hapless Bottom. "Now Dave," said Lady Russell soothingly, "you go home and have a nice long sleep. Come back to work tomorrow and I think you will find that everything is alright." He did and it was, and ever after Dave would say, "You know, the old man can't sack me!"'

A Place of Honour

From Russell's diaries and letters emerges a man of complex beliefs and drives. There is the fighting soldier who was also a man of culture, humanity and deep religious conviction. There is the idealist who wanted a society based on self-discipline, self-sacrifice and Christian ethics; the man who pledged while on war service to devote himself henceforth to the service of others. There is the maverick politician who refused to commit himself to the policies and beliefs of his party where they conflicted with his own. There is the would-be monetary reformer, and the relentless defence lobbyist who would see his warnings vindicated by the outbreak of another world war. There is the man who distrusted trade unions and left-wing politicians, but could describe himself as a convinced socialist. There is the soldier who served the State in two world wars, but would come to see State power and bureaucracy as potential threats to individual freedom.

Guy Russell was also a man of his time, in the main the first decades of the twentieth century. There was his hard line on the use of capital punishment in World War I, his ongoing antagonism towards conscientious objectors and pacifists, his support for exclusively 'white' immigration in the 1920s and '30s, and his firm belief in the superiority of the British race and culture.

Family records, however, reveal an active and affectionate family man who enjoyed his children; a man of strong moral principles who combined a good business brain with a seeming indifference to money and status. Family members recalled the strict but affectionate father who challenged his offspring to face and overcome their fears; the hard-riding practical farmer who loved planting trees, collecting wildflowers, and the vivid colours of a Hawke's Bay sunset.

They remembered the man who displayed the manners and sensibilities of the upper middle-class English gentleman of his time, and his disdain for those he considered ill-mannered and ill-bred.

They recalled the man with a strong social conscience who nevertheless had no tolerance of the work-shy or those who could not stand up to life's hard knocks.

Major-General Sir Andrew Russell will be remembered most as a military commander of the first rank, who led New Zealand forces for four unbroken years of war. He will be remembered for the 20,000-strong division that under his leadership became one of the finest in the British armies that fought on the Western Front. He will be acknowledged for his persistent lobbying of governments on behalf of his returned soldiers in the 1920s, and against defence cuts at a time of growing international instability in the 1930s. For his outstanding leadership abilities and moral courage, for his strength and breadth of mind, and for his will to put duty and the national interest before self, he deserves an honoured place in his country's history. He may yet be recognised as its greatest soldier of the twentieth century.

Acknowledgements

Many people have helped me through the long gestation of the Russell story. First and foremost were John and Phillida Russell, the present owners of Tunanui. Their willingness to open their family archives to me, and their ongoing hospitality, are what made this biography possible. Military historian Dr Ian McGibbon gave me much sound advice and support over the ten years the book took to complete. Lieutenant-Colonel Terry Kinloch lent me an early manuscript of his *Echoes of Gallipoli*, Stephen Clarke, executive director of the NZRSA, his unpublished history of the association, and Hilary Haylock material relating to her father's service on the Western Front.

Published authors John McGibbon, Redmer Yska and Graham Langton provided advice and helpful comments on draft manuscripts. The childhood memories of Rachel Russell, Mary Cave, Carol Marie, Tom Lowry and Nan Simcox helped me create a picture of the complex personality and family man that was Guy Russell. The professionalism and friendly support of the staff of the Defence Library, in particular Carolyn Carr, Katrina Willoughby, Mary Slatter and Joan Keate, were of great assistance, as they have been to many another military historian. To all of these, and to my lovely partner, Barb Freeman, for her outstanding editorial and IT skills, my grateful thanks.

Notes

Preface

1   Colonel H. Stewart, *The New Zealanders in France*, p. 614

2   *NZ Defence Quarterly* 23, Summer 1998

3   Ibid, p. 26

Introduction

4   C. Pugsley. *Gallipoli: The New Zealand Story*, p. 274

Chapter 1

5   R. Gambrill. 'Russell Family Saga', Vol. 3. Alexander Turnbull Library

Chapter 2

6   R. Gambrill 'Russell Family Saga'. Vol. 1. Alexander Turnbull Library

Chapter 3

7   Dixon N. *On the Psychology of Military Incompetence*, p. 54

8   Ibid, p. 234

9   Ibid, p. 53

10   Ibid, p. 234

11   Ibid, p. 234

Chapter 4

12   Keith Sinclair. *A History of New Zealand*, p. 171

13   Michael King. *The Penguin History of New Zealand*, p. 270

Chapter 6

14   T. Kinloch. Echoes of Gallipoli, p. 25
15   Briefing paper: Conference on Naval and Military Defence of the Empire 1909. Russell family papers.
16   I. McGibbon. *The Path to Gallipoli*, p. 209
17   T. Travers. *The Killing Ground*, p. 43
18   W.H. Oliver. *The Story of New Zealand*, p. 166
19   I. McGibbon. *The Path to Gallipoli*, p. 203
20   O.E. Burton. 'A Rich Old Man'. Unpublished MS, p. 390
21   C. Tobin. *Gone to Gallipoli*, p. 10
22   P. Baker. *King and Country Call*, p. 11
23   C.Pugsley. *The Anzac Experience*, p. 208
24   Letter to Defence Minister Sir James Allen, 16/12/14

Chapter 7

25   Major H.H.S Westmacott. *Memoirs*, p. 1704
26   Letter to Allen, 17/1/15
27   Letter to Allen, 25/3/15
28   C. Pugsley. *Gallipoli: The New Zealand Story*, p. 186
29   C. Mackenzie. *Tales of a Trooper*

Chapter 8

30   C. Mackenzie (ed). *Chronicles of the NZEF: 'Peregrinations of a Trooper'*, p. 199
31   T. Kinloch, *Echoes of Gallipoli*, p. 124
32   C. Pugsley. *Gallipoli: The New Zealand Story*, p. 216
33   Letter to Allen, 16/5/15
34   W.B. Fitchett, *RSA Review*. May 1958
35   C. Pugsley, *Gallipoli: The New Zealand Story*, p. 222
36   C.G. Nicol. *The Story of Two Campaigns*, p. 43
37   C. Pugsley. *Gallipoli: The New Zealand Story*, p. 226
38   T. Kinloch. *Echoes of Gallipoli*, p. 136
39   Ibid, p. 148
40   Ibid, p. 155
41   Ibid, p. 156
42   N. Boyack. *Behind the Lines*, p. 58

43   F. Waite. *The New Zealanders at Gallipoli.*

44   General Sir Ian Hamilton. Gallipoli Diary, p. 358

Chapter 9

45   T. Kinloch. *Echoes of Gallipoli*, p. 205

46   Major A.H. Wilkie. *Official War History of the Wellington Mounted Rifles Regiment*, p. 46

47   P.A. Pedersen. *Monash as Military Commander*, p. 113

48   C. Pugsley. *Gallipoli: The New Zealand Story*, p. 304

49   Sir Alexander Godley. *Life of an Irish Soldier*, p. 187

50   Letter to Russell, 13/3/17

51   T. Kinloch. *Echoes of Gallipoli*, p. 228

52   C.E.W. Bean. *Frontline Gallipoli*, p. 155

53   C. Pugsley. *Gallipoli: The New Zealand Story*, p. 318

54   General Sir Ian Hamilton. Gallipoli Diary, Vol. 2, p. 130

55   Letter to Allen, 24/8/15

56   Sir Alexander Godley. Report on Operations, 11–31 August 1915

57   Colonel A.C. Temperley. *A Personal Narrative of the Battle of Chunuk Bair*, p. 18

58   Robert Rhodes James. *Gallipoli*, p. 269

59   Les Carlyon. *Gallipoli*, p. 486

60   Robert Rhodes James. *Gallipoli*, p. 309

61   C. Pugsley. *Gallipoli: The New Zealand Story,* p. 319

62   C.E.W. Bean. *Anzac to Amiens*, p. 167

63   P.A. Pedersen. *Monash as Military Commander*, p. 125

64   J. Laffin. *Damn the Dardanelles,* p. 197

65   O.E. Burton. 'A Rich Old Man'. Unpublished MS

66   Colonel C.G. Powles (ed.). *The History of the Canterbury Mounted Rifles 1914–19*, p. 67

67   Letter to Allen, 10/11/15

68   P.A. Pedersen. *Monash as Military Commander*, p. 123

Chapter 10

69   Letter to Allen, 24/4/15

70   C. Pugsley. *The Anzac Experience*, p. 83

71   C.E.W. Bean. *Gallipoli Correspondent*, p. 182

72   Letter to Godley, 12/1/17

73   C. Pugsley. *Gallipoli: The New Zealand Story*, p. 348

74   O.E. Burton. 'A Rich Old Man'. Unpublished MS. ATL

75   T. Travers. *Gallipoli 1915*, p. 133

76   Ibid, p. 176

77   C. Pugsley. *The Anzac Experience*, p. 76

78   Letter to Guy Russell, 25/3/35, Russell family papers

79   C. Pugsley. *Gallipoli: The New Zealand Story*, p. 335

80   F.M. Cutlack (ed.). *War Letters of General Monash*, p. 102.

81   J. North. *Gallipoli. The Fading Vision*, p. 100

82   Letters to Allen, 21/11/15 and 22/12/15

83   C. Pugsley. *The Anzac Experience*, p. 14

Chapter 11

84   C. Pugsley. *Gallipoli: The New Zealand Story*, p. 348

85   George Tuck. Diary 1914–19, p. 270. ATL

86   P.A. Pedersen. *Monash as Military Commander*, p. 129

87   Ibid, p. 130

88   C. Pugsley. *Haig and His Dominion Commanders: The Evolution of Professional Citizen Armies on the Western Front*

89   Sir Douglas Haig. War Diaries and Letters 1914–18, Letter to King George V, 9/5/16

90   M. Middlebrook. *The First Day on the Somme*, p. 48

91   Operations Report. NZ Division, May1916. ANZ

92   James Meek, 1886–1960. Unpublished MS. ATL

93   Lindsay Inglis. Diary, Vol. 1, p. 122. ATL

94   Ibid, p. 131

95   Miscellaneous war archives files. ANZ

96   Circulars: 2 Wellington Battalion, May–August 1916. ANZ

97   Ibid

98   C. Pugsley. *On the Fringe of Hell*, p. 65

99   Ibid, p. 296.

100   Letter to Allen, 17/9/16. ANZ

101   C. Pugsley. *On the Fringe of Hell*, p. 265

102   Ibid, p. 197

103   C. Pugsley. *The Anzac Experience*, p. 156

104   Ibid, p. 170

105   Lt A.E. Byrne. *Official History of the Otago Regiment in the Great War*, p. 108

106   Sir Herbert Hart. Diaries 1914–19. ATL

107   O.E Burton. 'A Rich Old Man'. Unpublished MS. ATL

108   Letter to Allen, 15/7/16

109   P. Griffiths. *British Fighting Methods in the Great War*, p. 52

110   J. Terraine. *To Win a War*, p. 192

Chapter 12

111   O.E. Burton. 'A Rich Old Man'. Unpublished MS. ATL

112   P. Fussell. *The Great War and Modern Memory*, p. 13

113   R. Prior and T. Wilson. *The Somme*, p. 216

114   Circulars: 2 Wellington Btn, May–August 1916. ANZ

115   Lindsay Inglis. Diary Vol. 1., p. 135. ATL

116   Letter to Allen, 18/9/16. ANZ

117   Sir Herbert Hart. Diaries, 16/9/16. ATL

118   Colonel H. Stewart. *The New Zealanders in France*, p. 88

119   Ibid, p. 94

120   Lt A.E Byrne. *Official History of the Otago Regiment in the Great War*, p. 125

121   C. Malthus. *Armentieres and the Somme*, p. 105

122   Lt A.E. Byrne. *Official History of the Otago Regiment in the Great War*, p. 131

123   A. Rhind. Diary. MS papers. ATL

124   Lindsay Inglis. Diary. Vol. 1, p. 208

125   Colonel H. Stewart. *The New Zealanders in France*, p. 119

126   Sir Douglas Haig. War Diaries and Letters 1914–18

127   C. Malthus. *Armentieres and the Somme*, p. 119

128   A. MacDonald. *On My Way to the Somme*, p. 264

129   Letter to Allen, 15/10/16. ANZ

130   Letter to Godley, 14/10/16. Russell family papers

131   Colonel H. Stewart. *The New Zealanders in France*, p. 120

132   O.E. Burton. 'A Rich Old Man'. Unpublished MS. ATL

Chapter 13

133   Letter to Allen, 25/12/16. ANZ

134   Ibid

135   C. Pugsley. *On the Fringe of Hell*, p. 170

136   Ibid, p. 171

137   Letter to Allen, 17/9/16. ANZ

138   Ibid

139   Letter to Allen, 7/11/16. ANZ

140   Ibid

141   C. Pugsley. *On the Fringe of Hell*, p. 116

142   Letter to Allen, 3/4/17. ANZ

Chapter 14

143   Colonel H.Stewart. *The New Zealanders in France*, p. 188

144   O.E. Burton. 'A Rich Old Man'. Unpublished MS. ATL

145   S. Westmacott. *Memoirs*, p. 344. ATL

146   Letter to Allen, 18/2/17. ANZ

147   C. Pugsley. *The Anzac Experience*, p. 224

148   Sir Douglas Haig. Diaries and letters 1914–18

149   Lindsay Inglis. Diary Vol. 1, p. 32. ATL

150   C. Powell. *Plumer, The Soldiers' General*, p. 182

151   S. Westmacott. *Memoirs*, p. 353. ATL

152   C. Powell. *Plumer, The Soldiers' General*, p. 182

153   Letter to Allen, 11/6/17. ANZ

154   Colonel H. Stewart. *The New Zealanders in France*, p. 205

155   C. Pugsley. *The Anzac Experience*, p. 228

156   Letter to Allen, 19/6/17. ANZ

157   Ibid

158   Letter to Russell, 28/8/17. ANZ

159   H.E. Holland. *Armageddon or Calvary*, p. 66

160   O.E. Burton. 'A Rich Old Man'. Unpublished MS. ATL

161   Hansard. Parliamentary debates, 17 and 21 August 1917

162   Letter to Allen, 7/11/17. ANZ

Chapter 15

163   J. Phillips, N. Boyack, E.P. Malone (eds). *The Great Adventure*, p. 145

164   Letter to Godley, 7/8/17. ANZ

165   Letter to Allen, 13/9/17. ANZ

166   Leon Wolff. *In Flanders Fields*, p. 148

167   J. Keegan. *The First World War*, p. 391

168 Letter to Allen, 28/9/17. ANZ

169 Letter to Allen, 4/10/17. ANZ

170 Letter to Allen, 7/10/17. ANZ

171 J. Keegan. *The First World War*, p. 393

172 War Diary, 1–31 October 1917. ANZ

173 Leon Wolff. *In Flanders Fields*, p. 236

174 Major R.A. Wilson. *A Two Years' Interlude*, p. 62

175 P.A. Pedersen. *Monash as Military Commander*, p. 200

176 Lt A.E. Byrne. *Official History of the Otago Regiment in the Great War*, p. 218

177 O.E. Burton. 'A Rich Old Man'. Unpublished MS. ATL

178 Letter to Allen, 7/11/17. ANZ

179 Letter to Allen, 16/10/17. ANZ

180 Letter to Allen, 7/11/17. ANZ

181 Ibid

182 Letter to Sir James Wilson. ATL

183 Lt A.E. Byrne. *Official History of the Otago Regiment in the Great War*, p. 228

184 Colonel H. Stewart. *The New Zealanders in France*, p. 279

185 C. Pugsley. 'Russell of the NZ Division'. *NZ Strategic Management*, Autumn 1995, p. 48

186 G. Harper. *Massacre at Passchendaele*, p. 103

187 Letter to Russell, 29/1/18. ANZ

188 War Diary. NZ Pioneer Battalion, 1–31 October 1917. ANZ

189 Lindsay Inglis. Diary, Vol. 2, p. 61

190 T. Wilson. *The Myriad Faces of War*

191 Leon Wolff. *In Flanders Fields*, p. 253

192 Prior & Wilson. *Passchendaele: The Untold Story*, p. 200

193 O.E. Burton. 'A Rich Old Man'. Unpublished MS, p. 170. ATL

Chapter 16

194 O.E. Burton. 'A Rich Old Man'. Unpublished MS, p. 168. ATL

195 B. Pitt. *The Last Act*, p. 64

196 O.E. Burton. 'A Rich Old Man'. Unpublished MS, p. 171. ATL

197 Ibid, p. 172

198 T. Seddon MP. Seddon Family Collection. ATL

199 Ibid

200 Operations reports (NZ Division) October 1917–February 1918. ANZ

201 Letter to Allen, 6/1/18. ANZ

202 Letter to Godley, 7/1/18. ANZ

203 Letter to Allen, 28/9/17. ANZ

204 Letter to Allen, 24/11/17. ANZ

205 G. Harper. *Stopping the Storm: The NZ Division and the Kaiser's Battle, March–April 1918*, p. 30

Chapter 17

206 O.E. Burton. 'A Rich Old Man'. Unpublished MS, p. 178. ATL

207 G. Tuck. Diary 1914–19, p. 460. ATL

208 Letter to Allen, 3/4/18. ANZ

209 Ibid

210 Lindsay Inglis. Diary, Vol. 2, p. 103. ATL

211 Letter to Allen, 22/4/18. ANZ

212 G. Harper. *Spring Offensive*, p. 155

213 T. Seddon. Seddon Family Collection. ATL

214 C. Pugsley. *The Anzac Experience*, p. 285

215 Letter to Russell, 30/4/18. ANZ

216 Letter to Birdwood, 17/6/18. ANZ

217 Letter to Godley, 21/5/18. ANZ

218 Letter to Allen, 18/6/18. ANZ

219 Letter to Russell, 19/7/18. ANZ

220 Letter to Allen, 17/5/18. ANZ

221 Letter to Russell 19/7/18. ANZ

222 Letter to Allen, 4/7/18. ANZ

223 Letter to Allen, 9/8/18. ANZ

224 Letter to Godley, 4/9/18. ANZ

225 Ibid

Chapter 18

226 G. Harper. *Spring Offensive*, p. 122

227 G. Harper. *Dark Journey*, p. 349

228 Letter to Tom Seddon, 13/8/18 Seddon Family Collection. ATL

229 Ibid

230 Diaries. Sir Herbert Hart 1914–19. ATL

231 *Chronicles of the NZEF*, p. 79. ATL

232 Ibid

233 Colonel H. Stewart. *The New Zealanders in France*, p. 500

234 Diaries. Sir Herbert Hart 1914–19. ATL

235 J. Terraine. *To Win a War*, p. 143

236 *Chronicles of the NZEF*, p. 154. ATL

237 Letter to Allen, 16/9/18. ANZ

238 Ibid

239 *Chronicles of the NZEF*, p. 153. ATL

240 C. Pugsley. *On the Fringe of Hell*, p. 280

241 J. Terraine. *To Win a War*, p. 206

242 M. Gilbert. *The First World War*, p. 501

243 Diaries. Sir Herbert Hart 1914–19. ATL

244 T. Travers. *How the War Was Won*, p. 179

245 C. Pugsley. *The Anzac Experience*, p. 289

246 Letter to Russell, 18/12/18. ANZ

247 Lindsay Inglis. Diary, Vol. 2, p. 208. ATL

248 *Chronicles of the NZEF*, p. 279. ATL

249 R. Gambrill. 'Russell Family Saga'. Vol. 5. ATL

250 Lindsay Inglis. Diary. Vol. 2 p. 221. ATL

251 Russell family papers, Tunanui

Chapter 19

252 R. Gambrill, 'Russell Family Saga', Vol. 5

253 Manifesto 1920. National Defence League. Russell family papers.

Chapter 20

254 J. Phillips, N.Boyack, E.P. Malone (eds). *The Great Adventure*, p. 231

255 Letter to Sir James Wilson, 21/10/17. ANZ

256 R. Gambrill, 'Russell Family Saga', Vol. 4, 1919–60. ATL

257 *Quick March* (NZRSA official magazine), 21/7/21

258 S. Clarke. 'A History of the NZRSA'. Unpublished MS.

259 Ibid

260 Ibid

261 Ibid

262 Ibid

263 Ibid

264 Eulogy, December 1960. Russell family papers

Chapter 21

265 Letter to Seddon, 13/8/18. Seddon Family Collection. ATL

266 Letter to Allen, 30/7/19. ANZ

267 Group Captain Edward King. *Autobiography*, Chapter 1

Chapter 22

268 National Defence League policy statement. Russell family papers

269 Letter to sisters, 28/7/28. Russell family papers

270 Ibid

Chapter 23

271 National Defence League policy statement. Russell family papers

272 Memorandum. Russell family papers

273 Manifesto released under names of the four colonels, May 1938. Russell family papers

274 R. Gambrill, 'Russell Family Saga'. Vol. 4, 1919–60. ATL

275 Ibid

276 Russell family papers

277 G. Hensley. *Beyond the Battlefield*, p. 48

278 British Israelites brochure, 1/3/27. Russell family papers

279 Letter to Russell, 14/1/31. Russell family papers

280 *Dictionary of New Zealand Biography*

Chapter 24

281 M. Bassett & M. King. *Tomorrow Comes the Song: A Life of Peter Fraser*, p. 203

282 Letter to Tom Seddon, 29/12/50. Seddon Family Collection. ATL

283 War Council papers, January–July 1942. ANZ

284 F.L.W. Wood. *The New Zealand People at War*, p. 213

285 Ibid, p. 194

286 G. Hensley. *Beyond the Battlefield*, p. 92

287 Briefing papers supplied to Russell as Inspector-General of Military Forces. Source unclear, but probably NZ Army HQ. Russell family papers

288 Ibid

289 Tactical exercise briefings. Russell family papers

290 Report to Chief of General Staff, 6/11/40. Russell family papers

291 R. Gambrill, 'Russell Family Saga', World War II (1940–45). ATL

292 Report to Minister of Defence, 30/6/41. Russell Family papers

293 Letter to Chief of General Staff, 16/12/41. Russell family papers

294 Ibid

295 Letter to Fraser, 19/6/41. Russell family papers

296 F.L.W. Wood. *The New Zealand People at War*, p. 222

297 Ibid

298 Letter to Russell, July 1941. Russell family papers

299 Letter to Russell: Russell family papers

Conclusion

300 I. McGibbon. *Dictionary of New Zealand Biography*

301 G. Harper, *Kippenberger: An Inspired New Zealand Commander*, p. 13

302 Ibid, p. 15

303 Major-General Sir Nevill Smyth, 'The Span of Years: Russell Family Saga', Vol. IV

304 W.B. Fitchett. 'Tribute to Sir Andrew Russell', *NZRSA Review*, May 1958

305 Gertrude Russell. Letter to Milly, 29/10/15. Russell family papers, Tunanui

306 T. Travers, *The Killing Ground*, p. 20

307 C. Pugsley, 'Russell of the NZ Division', *New Zealand Strategic Management*, Autumn 1995

308 H. Stewart, *The New Zealanders in France*, p. 615

309 E.J. Leed, *No Man's Land: Combat and Identity in World War I*, p. 100

310 C. Pugsley, *On the Fringe of Hell*, p. 300

311 P.A. Pedersen, *Monash as Military Commander*, p. 143

312 C. Pugsley, *NZ Defence Quarterly*, Summer 1998, p. 29

313 G. Harper, *Dark Journey*, p. 469

314 H. Stewart, *The New Zealanders in France*, p. 615

315 G.Harper, *Kippenberger: An Inspired New Zealand Commander*, p. 14

316 G. Harper, *Born to Lead? Portraits of New Zealand Commanders*, p. 67

317 Letter. Russell family papers, Tunanui

318 Ibid

319 W.R. King, Letter to Sir J.G. Wilson, ATL

320 H. Stewart, *The New Zealanders in France*, p. 615

321 R. Gambrill, 'Russell Family Saga', Vol. 1, ATL

322 E.J. Leed, *No Man's Land*, p. 96

323 N. Dixon, The Psychology of Military Incompetence, p. 348

324 P.A. Pedersen, *Monash As Military Commander*, p. 165

325 C.Pugsley, *The Anzac Experience*, p. 212

326 Russell family papers, Tunanui

327 L. Inglis, Diary. Vol. II, p. 128

328 Letter, 15/3/35, Russell family papers, Tunanui

329 R. Gambrill, 'Russell Family Saga', Vol. 5, ATL

330 Seddon Family Collection, ATL

331 C. Pugsley, *On the Fringe of Hell*, p. 300

332 B. Pitt, *The Last Act*, p. 67

333 N. Dixon, *The Psychology of Military Incompetence*, p. 324

334 Ibid

335 P. Baker, *King and Country Call*, Preface/Introduction

336 Letter to Dan Riddiford, 13/8/31, ATL

337 R. Gambrill, 'Russell Family Saga', Vol. 5, ATL

338 Ibid

339 Ibid

340 Letter to Sir James Wilson, President of the Board of Agriculture, ATL

341 R. Gambrill, 'Russell Family Saga', ATL

342 Ibid

Bibliography

Published sources

Baker, Paul. *King and Country Call*, Auckland University Press, 1988

Bassett, M. & King, M. *Tomorrow Comes the Song: A Life of Peter Fraser*, Penguin Books, New Zealand, 2000

Bean, C.E.W. *The Official History of Australia in the War of 1914–18: Volume 2*, University of Queensland Press, 1924

——*Gallipoli Correspondent*. Allen & Unwin, Australia, 1983

——*Frontline Gallipoli. Diary From the Trenches*, Allen & Unwin, Australia, 1990

Belich, James. *Paradise Reforged*, Penguin Books, New Zealand, 2001

Boyack, Nicholas. *Behind the Lines*, Allen & Unwin, New Zealand, 1989

——*In the Shadow of War*, Penguin Books, New Zealand, 1990

Brown, M. *Imperial War Book of the Somme*, Pan Books, London, 1996

Burton, O.E. *The Silent Division: New Zealanders at the Front 1914–19*, Angus & Robertson, New Zealand 1935

——*The Auckland Regiment NZEF, 1914–1918*, Whitcombe & Tombs, Auckland, 1922

Carlyon, Les. *Gallipoli*, Pan Macmillan, Australia, 2001

Cutlack, F.M. *War Letters of General Monash*. Angus & Robertson, Australia, 1934

Dixon, N. *On the Psychology of Military Incompetence*, Pimlico, 1994

Dunn, Capt J.C. *The War the Infantry Knew 1914–1919*, Jane's, 1987

Fussell, Paul. *The Great War and Modern Memory*, Oxford University Press, United Kingdom, 1975

Gilbert, Martin. *The First World War*, Henry Holt and Co, 1994

Grant, David. *Field Punishment No 1*, Steele Roberts, Wellington, 2008

Griffiths, Paddy. *British Fighting Methods in the Great War*, Frank Cass, 1996

Haig Sir Douglas (eds Gary Sheffield & John Bourne). *War Diaries and Letters 1914–1918*, Weidenfeld & Nicholson, London, 2005

Hamilton, General Sir Ian. *Gallipoli Diary*, Edward Arnold, London, 1920

Harper, Glyn. *Dark Journey*, HarperCollins, Auckland, 2007

——*Massacre at Passchendaele*, HarperCollins, Auckland, 2000

——*Spring Offensive*, HarperCollins, Auckland, 2003

Hensley, Gerald. *Beyond the Battlefield*, Penguin Viking, New Zealand, 2009

Hickey, Michael. *Gallipoli*, John Murray, 1995

Holland, H.E. *Armageddon or Calvary: The Conscientious Objectors of New Zealand*, New Zealand, 1919

James, Robert Rhodes. *Gallipoli*, B.T. Batsford, London, 1965

Keegan, John. *The Face of Battle*, Jonathan Cape, United Kingdom, 1976

——*The First World War*, Hutchinson, London, 1998

King, Michael. *The Penguin History of New Zealand*, Penguin Books, Auckland, 2003

——*New Zealanders at War*. Heinemann Reed, Auckland, 1981

Kinloch, T. *Echoes of Gallipoli*, Exisle, Auckland, 2005

Laffin, John. *Damn the Dardanelles: The Story of Gallipoli*, Doubleday Australia, 1980

——*British Butchers and Bunglers of World War I*, Macmillan Australia, 1989

Leed, Eric J. *No Man's Land: Combat and Identity in World War I*, Cambridge University Press, 1979

McAloon, Jim. *Nelson: A Regional History*, Cape Catley, New Zealand, 1997

MacDonald, Andrew. *On My Way to the Somme*, HarperCollins, Auckland, 2005

MacDonald, Lyn. *Somme*. Michael Joseph, London, 1983

——*They Called It Passchendaele*. Michael Joseph, London, 1978

——*To the Last Man*. Penguin Books, London, 1998

McGibbon, Ian. *The Path to Gallipoli: Defending New Zealand 1840–1915*, GP Books, 1991

Malthus, Cecil. *Armentières and the Somme*, Reed Books, New Zealand, 2002

Middlebrook, Martin. *The Kaiser's Battle*, Penguin Books, Harmondsworth, England, 1983

Moorehead, Alan. *Gallipoli*, Hamish Hamilton, 1956

Neillands, Robin. *The Great War Generals on the Western Front*, Robinson, 1999

Nicol, Sgt C.G. *The Story of Two Campaigns*, Wilson & Horton, Auckland, 1921

North, John. *Gallipoli: The Fading Vision*, Faber & Faber, 1968

Oliver, W.T. *The Story of New Zealand*, Faber & Faber, 1960

Pedersen, P.A. *Monash as Military Commander*, Melbourne University Press, 1985

Phillips, J, Boyack, N. & Malone E.P. (eds), *The Great Adventure*, Allen & Unwin, New Zealand, 1988

Pitt, Barrie. *The Last Act*, Macmillan, 1962

Powell, G. *Plumer. The Soldiers' General*, Pen and Sword Military Classics, 2004

Powles, Col. C.G. *The History of the Canterbury Mounted Rifles 1914–19*, Whitcombe & Tombs, Auckland, 1928

Prior, R. & T. Wilson. *Passchendaele: The Untold Story*. Yale University Press, 1996

——*The Somme*, Yale University Press, 2005

Pugsley, Christopher. *Gallipoli: The New Zealand Story*, Reed Books, Auckland, 1998

——*On the Fringe of Hell: New Zealanders and Military Discipline in the First World War*, Hodder & Stoughton, Auckland, 1991

——*The Anzac Experience*. Reed Publishing (NZ), 2004

Sinclair, Keith. *A History of New Zealand*, Penguin Books, Auckland, 1969

——*Walter Nash*, John McIndoe Ltd, Dunedin, 1976

Stewart, Col. H. *The New Zealanders in France*, Whitcombe & Tombs, Auckland, 1921

Terraine, John. *Douglas Haig: The Educated Soldier*, Leo Cooper, London, 1990

——*To Win a War*, Sidgwick & Jackson, London, 1978

Tobin, Christopher. *Gone To Gallipoli: Anzacs of Small Town New Zealand Go to War*, Bosco Press, Timaru, 2001

Travers, Tim. *The Killing Ground: The British Army, the Western Front and the Emergence of Modern Warfare, 1900–18*, Allen & Unwin, 1987

——*Gallipoli 1915*, Tempus Publishing, UK, 2001

Waite, Major Fred. *The New Zealanders at Gallipoli*, Whitcombe & Tombs, Auckland, 1919

Weston, Lt Col C.H. *Three Years with the New Zealanders*, Skiffington & Son, London

Wilkie, Major A.H. *Official War History of the Wellington Mounted Rifles Regiment, 1914–19*, Whitcome & Tombs, Auckland

Wilson, Ormond. *An Outsider Looks Back*, Port Nicholson Press, Wellington, 1962

Wilson, Major R.A. *A Two Years Interlude. France 1916–18*, Keeling & Mundy, Palmerston North New Zealand (n.d)

Winter, Denis. *Haig's Command: A Reassessment*, Viking, London, 1991

Wolff, Leon. *In Flanders Fields*, Longmans, Green & Co., London, 1959

Wood, F.L.W. *The New Zealand People at War*, Department of Internal Affairs, Wellington, 1958

Unpublished sources

Burton, O.E. *A Rich Old Man*. Unpublished MS. Alexander Turnbull Library

Clarke, Stephen. *A History of the NZRSA*. Unpublished MS

Correspondence: General Sir Alexander Godley, Hon Sir James Allen (1912–15). Archives NZ

Correspondence: General Sir Alexander Godley, Hon Sir James Allen (1915–18). WA 252/1 Archives NZ

Correspondence: Hon Sir James Allen, General Sir William Birdwood, Major-General Sir Andrew Russell (1914–20). Archives NZ

Diaries: Brigadier-General Sir Herbert Hart (1914–19). Alexander Turnbull Library

Diary. Lindsay Inglis. Vols 1 & 2. Alexander Turnbull Library

Diary. George Tuck 1914–19. Alexander Turnbull Library

Gambrill, R.F. 'Russell Family Saga'. Alexander Turnbull Library

Malone, Col. W.G. MS Papers. Alexander Turnbull Library

NZEF Operation Orders, Gallipoli. Col W.G. Braithwaite. Archives NZ

Operations Reports: NZ Division (1917). Archives NZ

Operations Reports: NZ Division (1918). Archives NZ

Personal File: Major-General Russell. Base Records, New Zealand Defence Force

Reports on Operations, NZ & A Division. Archives NZ

Rhodes, Capt Tahu. Diary, Vols 2/4. Alexander Turnbull Library.

Riddiford Family Papers. MS papers 5714. Alexander Turnbull Library

Reports on Operations, NZ & A Division. Archives.

Routine Orders, Brigadier-General A.H. Russell, Commanding No. 4 Section. Archives NZ.

Sari Bair Operation File. Archives NZ.

Seddon Family Collection. MS papers 1619. Alexander Turnbull Library

Temperley, Col. A.C. 'A Personal Narrative of the Battle of Chunuk Bair, Aug. 6–10 1915', Queen Elizabeth II Army Memorial Museum

War Council papers, January–July 1942. Archives NZ

War Diary: HQ NZ Mounted Rifles Brigade. Archives NZ

War Diary: NZ & A Division. Archives NZ

Articles

Harper, Glyn. 'Stopping the Storm: The New Zealand Division and the Kaiser's Battle, March–April 1918', *New Zealand's Great War*, Exisle Publishing, Auckland, 2007

McGibbon, Ian. 'The Shaping of New Zealand's War Effort, August–October 1914'. *New Zealand's Great War*, Exisle Publishing, Auckland, 2007

Mackenzie, Clutha (ed.) *Chronicles of the NZEF 1917–18*, Gordon and Gotch, London

Pugsley, Christopher. *Russell of the NZ Division*. NZ Strategic Management, Autumn 1995

——'Russell: Commander of Genius'. *New Zealand Defence Quarterly*. Summer 1998

——'Haig and his Dominion Commanders: The Evolution of Professional Citizen Armies on the Western Front'. *New Zealand's Great War*, Exisle Publishing, Auckland, 2007

Simkin, Peter. 'Co-Stars or Supporting Cast? British Divisions in the "100 Days", 1918'. *British Fighting Methods in the Great War*, Paddy Griffiths, Frank Cass, 1996

Index